MW01278638

TRAVELS IN WONDERLAND

TRAVELS IN WONDERLAND

a memoir by

Ulla Ryghe

conundrum press / Montreal

'My candle burns at both ends;
It will not last the night;
But ah, my foes, and oh, my friends —
it gives a lovely light.'

— 'First Fig' by Edna St. Vincent Millay, *Poetry* 1918

© Ulla Ryghe, 2008

Cover photographs by Daniela Sneppova
Author photograph by Judith Brand
Cover design by Ulla Ryghe

Library and Archives Canada Cataloguing in Publication

Ryghe, Ulla   Travels in Wonderland / Ulla Ryghe.

ISBN 978-1-894994-31-6

    1. Ryghe, Ulla. 2. Story editors (Motion pictures)—Canada—
Biography. 3. Ryghe, Ulla—Travel. 4. Cyprus—Biography. 5. Teachers—
Canada—Biography. I. Title.

PN1998.3.R495A3 2008   808'.027092   C2008-900803-0

Dépot Legal, Bibliothèque nationale du Québec

Printed and bound in Canada on 100% recycled paper.

Distributed by Litdistco: 1-800-591-6250

First Canadian Edition

The opinions expressed in this book are exclusively those of the author and
do not reflect those of the publisher or any of its affiliates.

conundrum press
PO Box 55003, CSP Fairmount, Montreal, Quebec, H2T 3E2, Canada
conpress@ican.net
www.conundrumpress.com

conundrum press acknowledges the financial assistance of the Canada
Council for the Arts toward our publishing program.

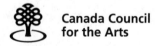

Canada Council   Conseil des Arts
for the Arts   du Canada

TABLE OF CONTENTS

A VERY STRANGE PLACE

Quietly I opened the door and stepped into the long, narrow corridor that led from the dining room down to the kitchen. In contrast to the silent rooms behind me, Cook's domain was filled with all sorts of sounds, and magical things took place there all the time. But halfway down the corridor my path was blocked. Just past the door to my mother's room, down on her knees, the ends of her big grey apron tucked into the lining of her skirt, Cook was polishing the floor with a milky liquid. Silently I moved towards her towering behind when a wet hand came up.

'Where do you think you are going?'

My yearning for company cold-shouldered, my resentment took hold of my right leg, and I kicked the bucket. Hard enough for it to overturn. Cook emitted a muffled cry and struggled to her feet while the white sea started to form a river down the narrow corridor. The commotion had caught my mother's ear, and she appeared, said something to Cook, grabbed my arm, and yanked me into her room, closing the door behind her. With my back turned, I could hear her open the door to her en suite and then the next one that led to her wardrobe. When she returned she held her riding whip and pulled me down over the tabouret in front of the grand piano. My ears heard its whine before I felt the whip hit my bum. A couple of smacks, and I was sent to my room.

This sort of violence had not happened before and was never repeated, but it brought to the surface an intuition that was not new: my mother did not like me. Her indifference had not hurt, but the hugs and kisses she administrated when there was an audience made me uncomfortable. I always tried to wiggle away. At five I was not acquainted with either the word 'ambiguity,' or the meaning of it, and I was not yet old enough to have been indoctrinated with the fancy that parents love their children and vice versa. I liked Mormor and Morfar, my mother's parents, but others — like Farmor, my father's cold and critical mother —

I did not, and thus it seemed natural to avoid them.

My relationship to Cook was somewhat ambiguous. My brother and I were noisy and messy, and I think she endured us more than she liked us. The forbearance her Christianity imposed on her was certainly in our favour, and most of the time, as long as I sat on my chair, she tolerated my presence in her kitchen. She came and went. From the pantry she brought the winter-eggs she had fished out of the big bucket filled with jelly, grey waterglass, and rinsed the slime off the shells before cracking, in one precise move, each egg against the rim of a cup. She would pry the two half shells apart and let the white and the yolk slip into the cup, smelling the contents, and only then let the egg slide on top of the flour in her big bowl. I never tired of watching her expert hands perform the routine, but from time to time she wrinkled her nose, and I could also smell a foul odour before the contents were tipped into the sink where they went down with a funny, sloughy sound. Patience was from time to time rewarded after the cream had finally formed its stiff tops and Cook would hand me the beater to lick. When a sponge cake had been poured into its breaded form, recompense for good behaviour was having a not-completely-scraped bowl being pushed my way, but as I would learn, Cook, like other grownups, also had her puzzling principles.

The day she found me chewing on potato peels she got very upset, and with an anger she had never before displayed, sent me out of her kitchen. The peels — curiously spotty and dark but on the other side just pale white — curled off her big hands and formed ringlets on the brown paper. As each peeled potato was dropped into the cauldron the mountain grew before my eyes, and when Cook turned to the stove, I leaned over and grabbed some of the serpentines. They were crunchy and nice to bite into, but the taste was floury and unpleasant. Not at all as nice as apple peels, and when I munched on *them*, Cook did not get angry. Grown-ups were indeed difficult to understand. As an adult, I have more than once wondered about the genesis of her outburst.

The next attempt to satisfy my taste-curiosity could have had more dire consequences: I swallowed a small handful of pills that contained arsenic. My mother had been prescribed some strengthening pills, and between meals the pillbox was kept where we children could not reach it. At mealtimes the little glass container was placed at my mother's cover, and we had been firmly told never to touch it. One morning, passing through the dining room, where the table was set for breakfast, I saw the forbidden object, and although my inner eye can clearly 'see' what then happened, I have no visual memory of it. Curiosity overcame obedience and a small handful of pills landed in my mouth before I replaced the lid and pushed the vial back to its proper place. When I came into my mother's room, she sent me to the kitchen to tell Cook that we were ready for breakfast.

The dining-room table stood on a big multicoloured Oriental carpet that covered most of the floor. If nothing more exciting was on offer, I used to squat on it and let my finger trace the winding patterns of each colour. When my mother entered the dining room, she, against all odds, spotted one of her tiny grey arsenic pills that had fallen on a small red square. Pandemonium broke out! My brother and I were questioned; he denied any knowledge and so did I. He was believed; I was not. A quick count showed that approximately twenty pills were missing. My mother got on the phone to our family doctor, but he had gone on a holiday, and the two other doctors she tried had done the same as it was only a day or two before Easter. My father was away and only expected back later in the day. Finally, she got hold of one of her older cousins who instructed her to call for a taxi and give me some hot milk while he would let the hospital know of our impending arrival.

I had never liked milk, and hot milk was even worse. I had no idea of the scope of my misdeed and did my best to avoid the glass, but Cook forced my mouth open and poured while my mother held my arms and managed to put on my coat and hat. The taxi arrived, and the driver was told to drive the quickest possible way to the hospital. He did his best but had not gone far before being stopped by a policeman, fortunately one with a quick mind; he hopped on the running board and kept his hand on the horn all the way to the hospital while the driver pressed his gas pedal. I do not think I have ever enjoyed another taxi ride as much as I did this one! What followed was less enjoyable.

Two nurses were waiting for us outside. They grabbed me under the arms, and I was heaved up the wide stone steps and taken inside to a room where a doctor with hard hands shoved a thick red rubber tube down my unwilling throat. It was only when my stomach was pumped empty that my coat and hat came off. I was undressed and put to bed, and then my mother left. My aching throat kept me in place for a while, but then the temptation to investigate the sounds that drifted in through the door left ajar must have become too much. A barefoot little figure in a long white gown trotted down a long corridor and was not caught until after passing through two sets of big swinging doors. I was brought back to my room, but never one to be easily discouraged I repeated my investigation — although in the opposite direction. Not that it changed a great deal! Captured for the second time, I was moved to a room across from the nurses' station, and bars were put up around my bed. The following morning my parents came and fetched me, and the next day the usual Easter eggs did not materialise. The concept of cause and effect started to gain some meaning.

In the Swedish version of a Victorian lifestyle's dutiful adherence to conventions, mine was a lonely childhood without playmates. Furniture, as well as the living, had their given place and respectability was held above anything else. All had to be ordered and spotless so that the door at any time could be opened to a visitor without risk of losing face. Although their homes had widely different atmospheres, my parents came from very similar bourgeois backgrounds. My father was the eldest son and had a sister and a younger brother. His father died when I was still a child, but I remember him as a short, moustached, gentle man domineered by his wife and daughter. My grandmother, addressed as Farmor, was constantly critical, and with her airs of pretension, never showed any warmth. As a role model for her children, she had certainly not done very well. Both my father and his sister lacked lightheartedness and spontaneity, while miraculously their younger brother possessed both qualities. In her mother's opinion, none of her daughter's suitors had been good enough, and my aunt aged as an unmarried, embittered copy of her mamma. My father seemed to endure them — rather than like or love them — and I was well into adulthood before I realised what an enormously strong sense of responsibility permeated his being. As his daughter, I too got my fair share of it.

At the end of an evening visit in order to tell my parents that my eleven-year long marriage had come to an end, my father saw me to the door with the parting words: 'I hope you remarry soon.' I walked away hurt, angry and offended for I had, after all, stood on my own two legs for some good fifteen years, but he did not see it like that. Whether or not I accepted or refused his money, until the day when I married, I would be his charge. If I dissolved my marriage, he and I were back to square one and he had to shoulder yet another obligation. Because my father had been among the first civilians to fly an aeroplane and drive a car, I — without much logic or psychological insight — expected him also to have some less rigid ideas. But he sadly conformed to the all too common idea of his time: women hovered on a lower stratum, had to be constantly supported on all levels, and could not be trusted to make sound decisions. Even when I was old enough to cross a street on my own, when out walking with him I had to endure his firm grip on my arm at every crossing.

My father always referred to his secretary and his female accountant as 'The hens.' I was probably fourteen or fifteen years old the day I finally boiled over. Above the big brown leather sofa in his office hung two oval photogravures in imposing golden frames. They were portraits of his father at a younger age, and of an uncle I had never known. To me both men looked very old and mysterious and as long as I can remember, these portraits had always fascinated me. I was sitting beneath them, and at his desk my father was reading through and signing the day's letters. His secretary had obviously made a mistake in one for I heard his usual, 'Oh, these hens!' I had now for some time comprehended the impact of being the speaker of veracity and opened my big mouth. 'How can you ever expect anything else with the way you have always treated them?' My father lifted his head and silently looked at me for a very long moment. I would have given my weekly allowance for his thoughts, but he only looked puzzled.

At face value I think my parents would have passed even the most rigourous mien of their epoch, but that did not prevent them from being poor teachers, and they could not understand why I was so lacking in social graces. They must have counted on osmosis but I know better. When once, their patience exhausted, they asked, 'Why can't you behave?' I told them my truth, 'You have never taught me how!' They looked at each other in total bewilderment. My mother and I for most of our lives lived in some sort of armed neutrality, but I had from early on done my very best to please my father. Without meaning to or even understanding what was happening, I was en route to becoming a puppet of my father's liking. Because of his interest in novel technology, he erroneously thought of himself as a very modern man, the epitome of openness, understanding, and freedom of choice, when in reality he was a narrow-minded dandy, typical of his time and upbringing. Within these limitations he also had some admirable traits, but before I saw them, I myself had a lot of growing up to do. My epiphany finally came a day when, unable to make up my own mind, I asked his advice and got the answer, 'You make your own choice, but you know what I would like you to do.'

Helpful? Hardly! Psychologically acceptable? Not to a child who would have stood on her head if that were to make her more loved. Although I had seen examples of it, I was not old enough to understand that my father was gravely lacking in psychological insight, and his answer was deeply troubling. On the other hand I knew what the word 'blackmail' stood for and what I had just experienced was in my childish head and heart one kind. I made the 'wrong' choice, and although there was not even any criticism, the event seemed to have set in motion a thought process: What sort of person would I become if I continued to try to be liked all the time — Petrushka's manipulated puppet or my own person? In youthful exaggeration I concluded that I was all alone. Time only partly modified that notion as I eventually found that I could, with some luck, get help and advice on many things, but when it came to the really hard questions, I *am* alone.

My father was inventive in a very practical way, and he would probably have been an excellent engineer, and a much happier human being, but due to the rules of the time, being the eldest son, he followed a pattern, or more likely was pressed into following it, and entered the family firm. After his father's premature death, the firm ceased to exist, and eventually he joined his father-in-law. Economically he did very well for himself, but he was not a happy man. An appreciative and adoring wife might in some measure have made up for his mother's shortcomings, but he unfortunately married a complicated, immature young woman who in some respects would be playing in her dollhouse all her life. My mother — the pretty middle sister of three girls — without a doubt had had an upbringing strictly following the dictates of the time. Her older sister had chosen to study law, and in due time gained attention as Sweden's first female judge in a district court. Her younger sister became a home economics teacher but my mother showed no interest in any such undertaking. More than anything else she yearned for a release from the strict rules of her home — mistakenly thinking that marriage would be the means. After having sent her to an excellent cooking school and satisfied that she was well capable as a hostess and homemaker, her parents let her have her way at the age of twenty. I doubt she had any realistic understanding of what she was getting into, and my father might have been good-looking, charming, and approved by her parents, but he was her senior by eight years and very set in his bachelor ways.

Her time of 'freedom' did not last even a full year before she became pregnant with my brother, and although there was help around the house, she was exhausted and up to her ears. With a nine-month-old baby on her hands, she found herself pregnant once again but not wanting the child, she resorted to some home remedies supposed to bring on an abortion. Nothing of the sort happened, and in due time she gave birth to an unwanted daughter. Things might have been somewhat easier if the baby had grown into a sedate little girl that resembled what she could remember of herself as a child, but her daughter was a tomboy with no interest in dolls — only a hankering for her brother's Legos, trains, and tool kits. My brother defended his possessions best he could, but when we were little I was the stronger one, and we fought more than we played.

My sole memory of a partnership dates from when I was eleven or twelve years old and returned home after an appendectomy. Then we played hospital for a while; my brother was the surgeon and I was the nurse. His tool kit provided the instruments and my normally neglected dolls suddenly became very useful as patients. However, when the last doll was mutilated, the game was over. My father did not take our destruction very seriously, but my mother was exasperated. Her first-born being her favourite, certainly it must all have been my wicked idea! Towards the end of her life she finally came out with it saying, 'I am afraid of you.' It was no news to me, but I was curious about when that feeling first emerged: at my unwelcome birth, when the riding whip once came out or when I caught her with a lie, but never said anything. It fascinated me to look at her face where the mouth proclaimed one thing, and the eyes told another story. It was a game that started early in life, and it still intrigues me.

My Great-grandmother on my mother's side was born in Strasbourg, France, and as a young bride-to-be, had come to Copenhagen, Denmark. She had six children who survived, but in the long run the marriage was not a happy one. Although they never divorced, at some point the husband moved out, and they lived separated from each other until death gathered them under one headstone. My grandmother was the second child, and I do not know what sort of life she had before her married one in Stockholm. Her mother must have been able — in spite of her marriage difficulties — to create a stable and loving home, for my grandmother remained close to her birth family and regularly took her three daughters — and later her grandchildren — to visit their Danish aunts and uncle. The subject of separation was not for small ears, and it was never talked about in front of the grandchildren. My mother told me she did not even realise, until she was almost an adult, that her grandfather moved back in with his wife and children only for the duration of their visits, then disappeared back to his own place when they had left.

My grandparents' marriage was a happy one, and although they had started out in modest circumstances, they had done well for themselves, and the atmosphere in their big home was warm and cheerful. Morfar had the lighter temperament of the two, and he was our childhood's big teddy bear, always ready for stories and play, while Mormor was more muted. But she also had her playful side, and as Mormor to her grandchildren, she was without any doubt less a disciplinarian than she had been as the mother of her own daughters. There was always an expectation of polite show, but in this home it was easy to put your best foot forward, not least because you knew that effort had its rewards! Mormor had decided that I needed to learn the alphabet and had given me a small table and chair in the music room but most of the time, after a short while, I would move to another place. Under the grand piano lay the snow-white pelt of a polar bear with a big, stuffed head. His two glass eyes never blinked, and you could without risk let your fingers slide up and down his yellowish tusks. Curling up on top of the soft pelt was much more attractive than sitting on a chair in front of a table and Mormor, who had a blessed sense for the essential, never scolded me for I had taken my alphabet book with me and studied it. When she found me, she would invariably inquire if the polar bear was not hungry? He always was, and she and I went into the dining room where she opened the doors to a big dark, richly sculptured buffet. My eyes went straight to one of the upper shelves and the white paper bag adorned with a small rococo figure in green, pink, and black. It came from Stockholm's best confectionary, and throughout my whole childhood and beyond, their bags stayed the same as did the delicious chocolates. A proper upbringing meant that you stuck your hand in the offered bag, grabbed one piece and withdrew it, saying, 'Thank you' before putting the piece in your mouth. I had a very sweet tooth, but nevertheless, some pieces *were* more desirable than others, and Mormor knew her grandchild.

'Are you sure it is the polar bear's favourite piece?' Miraculously the polar bear and I always seemed to have the same taste, and if I was shaking my head, Mormor would extend the bag and allow me to drop the piece back before she gave it a shake and offered it for a second time. With the bag still in her hand, she followed me into the music room and watched while I placed the chocolate between the tusks. Then I heard her turn and walk back into the dining room where she returned the familiar bag to its place. The sound of the big doors closing was followed by Mormor's fading footsteps, and it was time for the polar bear to give up the coveted delicacy. Mormor never forgot to ask later if the meal had been to his liking, and no matter how often the game was repeated, I always loved it.

PURGATORY WITH
SUMMER VACATION

From early on, my speech pattern was a concern because my tongue refused to pronounce certain sound combinations, and not even Mormor's patience had any effect. Before school started, I was finally sent to a specialist who, whatever the pathology, to everybody's relief successfully trained me. All the same, what followed was fourteen years of misery. I obviously suffered from dyslexia, but as the affliction had not yet found its way onto the medical charts, the presumption was, when I inverted letters and could not spell and read properly, that I was either inattentive or lazy — or both. It was of course a chicken-and-egg situation, but at the time the outcome was always scrambled eggs.

I was seven years old and had been enrolled in a very reputable private school governed by two elderly ladies who were sisters. They were always dressed in long dark skirts and white high-necked blouses and wore their grey hair in identical tight little buns. Although they did not teach any longer, nothing escaped their eyes and ears and every morning when we entered, they were there to greet us and encourage calm and concentration. I attended the school toward the end of its existence, but the ladies still honoured their initial ideas about what constituted good teaching: no more than fifteen pupils in every class and whatever your age, learning-expectations were high. The first year the classes were from nine to three o'clock with three batches of homework. I was hardly a stellar student but muddled through until in my second year I met my Waterloo. From day one, reading lessons were dreaded more than any other, and when my turn came, I wiggled out of my desk and stood up beside it, holding my book with a clammy hand while my index finger followed the lines word by word. Without any inflexion, I hesitantly pronounced every single word in a story about a mouse that had made its way into the larder. The Swedish word for larder is *skafferi* with the accent on the *i*. To my bad luck, the word came at the end of a line and was hyphenated: *ɉkaf-feri*. I read the parts as two separate words with no idea of what they meant.

Fourteen kids laughed their heads off, and before our teacher had restored some resemblance of calm and order, one of the sisters opened the door and entered. I faded back into my desk, and from then on reading lessons had moved to Purgatory — not temporary, as religious belief will have it, but everlasting. Homework was not much different, and although my mother was a perennial trainer of young housemaids, the two of us did not make a compatible team. Insecurity and fear always made my dyslexia break out in full bloom, and every afternoon became a disaster. Finally a tutor was hired, and although the cost was resented — it was after all during the Depression — it brought some relief to us all. I remember not liking her very much, but that might well have been because she and the detested homework got a dash of the same paintbrush. One day when we were unusually late, she was invited to stay for dinner, and when my father had a glass of schnapps he offered her one too. I was sent to the sideboard to fill it and did as I was told — only there were two bottles standing there — the schnapps and the foul-tasting cod-liver oil, and both contents were colourless. My father, of course unaware of what I had been up to, mischievously challenged the tutor to drain her glass, and the face she pulled with her mouth full of cod-liver oil was well worth being sent to bed on an empty stomach.

Eventually bureaucracy came to my aid. Unless the sisters brought their class sizes up to twenty pupils they would lose the government subsidy, but as they would not compromise their principles, and as they were close to retirement anyway, they decided to close their school.

I spent the following seven years in what was labelled 'a modern school' with vastly different ideas, among them no homework at all! It made life easier, but these years also fell short in providing me with a solid base of learning, or the skill to concentrate. I must have learned something, but surely not enough to graduate from dumb to less dumb! Unaware of the future consequences, I contentedly spent my after-noons in the sizeable parkland, Djurgården, where you could walk, bike or ride all year long and go skiing and skating in winter. The name dated from the time it had been the deer-hunting ground for the king and his entourage. The school for the blind resided there, in a huge red-brick building, and further out there was a restaurant with a great reputation. In adolescence their famed winter sledge parties occupied my unfulfilled romantic dreams. Mounted police patrolled the area on friendly big horses, and during the school year it was the substitute for Ulfvik, a place I loved.

Ulfvik was Mormor and Morfar's summer house some twenty kilometres from Stockholm, at the seaside. They had bought it the same year I was born and I spent all my childhood and early teenage summers there. Parental supervision, as well as dress code, eased up, and my grandparent's factotum, Eklund, who lived in one of the houses all year long, was the one who taught us to garden, to set nets, to smoke fish for Sunday lunch, and to use tools properly. My father had laid down the law once and for all: children who could not swim were not allowed in the rowboats or even near the water's edge, and even when we could swim, life jackets were obligatory when out on the water. Mormor taught us swimming in the bathhouse basin, and with all the pleasures looming, I learnt it in a very short time. When we were old enough, it was my grandmother's expectation that we should help in the fruit and vegetable gardens, but that was never a chore. I think Eklund, who had grown up on an island further out in the archipelago, had an existence to his liking, and he was patient and kind. In my memory he never aged, and I do not think I ever knew his first name. Disorder among his tools led to firm but gentle reprimands, and there was only one place that was prohibited: the dark, cool ice house. If he ever caught you sliding down the damp side of the sawdust mountain, you got evicted without any ceremonies, and Eklund would remain tight-lipped for a day or two.

In winter, when the ice was thick enough, he went out with his special saw to cut big square blocks that he then dragged up to the ice house. They were laid out like a pyramid with sawdust on top of each layer and along the sides. In summer, wearing what looked like a big black leather apron put on backward, he would make his weekly tour with one iceblock for each household. He grabbed the big block with enormous tongs, heaved it from the wheelbarrow to his back, and walked off with it to the icebox where he would slowly and expertly slide it into place. With time the procedure of course lost its fascination, but when I was still a child I would not miss that tour for anything.

Fetching the milk from the nearby farm was another obligation but seldom felt like one. In the afternoon, with a milk can dangling on the handlebar, I biked up to the farm, and if I came early enough, I would go out with the cowherd and help him get the cattle in. On very lucky days, one or two workhorses had also been left in the pasture, and he would hoist me up for a bareback ride to the stable. Waiting for the cows to be milked, a tour down to the sunless shed where all the garden produce was sold, was another pleasure. I loved all the different colours of the vegetables, but nothing could beat the sweet smells during the berry season. Once the warm milk was poured into my can, I knew that I had better turn my wheels homeward, for Cook liked the milk to still be warm when she poured it into a big bowl and put it down in the cellar overnight. First thing next morning, she would skim off a layer of pale yellow cream that promised a Sunday dinner dessert of sugared berries topped with whipped cream. The forests around Ulfvik were rich in mushrooms and an abundance of lily-of-the-valley grew wild. Everybody had his or her own secret places for picking, and they were jealously guarded. For her birthday, on June 13, it was a tradition to fill Mormor's house with the white, sweet-smelling flowers and every year carried the same worry; an early spring and you risked that they would be at the end of their season, or a late one and they would still be in bud. Some years were, as with the mushrooms, better than others, but I can not recall one single year when we were not able to bring home armfuls that filled the house for days with their delicate scent. Family and friends would arrive by boat or by car, and the big dinner was invariably the same: cooked salmon; delicate, small, roasted spring chickens with fresh vegetables; and homemade ice cream with berries.

But even this paradise had its serpent. Darkness had always frightened me, and when I was old enough to babysit my sister, younger by eight years, I was terrified from the moment our parents left the apartment. I curled up in a big wing chair in the living room and would not move until they came back. As nothing frightening had ever happened to me in the dark, there was no rationale, but that did not change anything and as I stayed silent my parents did not pick it up. At Ulfvik, the nights were darker than in the city, and when dusk fell I went inside and stayed there. From time to time, my mother would send me on an errand down to my grandparent's house after dark, and I ran as fast as I could. My big fear was that Mormor, not knowing that I was on my way, would turn off the light which shone dimly on the path between the two houses. I would have been about fourteen when it finally happened, and I remember standing there in the dark, paralysed by the biggest fear ever and unable to move. After what seemed like an eternity, it was as if the terror slowly started to seep out of me. Where this sudden sanity came from I did not know, but it made me ask myself *what* it was that I was so afraid of? The sounds that had sent me into this panic were only the wind in the trees and some small critter crawling through the dry undergrowth! There really was nothing to be afraid of, and finally common sense worked its blessed exorcism.

Although the change of school had abated academic expectations, my poor reading skills continued to brand me as the class dunce. My new teachers' softer approach, however, helped to calm the panic and it made school more tolerable. There was another girl in the class who also — although not for the same reasons — was a loner. In contrast to me, her marks were high, but she stood out because, owing to some heart trouble, she was exempt from gymnastics and sports. We became best friends, and for the next few years I spent considerable time in her home. Ingrid had no siblings, and since her father was an officer in the navy, she and her mother were often alone, but that did not affect the always lively and pleasant atmosphere in their home. In contrast to my own family, all three were avid readers, and their interest in and familiarity with books slowly, slowly had an impact, not least because I was treated as a second daughter. What so far had always been a chore, with time became pleasurable. I have stayed a slow reader, but books eventually became my friends and companions.

Even before I met her, Ingrid knew that she was destined to become an artist, but I had so far not given much thought to my future, and I do not think my parents had either. The feelings of relief and joy that my Ulfvik summers begot were probably what eventually led me to believe that I would like to become a farmer. I realised I would have to go to Agricultural College, and as part of the university system it necessitated upper secondary school exams, something my present school did not have. My father warmed to the idea of eventually becoming a gentleman farmer with his daughter running the show, and so started some tumultuous years with recurrent failures, setbacks, and changes of schools. The incongruity in course planning, between my present school and one I would have to move to, was alarming and for the first time, the price of seven years of intellectual slumber was written on the blackboard: I was one year behind in both physics and mathematics, and having had French as my first foreign language, I lacked three years instruction in English. Immediate, rapid and effective learning was badly needed and it was executed during the summer of 1940 in a boarding school outside Stockholm. The ordinary students were away on their summer holiday and we were only about a dozen adolescents, all with similar needs. To fill my lacunae was a Herculean job, and my teachers were driving me hard. That, however, led to a welcome discovery: what I had lacked was not intelligence but motivation. Once that become clear, I could work miracles — only small ones — but, to me still miracles.

Another welcome discovery was the enjoyment of company, that my profound shyness, to an alarming degree, had kept me away from. The school was very quietly — and my guess is, totally unofficially — housing a number of British airmen who had been downed over water or German occupied Denmark. Rescued and smuggled into neutral Sweden, they were only waiting to be flown back to England and bored stiff by the inactivity imposed on them. I mostly met them at meal times, but they quickly took great pleasure in broadening my English vocabulary. My appalled teacher was, to put it mildly, unhappy, as most of it was a language I should not learn, but all the same, the sheer fun of the naughtiness certainly worked. In autumn I had to pass a test to get into my new school. I managed physics and English but failed in math, and then followed a year of such dedicated studies that when spring term ended, I not only had caused damage to my eyes, but also had a tendency to faint if I got up from a chair too quickly. My mother finally noticed that something was wrong and marched me off to the family doctor. The outcome of that visit was another change of school, with a repetition of the last class. As was the intention, it became an easy year, but also a very boring one.

In the summer of 1939, presumably hoping to put some social polish on me, my father had enrolled me as a sea cadet, and it had been my first experience of any group activity outside school. What he had overlooked was that at fifteen I was by four or five years the youngest among the twenty girls on board, and we did not have much in common. They quickly formed coteries, and not to be included was fine with me, particularly as the captain and his crew were friendly and accepted me hanging around when I was not on my watch. They treated me as an adult, and in their company I probably learned more about navigation than I otherwise would have done. We sailed a beautiful wooden ketch, very different from the small boats I was familiar with, and I loved every minute of it. A long-distance sailing across the Baltic was the finale to our training, and when we dropped anchor in Gdansk, we did so as guests of the Polish navy. Their sailing ship *Dar Pomorza* was moored close to where we had anchored, and in comparison, we looked very small indeed. On our second day, the Polish cadets took us sightseeing, and at day's end we were given the tour of their ship and then dined onboard. The after-dinner dance had just started when we, without any explanation, were told to return to our ship and ordered to set sail immediately. Carrying regulation lights, we soon sailed out of the harbour, setting course for Copenhagen, Denmark. During the long night's sailing, we did not meet one single ship, but repeatedly saw lights coming up at the horizon and then quickly be extinguished. What we girls did not know was that the sabre-rattling that had gone on for months in Europe had, while we were at sea, become something much more serious. The second day after our hurried departure the bombs started to fall on Gdansk. Eventually we would learn that these mysterious lights we had observed belonged to a part of the German navy readying themselves to attack the city. Some time later, against all odds, I again met my dance partners from *Dar Pomorza*. With Polish flourish — and probably a great deal of luck — the ship had succeeded in getting out of the harbour unscathed and, without being attacked, sailed across the Baltic and up to Stockholm, where she would grace the inner harbour below Skeppsholmen for the next six years.

The Nazis occupied Denmark and Norway, and between a rock and a hard place, Sweden chose neutrality. We lacked enough military might to defend all our territory, and the government estimated, probably correctly, that we would be of greater assistance to our Scandinavian neighbours if we avoided occupation. In some small way, my family experienced the acumen of that thinking when some previously unknown distant relatives arrived from Denmark. They had been smuggled over by a fishing boat, and their baby had for security reasons been anaesthetised, but the dose had been dangerously strong. The mother stayed with us while the baby was in hospital, but once she was beyond danger, they disappeared from our lives and her husband, who belonged to the Danish underground, we never met.

The next surprise came from Norway in the shape of a sister and a brother who were distant cousins of my father and who until now had been unknown to him. The sister arrived first — frantic, as she did not know where her brother was or what had happen to him. Both belonged to the Resistance, and at the end of a day, leaving her workplace in Oslo, she had been whisked away and then smuggled over to Sweden. The Nazis had somehow found out about them and during that same day had occupied the house they shared in an outlying area of Oslo. The brother had left work before he could be warned and was already on his way home. His neighbours, who had seen the Germans arrive at his house, were almost hysterical, as they could not warn him without risking being seen doing it. Finally they came upon the idea to place lit candles in all their front windows, something they would normally only do at Christmas. To avoid any suspicions, they invited over a couple of 'safe' neighbours and staged a party.

The ruse worked, for when her brother passed and saw this unusual display, he understood that it was some sort of a warning, and although he did not know of what, he bypassed his own house and continued to walk for most of the night. He never revealed how and where he had been able to find the necessary clothing, but then managed the long hike through the forests and over the border mountains; a foot-slogging that did not end until he reached Swedish territory. When he arrived in Stockholm, his sister left us, and that was the end of my family's contact with them.

However, the lack of interface did not comprise all hands, for the brother and I did from time to time have short meetings. Luckily my parents never found out. If they had, all hell would surely have broken loose, as from time to time, I acted as a courier carrying documents in my schoolbag from one person to another in the city. I do not think it was an undertaking fraught with much danger and I seriously doubt that if there had been any great risks, my Norwegian relative would have used me. I of course never mentioned it to anybody, but I do remember feeling trusted, and that did my self-esteem a world of good. Eventually my newfound relative got his transport to England, and I never heard from him again. Or did I? Towards the end of the war, the mail one day brought a brown envelope with a Swedish stamp, and the parcel came from a publishing house. Inside was a book written in Norwegian by a Bjørn Stallare, and the preface informed that the short vignettes, giving glimpses of life in Oslo under the German occupation, had first appeared in *Norsk Tidend*, printed in England for the Norwegians there. In 1943, a Swedish publisher assembled the content into a book. There was no card and 'Bjørn Stallare' was obviously a pseudonym, but was it one for a man I had met, or was the book just a small token from a distant, thankful relative?

As an adult, I have more than once been astonished over how cocooned Sweden was during the war — and in many respects continued to be for as long as I had daily contact with my native country. I can only assume that the Depression lowered some sums in my father's company books, but I remember beggars coming to the kitchen door. With his suspicion that money would only go to buy alcohol, my father refused to give cash, but Cook had been instructed to give them food. The assumption must have been correct, at least partly, for on and off she found her sandwich packs left on the windowsill in the steep staircase. What I can not remember are any changes in our daily lives, and except for the obvious, I have that same feeling about the war years. The fact that I physically had been so close to the outbreak of the war did not really affect me, and fear was still mostly an abstraction. Stockholm of course had, like all other capitals, its fair share of espionage activities, and without ever — at least to my knowledge — being troubled by it, we happened to live in close proximity to these hubs. The British rented some apartments on the south, posher side of our building while the Germans had a spy, central on the north end facing a small, narrow street. The discovery that my father had a pistol in his night table drawer, at the time did not mean anything to me. What I of course did note was that, together with a multitude of other imports, oranges, bananas, and imported chocolates disappeared from the shops. When my sister after the war saw a banana again, she did not know what it was, or how to eat it. Textiles and certain foods were rationed, and my mother had to find hitherto unknown substitutes to keep us fed, but even if people complained, this must have been luxury compared with what the rest of Europe had to contend with. My parents listened to the radio and kept one daily newspaper, but I do not think that for most people — myself included — the raw reality was either well understood or keenly felt; at least not until the war was over. When the first pictures from the European concentration camps became available for publication, part of the press deemed them too offensive. The inside opinions differed, but, at some papers, it went as far as strike threats — for or against — but that was something I only learned about much later.

As a child I had no talents that directed me in any specific way and even when an awakening ambition started to make me more diligent, my handicaps notwithstanding, it never entered my mind that there was anything I could not become. Where this certitude originated I do not know for there were no role models in my immediate family. My aunt might have qualified, but when I was five or six years old, she had left her legal profession for marriage and motherhood. One of the conditions for acceptance at the Agricultural College was an apprenticeship period on one of their certified farms, and I figured that my long summer holiday would be a good time for getting this necessary practice. Making inquiries, I met with something unexpected: none of the farms wanted to take a girl, and I also discovered that so far the college had never had any female students. I doubt that 'glass ceiling' was even part of the language then and I had never heard of words like 'discrimination' and 'gender inequality.' All the same, now I suddenly stood face to face with these realities and I needed advice. As I could not see the use of asking my parents, I solved the problem by calling the College. The professor I spoke to must not have listened very attentively and, as a result conveniently killed two birds with one stone. On his phone was someone who wanted a summer job, and somewhere on his desk the problem to find somebody who could look after one of his scientific experiments over the summer still hung about.

Sven Hedin had been one of the last great explorers of his time and an internationally renowned specialist on Tibet and Chinese Central Asia. His book about Tibet had left me spellbound, and now at the College I learned that, during his last expedition in 1933-1935, he had collected a variety of cereal grains and brought them back to Sweden where the College started a multitude of tests to establish their different characteristics. To create a low-growing, frost-hardy variety, they were at this time cross-pollinating some of these cereals with Swedish ones, but the birds and the bees could not be counted on for scientific exactitude. The professor needed a reliable hand, but it was not until he

29

saw me in person that he realised that I was a schoolgirl and not the agricultural scientist he somehow had taken me for over the phone. Fortunately being of a sanguine disposition, he decided that, since I was standing in front of him, I could just as well have the job. For the next three months I walked in the fields day after day, feeling like God's secretary. A student, spending his summer at the College, was called upon to show me the ropes. He started by helping me to assemble the tools of my new trade: a pair of tweezers, a small brush, rainproof little bags, twine, tags, and pen and paper. I learned to judge when the ears were ripe, how to execute the pollination, and then to put a paper bag over the ears before taking down all the details about time, date, weather, and wind, etc. The boys who emptied the rat traps in the storage barns took a great pleasure in always keeping a sack of dead super-rats at hand, emptying it as close as possible to my feet when I passed by. Although I did not gratify them with the jumps and screams they so hotly hoped for, they never gave up. How could they know that I had seen Eklund empty enough rat traps at Ulfvik — although, admittedly, his catches had only been mice and certainly not grain-fed ones.

My student 'supervisor' was helpful in an unobtrusive way and also a good pal who introduced me to Uppsala. At the time, the university town appeared to be mainly populated by students and clergymen's widows who rented out their rooms in order to improve their small economies. My landlady satisfied her prying instincts by keeping close track of my comings and goings; if I came in after ten o'clock, it was a matter of debate the following day. My pal, of course, never came further than the garden gate, but that did not boost my goodwill.

The following summer, I was finally working on a real farm, thanks to the help of one of my classmates who came from a big property in the south of Sweden. He and his siblings only went to school in Stockholm, and he talked to his father, who helped land me a job. That it turned out not to be very pleasurable had nothing to do with the fact that the work was laborious, for I had always liked physical activity and had enough strength for it, but was solely on account of some wretched human behaviour. The farm was independently managed by a leaseholder who was a rather unpleasant character. I suppose that when asked if he would take an apprentice, he had not been able to resist the offer of two more hands for hardly any cost at all, and when dealing with his landlord, he probably also showed a more civilised side. Although totally absurd, in his eyes I came from 'the big house up there' and that was unforgivable! What made it so unpleasant was that I was never allowed to forget that I did not belong to their own class. Thus, it was the summer when I was introduced simultaneously to class strife and a cow shed with forty dairy cattle. The morning milking had to be finished before the milk truck pulled up at the farm, and then I had to take the herd out for grazing. A quick breakfast, then it was back to the shed to clear the dung and wash the milking machines, whereupon there was garden work waiting. I could not avoid joining the family at the midday meal, but for breakfast and supper I usually ate later than the others. The wife seldom bothered to keep the food warm, but between their hostility and cold food, I preferred the latter. In the afternoon, after more garden work, the cows had to be fetched, milked, and the heavy cans dragged to the cooler. When finally the machines were again washed, I could call it a day.

At midsummer, some spectacular rainstorms destroyed the power lines to the cowshed, and for the next forty-five days, there was no electricity. With no milking machines, my days started even earlier than before and lasted longer, for every cow was now to be entirely hand-milked, but that did not seem to worry my boss who offered no help. I was not going to give him the satisfaction of complaining, but at summer's end, it certainly was a relief to leave. He gave me a surprisingly good reference — that, as it turned out, I would have no use for.

During the following year, I thought long and hard about my future and finally decided to abandon my plans to go to Agricultural College. It had nothing to do with the experience of one dreary summer, but had its genesis on a much deeper level. My love for the 'country' life I had been afforded while growing up was real enough — and it made me a lifelong gardener — but the relief it offered had largely obscured the fact that I, to a substantial degree, was a city creature. I had with envy observed the country kids, half my age, with their instinctive knowledge of animals and farm work. For me it was not intuitive; I had to learn every bit of it, and although it was undoubtedly achievable, with my lack of natural ability the weight seemed very heavy. I had also started to go to concerts, museums, and art galleries, and as these opportunities had become more and more important, I now realised that becoming a farmer would not include such activities on a regular basis.

In spring I passed my written tests for my student examination but failed the oral and had to spend another term before I was allowed to try again just before Christmas. This time I made it and it was with enormous relief I said goodbye to a part of my life that had not only been filled with pain but worse, had not even left me with any clear idea of who I was and where to go next. Even so, after this last hurdle, I crawled out of the school system and was, if only in theory, ready for that very big expectation called Life.

TO BE OR NOT TO BE

At the time my understanding of psychology was not very developed, and I did not then see the irony in my father trying to press my brother to come into the company, as his father had done with him. The two did not get on very well, and my brother solved his problem by moving to Canada. For me it became the realisation that geographical distance could be something very useful. The announcement of giving up on the Agricultural College had not begot the blow-up I had anticipated, but one of the extenuating circumstances might have been my wish to still go to university. Although I had found Uppsala, but for my hostess, quite likeable, its relative closeness to Stockholm did not make it a good choice: yet Lund — in the south of Sweden — was sufficiently distant, preventing any expectations of homecomings during term. Even as naive as I was, I realised that I needed to present a less discourteous reason and I had an excellent one ready. I wished to take art history with Ragnar Josephson, who was a renowned professor, art historian, and writer, and, as it turned out, the very inspirational teacher he was rumoured to be. A family friend, an art historian working at the National Museum, was asked for advice and because he approved, my father was convinced. Assuming that I saw my future working at the Museum, this very kind man took it upon himself to put in a word for me, and without having asked for it, I found myself allowed to do the compulsory apprenticeship period even before the start of my university courses. The arrangement was a success on several levels. Most importantly, it allowed me to experience museum life from the inside, and without that knowledge, I might well have started on another career, that most likely in the end would also have been a mistake. But into the bargain, this was the summer when the Museum presented a big exhibition by Van Gogh, and to be allowed a prolonged period of time among all his originals was an immense experience. The crates had arrived overnight and were opened one by one in the morning, and the galleries — emptied for the exhibition — slowly filled with supreme colour and energy. So far, all I had seen of Van Gogh's paintings had been reproductions, and although some of them had been very good, this was something entirely different. The excitement of that morning would stay with me for a very long time. By the end of this rich summer, I went south and, not surprisingly, found that Lund in many ways resembled Uppsala. With great luck I was able to rent a small, newly built student apartment and thankfully did not have to be under the thumb of another landlady. Once was enough!

Considering my handicap, it was strange that literature had eventually become a pleasure and the only subject where I had been truly successful. For that I had the unusual teacher who blessed my last two years in school to thank. He hardly ever gave me back a composition that was not marked A+ for form and content, but also 'decorated' with his spelling corrections in red ink. Invariably he would make a note at the end of the essay citing the number of these mistakes, but then continue to laud the rest. My composition for the Student Examination followed the trend with an A+, although the tension of the moment had created seventeen misspellings! Miraculously enough, the external examiners left it alone. No wonder then that I would start with Literature, but I had also gone to Lund convinced that, after the all-too-long nightmare of years filled with too many, mostly uninspired, pedestrian lessons with little or no space for ideas, ahead of me lay 'free' studies — the pleasure of also thinking instead of simply learning by rote — but I had forgotten that oranges are not the only fruit.

Instead of the openness and human intelligence I had been used to, my professor in Literature was an old-fashioned disciplinarian and a pedantic, dry, and very boring lecturer. To everybody's misfortune, the class size was enormous, and unfortunately it had nothing to do with the love of literature, but was simply the sad by-product of the university laws: a BA had to be composed of a minimum of three subjects and carry a total computation of at least six marks. The result was that a crushing majority went for their last 'filling-in-point' in Literature — looked upon as an 'easy' subject. To manage his workload, the professor lectured for three hours one week and then gave written exams the next, a routine that continued for the whole term. What made me revolt was not the tediousness of it all but the one-sidedness; one week I had listened to how to interpret *Hamlet* and the following one, if I did not repeat exactly what I had heard, I did not pass!

After some time of this rote learning I had had enough, and lacking the savvy to know what I was setting myself up for, I approached the man and asked to instead be examined at term's end. Was I not satisfied with his teaching methods? I had not anticipated the question and without time to think did not come up with a passable answer. Not that it really mattered, for I had already put the hangman's noose around my neck, and when it was time, this man, with some sadistic tendencies, yanked at it. He had already detected my lack of 'knowledge' of birth and death years in the literary canon and started the exam by firing off ten such questions before he threw me out. For some reason, my brain has always had a deep aversion for retaining dates, and my practical side had long ago come to the conclusion that I could always look it up when I needed to be precise, so why bother? I thought that it was more important to know in what order the works had been created, and that was a question I could answer correctly. I did not register for Literature the following term.

Classical Archaeology was interesting enough, although a bit dry in the beginning, but Art History was passionate. Both subjects got a bit more of my time, but I am afraid Latin did not. The University had a strange edict saying that you could not take Art History without having had some Latin — how much was never disclosed — so every Saturday morning I joined a motley group of law students, future doctors, and the likes of myself, who all had succeeded in leaving school without any knowledge of the complexity of Latin grammar or how Caesar had conducted his wars. It was well known that there would be no final exams, and as it was really just *pro forma*, an attendance certificate was all we needed. The Professor giving the course knew that we knew, but he loved the language and made a truly heroic effort to share this love. A beanstalk of a man, he was full of humour and invariably good-natured. This was put to the test when I had played hooky one beautiful autumn Saturday morning and then, without warning, met him in the afternoon. He had given his morning lecture while I had fallen for an invitation to go for an early picnic lunch and a long forest walk. I had not been forewarned that we would both be guests at the same traditional Martinmas goose dinner on an estate in the country. The professor had obviously just arrived, saw me approaching across the courtyard, and loudly greeted me with, 'Salve Puella!' followed by a deep bow. Even with my rudimentary command of Latin, I knew that 'puella,' besides being used for 'pupil' also has a connection to 'pupil-la,'as in disciple, but also charmingly translates to 'the apple of my eye.' We had a very enjoyable evening.

A young theatre director from the nearby city of Malmö had started to form a small, informal theatre company at the University. I joined the group and we staged a number of plays, and we even, with considerable success, toured in the province. For some unaccountable reason, when I stood on the stage my shyness fell off me like a torn old rag. Stepping out of my old skin and entering that of a character was neither easy nor without pain, but the process had an enormously deep attraction. The more roles I appropriated, the more natural it felt. Compared with the ideas I had earlier entertained, this touched a much deeper and more fundamental level, and without obliterating the negatives, I in earnest envisioned it as a way of life. Nevertheless, old insecurities whispered: *Are you really capable?*

When a new academic year started, the Literature professor was on a sabbatical, and two younger assistant professors shared his duties. Still determined to include literature in my BA, I resumed my studies, and at the end of spring, got the marks I had aimed for. This examiner was thorough enough, but at the same time a pleasant human being, and once the serious part was over, he kindly offered me tea, and we had a cordial but serious conversation. I let on that I had always been very unsure of what to do with my BA, but it was a surprise when my host brought theatre into the conversation. He mentioned that he had seen our theatre performances and asked if I had not considered becoming a professional actress? To him it seemed evident, and for me it became the affirmation I needed and had been hoping for.

The theatre school at Dramatiska Teatern in Stockholm had a very good reputation, and the theatre itself, with an amazing assembly of talented actors and very gifted directors, was in a hugely vibrant period. It was far from easy to get into the school, and what I needed before anything else was a good prep school, and Stockholm had one. I paid my parents a visit and announced my plans. My father, with a very different outlook on things, threatened to stop paying my allowance, to which I said 'Fine' and left. The following day I saw Gösta Therserus at his theatre school, where I got accepted for the autumn term, and then set about to find a full-time summer job. It materialised at my uncle's office. He showed more understanding than his brother, but we were discreet about the arrangement. The last thing was to find somewhere to live and that turned out to be difficult. One of my former teachers who, in my last year at school, had let me borrow her small flat when she was away on holiday, once again came to my rescue, but that only took care of the summer. Unless you could pay 'key money' there was no hope to get your hands on even the smallest place. I placed an ad in the papers, offering my Lund apartment in exchange for something in Stockholm, and went back south. I saw my landlord who reluctantly, after a lot of arguing, agreed to let me proceed with an exchange, packed my things, and returned to my hometown, while in my heart I thanked Lund for the good it had done me.

My ad yielded only one answer, a hand-written note with an address but no telephone number. I made my way to the south part of town and found a surprise — or rather two. Surrounded by four- and five-storey bland apartment buildings squatted two low wooden houses, certainly a good hundred years old, and the address indicated one of them. Somehow reluctant to enter, I went across the street and stood looking for a while, and I could see somebody moving in an upper room. Eventually a man came out, approached me, and asked if I was the person who wished to exchange an apartment. He appeared to be in his middle twenties and clearly suffered a substantial hangover, but he did not emit any danger signals. I followed him up and from the landing entered a diminutive kitchen with a sink, a cold-water tap, and a short bench top with a two-burner gas cooker. Next came a small room with a round, white-tiled stove, and finally, facing the street, a slightly bigger room, also with a heating stove. The loo was down in the yard, and for the price of five kronor, the City emptied it once a month. That was it. To find something as antediluvian as this in 1950s Stockholm was almost absurd. Who was the landlord and had he given the exchange his blessing? When was this man, who still had not told me his name, thinking of leaving? He assured me that the landlord was a relative of his, and I did not need to see him as he had already given his permission, and as for leaving, he would be out tomorrow. Nothing of this sounded quite right, but I said that I would think it over and be back in an hour.

Out on the street I noticed a sign for a pottery store and went over and looked in the window. The display looked strangely familiar, and when I entered the workshop I also recognised the potter. She was Danish, and, together with her husband, had been a craft teacher at the boarding school where I had spent the summer that was the beginning of my wobbly way to graduation. Grete made tea, and in her opinion it was worth a try to get the little apartment across the street. I left with her telephone number and a promise to, in exchange for his keys and his lease, give this still-nameless man a note with my co-ordinates in Lund.

To my surprise, he did leave the keys, the lease, and an unbelievably dirty place. Grete lent me all the paraphernalia a real scrubbing demanded, and I rolled up my sleeves. After a couple of hours, a very angry man stormed in and dangled a paper in front of my sweaty face. I stopped scrubbing and looked at an eviction order — but not in my name. It took a while for him to calm down, and then we started to sort things out — sort of. He was the actual owner of the building but no relative of the tenant who had not paid his rent for a number of months and who had no right to sublease the place. I had to leave immediately. End of discussion!

Even a rudimentary roof is better than no roof at all, and with my back to the wall I managed to deliver a number of arguments in my favour. Look at what I was doing! Once the place was clean I was going to paint it, and it would not cost him a cent. Then and there I even offered him the rent money for the first month, and if I later defaulted, nothing prevented him from *then* evicting me from a clean and improved place. And for the cherry on the cake, I could give him an address where he could pursue the 'skunk.' The avalanche of all this logic had its intended effect: I was promised — and later received — a legally binding lease, paid my rent with commendable regularity, and I never saw my landlord again.

My furniture arrived from Lund, and it became, for a couple of years, a very cosy little place, although dreams of an inside loo and a shower were, not least in winter, a recurring fantasy. Creature comforts, however, nice as they are, would almost certainly also have made the place unaffordable. When my new address reached the post office in Lund, my mail was forwarded, and I found my monthly check from my father's office. It went back unopened, although I took the trouble to go to the post office and have them stamp the envelope so one could see that it had been returned from Stockholm. If he did not like my choice of career, I was not to take his money to reach my goal!

Conscious that when the theatre school started I would only be able to work on weekends and after class during the week; I knew I had better save as much as I possibly could, and I spent a very frugal summer. Came autumn my darling uncle kept me on with work that could be done after office hours, Saturdays I did cleaning jobs, and Sundays I cooked a week's worth of dinners for a family with four kids and parents who both worked outside the home. It was a heavy load, but almost all the students at the school were in the same boat, and although cleaning has never been one of my favourite jobs, my income was dependable. When the second term started, I had to make a choice of three roles suited for the auditions at Dramatiska Teaterns school. You were expected to perform without any makeup or props, on a naked stage, and with a student at the school reading rejoinders from the wings. If your part required it you were allowed the luxury of a chair! I would be miscast in any ingenue role, and my interest and liking had anyway always been for drama. After consideration, we agreed on parts from Strindberg, Lorca, and Shakespeare. The school only admitted five or six students each year, and the number of applicants was overwhelming — the culling between the first and second tests, draconian. Shakespeare's Cordelia from *King Lear* took me to the second, and Lorca's Yerma to the third, where I performed Strindberg's Queen Kristina, my favourite role among the three. After some horrible waiting time, I was called up and told that I had not made it into the school, but that I was welcome back the following year, and then should 'show more of myself and less of my teacher!' It was brutal, but even worse, it left me totally clueless. The local theatres in Malmö and Gothenburg also had schools, but they had already done their selections. The director I had met in Lund was my only contact in the theatre world, and he had left the theatre in Malmö and could not be found. Another year of preparation did in itself not deter me, but where would I find the guidance? Gösta Therserus 'offered' to let me continue at his school, but after what I had been told, what was the use of that? On the grapevine, the reputation of the two other theatre schools in Stockholm was not promising, and a visit to each of them seemed to confirm it. I was completely cornered and could not see *any* way out. Any other setback or misfortune I had suffered was incomparable to this profoundly devastating defeat. Deeply scarred, I finally had to let go.

More than anything else, I needed time to think, and a six-month temporary employment at the Swedish Export Association's library afforded just that. Although import and export to me seemed to have precious little to do with the subjects I had pursued, it was my academic background that landed me the job. But never mind; it was thankfully not even close to theatre, and if the job did not exactly pour balm on my wounds, it was a welcome distraction which demanded my full and undivided concentration. A chance meeting in the library finally made my life slowly take a turn for the better. L. was a senior journalist at a prestigious newspaper in another city. Since he was on an extensive research job, he was frequently up in Stockholm, and we developed a relationship with mutual benefits. He was in what appeared to be the last stage of a very messy marriage and could do with a lover who did not expect a marriage proposal. His easy company, rich on human and intellectual qualities, did me a world of good, and he even took my need to lick my wounds with admirable patience. He also one day altered my future life by saying: 'Don't you realise that you would be a very good journalist?' I looked up in astonishment for *that* had never crossed my mind.

I was not yet ready to jump into anything new, but what he had said stayed with me, and I started to analyse what in my studies had really made me enthusiastic and what had not. Searching for the facts excited me, and I liked the ordering and sorting-out process, but once the pattern was clear and understood, I wanted to move on. It amused me to speculate over different possibilities, but I had no illusions about having a scientific mind and could not see anything wrong with that. Possibly for the first time, I was able to look at myself without attributing a value system where 'good' and 'bad' were the bookends with very little in between. Growing up the way I had must have inflicted more harm than I had realised. Eventually the person I had replaced at the library came back from her maternity leave, and my time was up. The seed L. planted had by now germinated; some research divulged that there was an academic course in journalism given in Stockholm. If, over the summer, I could get three month's newspaper practice, I would be eligible.

THE DRIVING FORCES

My job at the Swedish Export Association and L.'s recommendations helped to land me a summer job at *Sundsvalls Tidning* in northern Sweden. With my apprenticeship still a couple of month away, I looked around for another short-term job. To apply for a job at the *Gazette* when you suffer from dyslexia might look like madness, but it was not an idea originating in fool's paradise. At some point I had discovered that, when in doubt about the spelling of a word, if I wrote down the alternatives, I would see which one looked to be correct. The method was not 100% foolproof, but time and repetitive use made for a surprising success rate. While writing, I still inverted letters, but when proofreading that was something I would detect, so — without mentioning my handicap — I sent in my application. After three months and without any mistakes to my name, I left the *Gazette* and went north to see the midnight sun for the first time in my life.

Sundsvall was a relatively big, predominantly industrial town and the paper a family concern: the owner was also the editor, his wife covered Food and Mode and the two other journalists were family friends as well as old hands at the paper. I had been invited to board with one of them. People were very friendly, and I was gently eased into the group and taught the alphabet of my future trade. When it was discovered that I did not have a driver's licence, I was sent off to driving school, with the paper covering the costs. My teacher was an air pilot, moonlighting as a driving instructor, and as I had never been behind a wheel, I could not have asked for better teaching. The first day he took me halfway up a very steep hill, switched off the engine, and asked me to start the car. My panicky foot on the gas pedal generated a lot of noise, but we only slid backwards until I was made to use my ears and listen to the engine sound, gently balancing my two feet between the gas and the brake pedals and simultaneously operating the hand brake. After nine more lessons, I passed my licence test.

The following Sunday, I was handed a camera and a map, put behind the wheel of one of the paper's big Mercedes, and sent off to take a picture and do an interview. My destination was a small holding in the middle of endless woods, hours and miles away from any other habitation. The object for my article was a seventy-five-year-old man on his first visit back to the two-room croft that he, as a fifteen-year-old, had left for America and the gold rush. He had slowly learned a new language, lived in a big city and lost almost all of his Swedish, but not his childhood memories. Alas, now the meeting between the reality and his sixty-year-old dream was not as sweet as he had expected. It was not a story that would ever have had much chance in a big city paper, but here in the province it was newsworthy. The summer was filled, especially on weekends, with these kinds of jobs, and they were immensely instructive. Come Friday, I knew that the only really boring job of the week would be mine: covering a lengthy list of parishes and taking down all the minutia that has such importance in small communities. As the only seven-day-a-week newspaper, *Sundsvalls Tidning* published on Sundays a wealth of obituaries, births, engagements, Sunday meetings, you name it. The necessity of names being correctly spelled was hammered into me from the day I arrived, and there was proof of the consequences of sloppiness! The paper had once or twice gained a subscriber made irate upon seeing his name misspelled by one of the other papers, and they did not wish for the same thing to happen to them.

My driving instructor had promised to take me up flying if I passed my licence test the first time, and he kept his promise. I had never been in a plane but took to his little two-seater like a fish to water. He again became my instructor, but now with a flying certificate in view. During the summer the forest companies were in great need of aerial fire controls, and they paid handsomely for this service. In practical terms, it meant that you could clock up your required flying hours for a minimal cost, and I spent as much time in the air as the newspaper work allowed. The written tests were more difficult, but I got through them one by one, and when the apprenticeship at the paper came to an end, I had started to fly solo and was well on my way to a certificate. Once back in Stockholm, it was a different situation. The costs were high, and when my studies started, there was neither time nor money for such high-flying pleasures.

To go back to university was not without a slight tinge of angst, but now, with a realistic picture of my future, the step had a relevance that earlier had been lacking. To start with, I felt that the teaching was thought-provoking and also often interesting, but fairly soon discovered that the content was academically conservative and quite narrow in its scope. A lack of vision permeated most of the teaching: the possibility of technical evolution was hardly talked about — even as a possibility. The tutoring was concentrated on the reporting side, while the equally crucial sphere of investigative journalism was hardly given any attention. Although at the time the expression was not yet coined, the idea of 'thinking outside the box' had not been on the course plan!

My work at the Swedish Export Association's library had alerted me to two things: that the economy and the technical evolution are the two forces that — whether we like it or not, or are even aware of it — exert the strongest pressure on our lives. I had never seen my own situation as a part of the whole, and I soon realised that around me floated a mass of the equally badly informed. My second discovery was that those who wrote articles on the subjects mostly did it in a heavy, uninspiring — and for ordinary people often unintelligible — language. Precious little was to be found that would attract and inform us, and we were the ones who really needed this information. Here was obviously an almost empty space, and I had no difficulty seeing myself filling it.

Although the class on the whole was intent as well as open-eyed, we were the products of a relatively isolated country, and for most of us it was a surprise to find that 'news' was not one and the same thing all over the planet. There was, however, not much proof that this startling discovery also provoked any thoughts about the differences and the sameness among races and cultures! When, on the subject *What Is News?* we learned that in Finland it was not unusual for the Monday papers to have a small notice with the caption 'Knifed over the weekend' containing nothing more than a list of names, our first reaction was one of superiority. At that time in Sweden a knifing, let alone several, was still newsworthy. Eventually, even Swedes would see the day when a changing economy, together with information overload, forced us to open our eyes to new realities. In an effort to give the amorphous 'news' a face, one of our professors put it to us that reader attention has much more to do with familiarity than with altruism. He held forth that Smith will be more interested in reading that a cat has sneaked into Brown's kitchen and made off with the dinner chicken, than that one hundred thousand Chinese have drowned in the Yellow River. Smith and Brown know each other, at least by sight, but neither has most likely ever met a Chinese person (we are talking about the 50s), and do not know where the Yellow River runs.

All this sounded reasonable, and it certainly confirmed my summer's lessons. Our language teacher fought an uphill battle, and although we did gain some valuable knowledge about writing our articles clearly and succinctly, we never made peace over the art and language of captions. We felt his rules were too square and did not make allowances for either the restriction of space, or our love for wordplay, and when no arguments — even these supported by figures — had any effect, the class spent a merry weekend fabricating a newspaper where all captions strictly followed his rules regarding content, but in doing so, they, as we saw it, sadly lacked all allure; our super additions undoubtedly added both life and colour, but the paper's right-hand-side was now a happy delirium of extended strips. Before spending time on comparing and criticising our handiwork, he made us make a 'normal-looking' edition. That old fox knew his trade, and to add insult to injury we then had to see him reduce our unorthodox version to prescribed lengths — the bite still buttonholed.

Through meetings with management and journalists from the Stockholm papers and intense use of their archives, we got a fairly good understanding of what we could expect after graduation. The big weekend supplements had, during the war, shrunk considerably, and even when the paper rationing was lifted, they did not come back to their old, fat formats. These supplements had been the bread and butter for a number of freelance journalists, but as they had been forced to look for other sources of income, freelance work for the daily papers did not exist on a regular basis. Female journalists were not common either, and the few who were around would normally be found in the kitchen and fashion sectors. The exception was *Dagens Nyheter, DN* for short. One of two competing liberal morning papers in Stockholm, it employed two high-profile female journalists: Barbro Alving, who wrote under the pen name Bang, and Pernilla Tunberger who, although she covered their food section, did it in a very unique way. Her weekly page, sometimes with reports from America and various corners of Europe, brought Sweden a new, more diverse, often simplified style of cooking. Her following was such that sectors of the food industry as well as the bigger grocery stores had to listen. The consumers now wanted French baguettes for their weekend dinners, and without any help from dentists or dieticians, Tunberger single-handedly arrived at reforming the Swedish bread baking industry. Sugars disappeared from most breads. New vegetables showed up on the grocery store shelves, spices multiplied. Dill, salt, and sugar got healthy competition. I admired Tunberger the journalist, and I cooked her recipes with enthusiasm, but professionally I had no wish to follow in her footsteps.

I was not to become a new Bang either. She was one of a kind: with a keen eye for human folly and weakness, a deep fondness for humour, and an elegant style. She was firm in her values and called a spade a spade. Bang came to our class only once, and although she made us laugh a lot, she also left us with clearly defined and lasting thoughts about our responsibilities. Another lecturer, somewhat younger than our ordinary teachers and noticeably different, was Hans Werner, also a *DN* journalist. He had started as a general news writer, but when I met him he had his own page 'Technology and Research' and his ambition was — in his own words — 'to write about what the expert does in a language that everybody can understand.' As well as a real understanding of how radically the Second World War had changed our world, and with no interest in living in any other, he also had a natural instinct for writing factually without being boring. As his and my own interests and ambitions ran in the same groove, we soon found each other compatible company, and lecture time extended into companionship that finally led to marriage.

Sundsvalls Tidning had mentioned that I would be welcome back as a proper journalist the following summer, and it was not only flattering but also tempting. It meant that I could take up flying again. If I hesitated, it was because the year had very seriously brought home the awareness that if I desired to swim against the current with any hope of success, I had to be a cracking good journalist. To go back to something I already knew was not an advancement, and when a summer job opened up at *Göteborgs Handels- och Sjöfarts-Tidning* — *GHT* or *Handelstidningen* in daily parlance — I knew it *was* a fabulous opportunity.

GHT was a liberal morning paper started in 1832, but it had very nearly come to its demise during the Second World War. Its legendary editor-in-chief, Torgny Segerstedt, had since the early 30s relentlessly fought for democracy, for freedom of the press, and against Nazism. During the war this not only led to conflicts with the official Swedish position of neutrality, but the widespread German sympathies in Sweden also made his subscribers abandon *GHT* in droves, thereby bringing it dangerously close to bankruptcy. Segerstedt never wavered in his beliefs and succeeded in keeping the paper going. Finally, halfway through the war, the Swedes started to see what Germany under Hitler really had turned into. In spite of age-old feelings of insecurity regarding Russia, more and more people started to turn in favour of England and USA and Segerstedt slowly got his readership back. The paper held a unique position in the Swedish news world, and a job there was priceless. Segerstedt was still at the helm when I came to *GHT,* and two of his long-time colleagues were working in the newsroom. One was the paper's only female general news journalist, who took me under her wing in a gentle but effective way. The other was the night editor, a short, white-haired man not often given to small talk. So when he one night, reading through my first big article, said, 'This is good,' it was music to my ears, although my eardrums were still aching.

Nobody had had the foresight to tell me that earplugs would be a good idea when I took on the assignment, so without any protection, I had, together with one of the sport journalists, spent two days at the summer's big, international car-racing event. My mission was to write 'an atmospheric piece for the first page' of the Monday paper. The cool drivers, the noise and the fumes, the presence of a fraternity that I had no prior knowledge of, the almost ballet-choreographed precision and amazing speed of work in the pit stops, the wives and girlfriends decked out in attire spanning from sedate to provocative, the hangers-on — it certainly had been 'atmospheric' and full of arresting material, but Sunday night it needed judicious selection and merciless sorting out. 'Edit' and 'paste' were not yet at our fingertips — you banged feverishly on your typewriter, read it through, and then used scissors and tape until at the very last minute when, with the deadline rapidly approaching, you *had* to dump your efforts on the old man's desk. The byline in next day's paper took me by surprise; it was the first time I saw my name in such large sized print. If I later could return to Stockholm with a respectable number of big articles to my name, it was in no small measure thanks to the guidance of these two knowledgeable and generous people.

Afternoon papers in general did not have a very good reputation, but in Stockholm *Aftonbladet* was an exception. P. G. Peterson, the editor-in-chief, had a reputation as a first-rate journalist and a demanding boss, but we had an easy rapport. He had liked what I presented him as proof of work, and when I returned to Stockholm, he started to give me a string of bigger articles for the paper's Saturday supplement. I could not have asked for better: Most of these articles meant interesting research work and enough time to really polish the writing. It also meant exposure; your name was up there in readable print, and as a freelance female journalist with interests that differed from the expected, it was something I needed.

My relationship with Hans Werner continued, and as he still lived at home I had also started to get to know his family. His father was a vicar, his mother a schoolteacher, and Hans was the oldest with two brothers and a teenage sister. It was a very busy household, but also one in which people genuinely loved each other and took pleasure in each other's company. I was effortlessly and very generously brought into the fold, and when eventually Hans and I got engaged, they all seemed genuinely pleased. Other people were less acquiescent, and the day after our engagement notice had appeared in the papers, we were both called in to our respective bosses. After the congratulations came the warnings. From *DN*'s point of view, I worked for a competitor, which of course was true, but *DN* was not in favour of employing married couples. They were presumed to put extra pressure on scheduling by demanding the same days off and simultaneous holidays! There was not much the paper could legally do, but Hans was given a firm warning to keep work and home life well separated. On my side, P.G. Peterson offered genuinely warm congratulations followed by fatherly advice. He also told me that his boss had demanded that he no longer employ me, an order P.G. had refused. As long as nothing untoward happened, he was not — for unjustified fears — letting go of what he considered a good journalist. That was the sort of backbone I thought I saw in the man, and it had been one of my initial reasons for approaching him. It felt good to see my judgement positively confirmed, and I appreciated to have been told.

Hans and I discussed the day's events, but as neither of us was compelled to either end our relationship and/or our occupations as they presently existed, we carried on as we had intended. Journalism was only one of our common interests, so we had little incentive to rehash the day's work at home and over the years neither of us ever encountered any problems. All the same, the idea that we could constitute a threat to each other's well-being, in the long run probably sedimented differently in the male and the female subconscious. It is possible that what had been said — especially to Hans at the time of our engagement — had become one small part, among several others, that caused the rafters to slowly split and finally, some eleven years later, caused the roof of our marriage to come crashing down.

SURPRISE, SURPRISE

Hans and I formed a very compatible foursome with one of my cousins and her husband, who had inherited the most charming qualities from a Swedish father and a Russian mother. When work allowed, we often spent Saturday evenings together over a good dinner and always stimulating conversation, but one specific Saturday turned into a disaster and all because of that cable-filled box that always promises so much but seldom delivers. My cousin had fallen for this latest toy that had not been on the Swedish market for very long. The dinner was as good and enjoyable as ever, but then for the rest of the evening she refused to switch the darn thing off, hoping, against her better judgement, that the next program would be better. For the very first time Hans and I returned home sadly disappointed and not very pleased, having been forced to assist at one of the never-ending birth efforts of Swedish TV.

My introduction to TV had thus not been very positive, but what eventually, against all odds, brought me back to it was the revelation that 'one image is worth a thousand words' was much more than a stock phrase; it *was* reality! For some time already, reader resistance to long articles had become very perceivable, and although you could use illustrations, shorter paragraphs, and other tricks to visually lighten the look, the need for even a minimum of explanations of complicated science still created lengthy articles. The readers for whom I was writing consequently often eluded me. I had grappled with this problem for quite a while before I finally saw a clear pattern. The readers were not very likely to change, and if they did, it would most likely be for the worse, *but* I was changeable. The print journalist was to become an image journalist! People bought more and more TV sets, but seldom reached for the switch-off button and here I saw a possibility to open their eyes and minds to the fact that there was far more to the atom than only the bomb, and that there might exist economic propositions even more creative than running away to the circus. I was convinced that, if you stopped making it look like 'illustrated radio,' TV could be a fabulously entertaining *and*, at the same time, informative forum. If it was informative, it could be 'educational,' and I could not, and still can not, see that in a negative light. 'Educational' and 'boring' are not inherently synonymous even if lack of knowledge and/or talent among program makers often enough makes it look as if they are. I was at a loss to understand why most of the time they did not exploit TV's mobility and inherent image richness, and eventually I made an appointment with the appropriate TV person. As soon as my lack of proper film knowledge was exposed, I was shown the door. I regarded the gesture as not only offensive but also utterly short-sighted. By then I knew that I had been able to learn a number of very different things, so why not film?

Svensk Filmindustri seemed the ideal place to work. They produced a weekly news reel, but I was told that it was not a money-maker and only kept going because of tradition. They were not prepared to let me work there even without pay, but offered me a job in their publicity department. As I could not see how this would teach me much about filmmaking, I tactfully declined and called the next studio — an act that would instantly transform me from established journalist to a pathetically unskilled assistant editor at Europa Film. The studio director negotiated my employment during this initial telephone call. On my first day at the studio, I understood that it was our conversation that had brought home how alarmingly close the start of Wic Kjellin's five-week summer holiday was. She was the studio's only editor; her absence would leave him not only without his factotum, but also with an empty editing room. I was asked to start the following day, but as I had some loose ends to tie up, I insisted on my need for another week. The morning I first faced Wic, it hit me that I had just five more days to learn the ropes!

Miraculously, I somehow survived those weeks without creating more than one catastrophe, and that one stayed a secret between me and the night watchman. One afternoon, somebody left me a big 16 mm reel and some instructions of what to do with it. Once finished, I lifted, in a very dangerous and totally unprofessional way, an unusually big and not very tightly spooled reel off the editing table. Before I could blink, the centre bobbin hit the floor, trailing with it a rushing serpentine of film. I finally came to my senses and plunked the rest of the 'cake' on the floor. That's where the night watchman found me hours later when he came to his station outside my editing room door. The open door, the lit room and a snivelling sound made him investigate, and it must have been a sorry sight because he sat down beside me and for quite a while helped to untwist the serpentine and force the bobbin back in place.

Wic had been a negative cutter[1] for some twenty years, and when I met her, she had been a film editor for about five. She was an honest and generous instructor, who with diligence taught me the basics, and if it was not exactly a time of watching fireworks, it certainly brought home how meticulous one needed to be. When I was not needed in the editing room she did not mind me trying my hands at other things. The studio also produced records and had a big music department, and I got a taste of more than just editing. When eventually I joined Svensk Filmindustri, where the structure was stricter and much tighter, I realised how lucky I had been.

The film and TV industries were not the best of friends so, when I sought employment at Europa Film, I had naturally been taciturn about my future plans. That I only intended this to be a three-month employment, after which I would go back to journalism and with the greatest glee make the TV bosses aware that I had added film knowledge to my other assets, was of course never mentioned. When autumn arrived it was completely unexpected to be told that the studio wished to keep me on for good. I knew that I had barely skimmed the surface of film knowledge and that my earlier estimation of the time needed had been somewhat optimistic, but at the same time I was also convinced that I had learned enough to be able to handle TV. I talked to Hans about my options, and he listened — attentively as always — but did not offer any personal opinions; it was my job and my choice.

Contrary to a good number of people in the milieu I came from, I did not see my hitherto zigzag route through life in a negative light —

quite the contrary. In my mind I had gathered skills and knowledge that were an asset, not the least for a journalist, and until now I had regarded this latest know how only as a natural addition. It had never crossed my mind that it might be the means to its own end. More than once I have counted myself lucky that L. had seen in me something I myself had not detected, and had helped to steer me into a field I very much enjoyed and obviously was good at. I was also now acutely aware of something new and very notable: this latest learning curve had been easier than any before. For the first time, the concept of 'learning' had dropped its up to now dominant, uniquely tough-donkeywork aspect, and 'intuition' and 'talent' had suddenly found some voice. It had been a surprise to me to see Wic, with all her experience, hesitating between different alternatives, yet I seemed to have an instinctive understanding of the best solution. I was both puzzled and fascinated by this discovery, but not yet entirely clear about what to do with it. I do not think I had the slightest inkling then, that the magic of images had already not only cast its spell over me, but had also put its claws into me.

I obviously had some soul-searching to do. Was I prepared to give up journalism and my wish to develop it on the TV screen? I had no unambiguous answer, but for some time, on and off I had started to feel that Hans and I had some sort of silent competition going on in the house — something that was not really good for our marriage. There were no concrete signs, only a slight unease on my part, and I asked myself if it would disappear if I did not return to journalism.

After much reflection, I wholeheartedly accepted the offer from Europa Film and would never regret it, but in due time I would also learn that not only had my instinct been correct, my action had only acted as a temporary band-aid. Hans' best friend — a man with considerable psychological insight — after our divorce, pointed out that the only two occupations that Hans would without reservations have accepted in a wife, were teacher or nurse! He was undoubtedly correct, but I all the same deplored my former husband's unwillingness to put problems on the table. Hans thought discussing them would make them even worse — I thought it would clear the air!

To me the laboratory was unknown territory, but one of the things I had discovered in Wic's editing room was how often her intimate knowledge of negative cutting prevented her from making mistakes that later in the process could have had very costly consequences. In my second year at the studio, the film industry endured a lengthy strike, and Wic and I had no work. All the same, we were expected to clock in at the studio every morning. Quickly fed up with doing nothing, I thought it was the perfect time to find out what the studio's laboratory had to offer and went to see the director. He listened patiently to my request, diplomatically called it 'an interesting idea,' and promised to think about it. Obviously he did not understand what I had to gain and did nothing at all. I finally made daily visits to his office, and when he could no longer stomach the sight of me, he grabbed his telephone, called the lab manager, and informed him that he could expect me the following morning.

For the next six months I made my slow but steady way through a film laboratory, mentored by a man who had spent his entire adult life there but who now was close to retirement. He still kept up his high demands and through uncompromising drills taught me every aspect of laboratory work — even hand-bleaching fades as they used to be done before mechanisation took over. I was not 'promoted' before he was satisfied with my work; this way I got a good understanding of what takes place between the editing room and the cinema. To have nagged my way into the laboratory was probably one of the smartest things I did during those two years, although it was not until later that I would fully understand how important it had been. Even at the shaky beginning, this specific knowledge enabled me to edit a work print in such a way that the negative cutting was never compromised. Equally important: I was never forced to take 'No' for an answer when human laziness pretended something could not be done. I *knew* what was achievable and thus was able to argue until I got what I wanted.

Advantageous as all this was, in 1959 it was clear that I had nothing more to learn at Europa Film and gave notice. However, I still wished to stay in the film business and started to look around. Calling

Svensk Filmindustri, I had better luck than the first time. Their chief editor was on sick leave, and by sheer coincidence, their assistant editor had been fired the day before! I was called to an interview with the studio director — a tall, pompous man who did not even invite me to take a seat — and who clearly was not at all happy with the mere thought of a female editor. With a non-functioning editing room, he was not left much choice and finally, barely concealing his reluctance, gave me a three-month probationary contract as assistant editor. My good performance obviously did not change his mind, and he showed the same lack of enthusiasm when he later had to tell me that I was on a regular contract.

So, was there in reality glass ceilings and discrimination in democratic Sweden? Officially no, as the law prohibited it, but the old, stale traditionalists found ways. You could, for example, not advertise for female negative cutters — it had to be for 'negative cutters' period. There are, however, many ways to skin a cat. Men still had higher pay levels than women, so when the ads lawfully mentioned the pay, no men applied, and negative cutting stayed a lower-paying female job. In the long time I spent in the industry, I have met one single man in that job — a very gifted Italian in a Montreal laboratory.

Nothing much happened in my new editing room until, some weeks later, Oscar Rosander came back. He had been at the studio for a long time, always worked on Ingmar Bergman's films and was regarded as the grand old man in Swedish film editing. He was without doubt very accomplished, but unfortunately I soon discovered that my new boss was less grandiose on the human scale. *The Devil's Eye* was in its filming stage, and as Rosander's assistant I did all the preparation work that comes before the serious editing starts. Negative cutters being among the neatest people in the land, one would have expected Wic's editing room to be dust and dirt-free, but it had strangely enough not been a very high priority. Consequently, I had never learned to make an effort to keep the work print in pristine condition. However, the perception that things were different at Svensk Filmindustri had made me ask Oscar Rosander if, as had been my habit, I could mark the scene numbers on the work print with a white grease pen? He told me it was okay.

The opening of *The Devil's Eye* takes place in hell where Don Juan, punished for his numerous seductions on Earth, is sentenced to encounter a never-ending line of very beautiful women who, alas, vanish as soon as he reaches for them. The set is sparsely lit, and all the walls hung with black velvet. When projected on a big screen the darker an image is, the more noticeable any imperfections will be, and my markings could hardly have been called diminutive. The result was disastrous. Rosander had been with Bergman long enough to know how such things drove him to distraction, and my boss seemed to have cleverly planned to get rid of me through Bergman's ire. Not that it made it more palatable, but I do not think Rosander's action was a result of misogyny, but rather was rooted in human insecurity. Competition scared him, and that was what he had feared since our first day in the editing room. That he could became his own victim had obviously not crossed his mind.

One night after the rushes[2] were screened, Bergman wished to look at the film's opening reel, and already tired after a long day's work, when — on the big screen faced with all the dirt I had unwittingly created — he lost his temper. In front of the crew, the people from the lab, the music director, and of course Oscar Rosander himself, Bergman lashed out at me, finally reducing me to tears. He then stormed out of the theatre followed by Rosander and most of the others. A couple of kind souls stayed back and tried to comfort me by pointing out that this was not serious, it happened to everybody from time to time, and in the long run, it meant nothing. I do not cry often or easily, but when I do…. All the kindness was virtually water off a duck's back, and I regardless continued my impersonation of Niagara.

The next day I was still red-eyed and puffy-faced, and when I passed the shooting stage, delivering a camera test to the cinematographer, Bergman noticed me. I heard a snide remark about my looks and reacted by telling the Director that I was prepared to apologise for a mistake and that he would in all likelihood be spared to see the same one repeated, but he was to leave my persona alone! Everybody froze. Bergman came up to where I stood, put his arm around my shoulders, and we started a long walk around the outskirts of the stage. I got an explanation for the outburst, an excuse for it, and had my initial glimpse of a man with a great curiosity about people, but a sometimes profound difficulty not to hurt them even though he may like them. We had had our one and only big run-in, and once the air was cleared and the rules set, we worked under a lasting, reciprocal respect for and trust in each other. Honesty is a complex notion with some uncomplicated facets, and as I had understood Bergman's need to know the reality, I took a very straight approach. Later, as the editor, if I had done something stupid — a maddening reoccurrence in the very beginning — I went and told him of my blunder. He would shake his head, tell me I was an imbecile, and that was it! I repaired my mistake, and I never heard about it again. It does not take a genius to understand how lies and subterfuge trigger uncertainty followed by insecurity, and most often *that* was what made Bergman explode. I was, I think, also well served by my notion that reasonable resistance is something we all need, and in that respect Bergman was not different from most other human beings.

Additionally, the incident in the theatre gave me a quick lesson about who was who in the laboratory. During the shooting period, the person responsible for the film was always present at the daily screenings, and for this one, as for all Bergman films, it was a man with a long service record and, I was told, one of Oscar Rosander's old pals. Also present was a young assistant, obviously being groomed, but I had never heard him say a word until the day after the debacle, when late in the day, after most people had already left, he turned up in my editing room. To begin with he made it clear that he had come on his own initiative, and then offered to take all my dirty film over to his department and, after hours, put it through their cleaning machine. This extraordinarily kind offer spared me hours upon hours of work, and from then on I used my grease pens in a very different way.

The following year, when *Through a Glass Darkly* was ready for editing, Rosander was again on sick leave. It was only supposed to be short, but it gave Bergman the opportunity he obviously had been looking for. Through the grapevine I had heard that on insistence from the company director, but without telling Bergman, Rosander recently had made some alteration to an edit. Bergman of course found out, and as he saw this as a betrayal of trust, something he would not tolerate, he had only bided his time. Now he grabbed the opportunity, insisting that he had to start working immediately and also that he wished me to take Rosander's place. This certainly raised a number of eyebrows, and I am to this day convinced that Bergman's choice was based on a mis-understanding! During my earlier laboratory practice, I *had* spent about a month in the negative-cutting department and thus was famil-iar with the routine, but it is not a job you master in that short a time. Bergman had obviously heard some rumours, and darting around as rumours do, the feather had become a whole bird. He thought I was a skilled negative cutter, and in his eyes they were people with nerves made out of steel. For him that had an appeal.

It is hardly the ideal situation to, at the same time supervise the edit-ing of your film, and have to train your editor, but that was the situa-tion Bergman had created. I had very limited experience, only basic skills, and was overwhelmed by the sheer size of a footage I clearly needed to learn to memorise. It is true that in the past my visual mem-ory had often saved me, but now, mysteriously, my brain seemed to develop into an immense, constantly growing sponge that effortlessly retained information. I slowly conquered my confusion, but thinking back on *Through A Glass Darkly*, I still see myself more as a pair of human scissors — guided by Bergman — than a truly participating edi-tor. We undoubtedly had a tough time, but by sticking it out, we not only made a film, but also laid a very solid foundation of trust and con-cord. My skills multiplied in leaps and bounds, and by the next year Bergman had much more of an editor at his side. From the very begin-ning, I noted that my remarks and/or suggestions always found an ear. The response was not always immediate, but sooner or later I was told 'let's try it' or 'I have thought about it, and I do not wish to do it' followed by his reasons. It was very instructive, and I admired that in the editing room Bergman was always more intent on getting it right than being right.

His way of looking at his footage formed a tremendous learning trajectory and, I am sure, was among the most valuable coaching during these years. He never wore glasses tinted with the rainbows of what his intentions had been, what he had wished to do, or what he hoped to find on the screen. He instead looked at every image with an acute attentiveness until he was sure of what *the image* was telling. When something did not add up, he lamented over the fact that, even after so many years of experience, he had not been conscious of the solecism at the time it occurred, and then we began to look for possible solutions that would mitigate it. Bergman's capacity to let go of self-indulgent and/or superfluous material was also remarkable, and I never saw him fall for the allure of an image even though he clearly loved it. Never again would I meet a director with the same degree of objectivity that made the Bergman years so blessedly free from the destructive self-indulgence other directors' work occasionally reveal. If I was asked to put together a compilation called *The City In Film*, the opening sequence from *The Deer Hunter* would have its given place, but I would not even think of destroying *Dancing On Celluloid* by including *The Deer Hunter*'s never-ending Ukrainian wedding. Who needs a documentary in an already overly long feature?

Science attachés were part of all the bigger foreign embassies in Stockholm, and they all had regular contact with Hans. He, as well as his weekly page, were highly respected, and consequently, when UD, the Swedish Foreign Office, decided to send their first Swedish science attaché abroad, Hans became their choice. Not one to ever trumpet forth from the roof either good or bad, he came home one evening, showing nothing unusual, but finally during dinner let out about a meeting he had had at UD that same afternoon. They had offered him this new post! It had not yet been decided if it was to be in Washington, USA, or Paris, France, but I was the one jumping up and down, congratulating him over and over again. When asked how I felt about moving abroad, I reined in some of my bubbly enthusiasm for a change. I thought of it as a tremendous opportunity, the sort of thing that probably only happens to you once in a lifetime, and in my mind it was an offer you simply could not turn down. With the professional 'luggage' I possessed, I did not have any doubts that I would be able to continue in my own field in either country. We did not have children who would be uprooted, and if it had been asked of me, I would have packed my bags the same evening. Only I was *not* the one who had the offer, and while assuring my dear husband that I would happily go with him, I stressed that it was his offer and his decision. No more was said, and for several weeks, increasingly itchy, I kept myself from asking. Then came the fatal dinner when, on its way to my mouth, a spoon filled with delicious green, sweet cicely soup fell out of my hand and made a mighty splash over the table. I had been wrong. My husband was bloody well able to turn down an offer of a lifetime! I could hardly believe what I heard, but Hans had just told me that he had said, 'Thank you, but no thank you' to UD. Why? He could not make himself move that far from his family! I chewed on his answer for a long time. It revealed an insecurity that he had never shown. Or had it been there all the time, but I had not seen it? It also brought with it the sad conjecture that I probably, after all, was not the wife he needed. Some years down the road, this finally was undeniable, and I insisted on a divorce.

THE BEST CURE FOR BOREDOM

Hell has no place in my belief system, but that does not prevent me from picturing what it would be like: never-ending repetition, without any further learning and/or insight. It would probably be completely exhausting to live a life without *some* repetition, but it must be kept to a minimum. The editing room is an ideal place for such requirements: you cut and splice pieces of film together, you roll up trims, log them, and put them aside, but that is basically the extent of the tedium. Each cut is a different choice, and only partly yours since it is —or should at least be — dictated by the actual images. When splicing two bits of film together there is in each piece *one* image that is the perfect one for your cut, and if you find it, you — humble servant of the footage — have made your cut almost invisible!

Bergman's editing room was the perfect place to learn and perfect this art, for nothing was ever done on a whim, rather every move was calculated to serve the whole. His 'kill-your-darlings' mentality was of course what made it possible in the first place, but at the core of the steady progress also lay his methodical way of working. The footage, in order to be manageable, needs to be divided up in separate reels, but they are still part of the whole, and in Bergman's editing room this was never forgotten. Before starting work on a new reel, the preceding one was always looked at in order for us to refresh our memory of its pacing and thus the editing progressed in a steady rhythm, starting at the film's beginning and carried on to its end and each time only a relatively *small* amount of film fell away. The process is like panning for gold; each round washes out more and more of the stones, the pebbles, and the sand until the gold — if there is any — glitters in front of your eyes. Cutting out chunks here and there, just because they *seem* to ask for it, is most often very destructive to the overall pacing, but if each cut is made in function of what came before and what follows, the rhythm inherent in the footage will be released. Our workdays also followed the same pattern year after year. Bergman arrived at 9:00 AM, and we started in the theatre looking at yesterday's reel(s) on the big screen. Even in Bergman's unusually well thought out and carefully organised film work, sequences had to change place and these screenings always brought that to our attention. The big screen also amplified ungainly cuts that the editing table's small screen had camouflaged. Back in the editing room I put the next reel on my table, and we started to go through it in stops and starts. I took notes of what was to stay and what was to go, and the number of reels we went through each day was merely based on how much work they each appeared to demand. Bergman usually left no later than noon, I took a lunch break, and then started to cut and splice.

When searching for the exact first and last frames in dialogue scenes, it is the rhythm, inherent in the combination of image and sound, that helps to guide you, but when you work with images initially filmed without synchronous sound, you are on your own. Movements in the image can be of some help, but it is not as useful as the rhythm of a soundtrack. I was not comfortable without it and either asked the sound department for some atmospheric sound that fitted the surrounding sequences, or talked to the composer of the film's music. If he could give me a preliminary tape it was even better, and it felt much more satisfactory than just 'blind' cutting of mute footage. As my editing table could only accommodate two sound tracks at the same time, I often had to ask the sound mixer to make premixes, and even if the request was a bit out of the ordinary, he was always the same kind and helpful colleague. Normally the film editor only attends to the dialogue tracks, and all the rest is taken care of by the sound and music editors, but Bergman had an understanding of my need for sound and was fully supportive. He always was. Whatever I did to learn more about my tools as an editor had his approval. There were no unions at the time, and the rules were set more by habit than by principles, and as long as Bergman was happy, nobody at the studio was prepared to rock the boat.

Until I came to this editing room, I had not known a great deal about sound, but I took real pleasure in working with it. The greatest discovery was to learn how the fusing of all the specific elements was done so that in the end the film resembled a big balloon filled with a gas composed of different elements. Because you had worked with them all, you knew what they consisted of, but when the balloon moved in the wind, they stretched the membrane and kept the balloon afloat but were no longer individually identifiable.

It would have been fun to sit down and compare notes with the editors who worked with a younger Bergman, but even without that, I was fully aware that *my* Bergman was using his considerable experience very wisely and not least yoking it with an admirable amount of discipline. Admittedly, most of the scripts for the films I worked on were written by himself, and I assume that behind the final script lay a visualisation process that had been driving the writing. That must be a great advantage when the camera finally rolls, and I am convinced that, if I was lucky enough to always start out with a manageable amount of footage and at the same time never lack anything of essence, his methodical and vast insight — together with Sweden's limited budgets — played an essential part. Not counting the time for the preparation work that went on simultaneously with the filming, the editing of image and dialogue was usually finished inside seven weeks.

There was no assistant in my editing room. Consequently, at the end of the day, it was up to me to roll up all the trims, mark them, and put them away in such a manner that they could be easily retrieved if needed. This job came at the end of already very long workdays, but since I realised that it helped me in training my image memory, in the beginning I did not really resent it. Later on my attitude changed somewhat, for I had become acutely aware of the fact that the *only* way to learn to become a skilled editor is by training under supervision. Once, on a work visit to one of the biggest film studios in London, England, I had great difficulty in keeping a straight face when the editor and I, after a morning screening followed by lunch, entered his editing room, and the first thing I saw was his five assistants lined up inside the door, sitting there on high tabourets waiting for their master. Sweden is still today a small country with a limited film industry (although the budgets seem to have swelled), but even in much bigger England, I thought five assistants was overkill; *one* would have made me very happy! What irked me most was not the absence of help, but the industry's lack of foresight. I guess it was in equal parts the result of being penny-wise and pound-foolish — Europa Film had not replaced me when I left — and that the powers that be seem to have conveniently, but erroneously, talked themselves into believing that there was no need to train film editors. Their narrow reasoning was served by the fact that the television industry had started their own training, but precious few of these editors ever transferred to the film industry.

Outside of the periods when he was filming, Bergman and a small group of friends and co-workers came together once a week to look at films and this way we saw a great number of films from different countries that would never have appeared on the commercial circuit. The man who imported Russian films had our great appreciation; through him we were able to screen some remarkable films steeped in an emotional perspective very different from ours. The Russians had also, during the war, captured some territory where advanced film laboratories were located and they had started to experiment with colour film. The results were uneven, but when they were good, they were exquisite! Equally interesting, although most of the time far too garish for my taste, were the offerings from America. Also, the French director René Clement made, I think, a remarkable first when in 1956 he filmed *Gervaise* on colour negative but printed it on black-and-white stock. The method rendered Emile Zola's depressed, poor, smoky Paris of late 1800 an authenticity and strange beauty that gave food for thought. I sussed out what was on offer, and then Bergman and I composed the evening's program, but when we started I am afraid we acted like kids in the candy store. We jammed in far too much, but some not too. discreet snoring soon told us that we had to limit ourselves to one, or at the very most, two short films followed by one feature.

The work time with Bergman was blessedly free from unwanted disruptions. No incoming telephone calls, no uninvited guests, and hardly ever any invited ones either. It was not until I emerged into the 'real' world that I understood how 'spoiled' I was, although I do not see it in that light, as effective editing demands a high degree of concentration. I do not think you can successfully multitask when at the editing table. Those were Bergman's needs as well, and the last week of shaping routinely took place away from the demands and the distractions of the studio. We went to Dalarna some 300 km north of Stockholm. The province was rich with echoes from his childhood; Bergman's maternal grandparents had lived there, and as a child and adolescent he spent periods of time with them. His maternal grandfather worked for the railways, and for the boy it must have been a great adventure to be allowed to accompany him when he went to inspect the line on his trolley. No wonder Bergman had a lingering love and an eye for big, smoke-billowing trains! All exteriors and some church interiors in *Winter Light* were filmed in this same landscape.

Siljansborg was a big, old-fashioned hotel known for its good table and its beautiful surroundings. People who could afford it would come there to recuperate after operations, family dramas, and the like, but although we did not fit into any of these categories, the director, the actors, and the whole crew were billeted at the hotel. Table and editor were together shipped to all exterior locations where the editing room replaced the studio cinema for screenings of the daily rushes. At the studio, my editing table had been given a makeover. Solderings were replaced with electrical contacts, boxes were constructed for the different parts of the table, and I got very good at assembling it, taking it apart, and packing it up for transport back to Stockholm. I had been given a crash course in the simpler repairs of its 'entrails,' and technical charts, soldering equipment, and a toolbox became part of my luggage. One room at Siljansborg had been transformed into an editing suite, and when we went back to Stockholm, the installations were left in place. When Bergman and I went there for that last week of 'fine-tooth-comb editing,' we also used the editing room as our evening entertainment zone. Now we took revenge on the drowsy, and it was not unusual for us to delight in several shorts and two feature films even after the daylong focus on 'our' film. If you are hooked, you are hooked, and there are only a few things in life as relaxing as looking at films, where you are not part of the problems, only the grateful recipient of inspiration and ideas.

I shared Bergman's fondness for Siljansborg — how could you not? No household chores, no need for shopping, good food appearing in front of you at every meal, an hour's daily walk in nature, and first and last film, film, film. As it is, I also had ulterior reasons. When we filmed *Winter Light*, I made the acquaintance of a man who, over the years, afforded rare but much enjoyed company, and who eventually showed a generosity I had done nothing to earn. It was only our second day at Siljansborg, and since the crew was on location, I had a solitary lunch in an otherwise empty dining room. When he entered there was something familiar about this tall figure with a mane of dark hair and strong features, but it took me a while to figure out that I recognised him from a photograph. He was a well-established architect from the south of Sweden and the owner of a substantial sculpture collection that I had read about. What, however, struck me most that day was not his good looks but the nimbus of melancholy that surrounded him. I think we both soon realised how ridiculous it was with the two of us at separate tables at each end of this big dining room, and after a couple of days we asked to be seated together. His conversation was not limited to architecture and art, but was wide-ranging and always interesting, and I think we both enjoyed our lunches. The filming finished, and I returned to Stockholm, but six months later he called me at the studio. He was in town for a couple of days and invited me out for lunch. This habit continued for some years; we met for a stimulating conversation and a good lunch. As our conversations never alluded to the personal, I never got even the vaguest idea where this aura of melancholy was rooted.

When I first started to talk about a divorce, Hans did not want to hear about it, and it took both time and the intervention of his best friend before he agreed. We were by then living in our own house, but even our best efforts to sell it in such a way that we each got an apartment did not succeed. Eventually we found a buyer who could provide an apartment that suited Hans, and I said 'let's take it.' The only way to find an apartment in Stockholm was still to pay 'key money.' It was not legal, but the law turned a blind eye, so your real problem seemed to be that you never knew who you were dealing with. Would you really get what you had been shown, or would the scam artist take your money and disappear? I was not even sure that my part of the sale of our house would buy me anything at all, nor did I know how to get in contact with this black market. Realising I could not take this stalemate much longer, I decided to put my furniture in storage and rent a furnished room until I could figure something out.

My architect friend made one of his Stockholm visits around this time and we, as usual, had lunch together. I did not mention any of my problems, but he must have sensed that something was not quite right and very gently made me put my problems on the table. At the end of our lunch, he excused himself and left to make a telephone call, came back, and asked if I had time to go and look at an apartment! I was speechless. An hour later I was the tenant of an affordable, sunny, pleasant one-bedroom apartment opposite a park. I had a signed lease, the keys, and a bank account number to which I would pay the 'key money' — once I had my share from our house sale. When the time came, I realised that the bank account was the architect's. He had not only negotiated a reasonable sum on my behalf but also paid it in my name. You can not write thank you notes to bank accounts, and no other lunch date ever gave me the opportunity.

'CURIOUSER AND CURIOUSER!'
cried Alice[3] — and so did I!

'Experimental' is not the first word that comes to mind when talking about Bergman films, but while in principle retaining his narrative style, Bergman was constantly exploring and pushing the limits of conventional and/or established wisdom. All over Europe, the 60s became a time for change, but while innovations during later decades would basically be technically driven, at this time it was creative thinking and intellectual curiosity that brought about the mutation — not the least in Bergman's cinema. Take a look at the scene in *Through A Glass Darkly* where Karin, after she has seen her father and her husband off on their fishing trip, sneaks up behind her brother and snatches the magazine with nudes he has been ogling. Minus jumps up and, trying to retrieve his precious substitute for Latin grammar, runs after his mocking sister. The chase has a great swirl and high pace to it, but this is not the result of an excellent editing job manipulating a multitude of shots from different angles. Conservatively, we were taught that when filming from a different angle, unless it was a travelling shot, we had to stay inside a 180 degree part of a circle, and for the reverse shots, a move of less than 180 degrees was prescribed.[4] This sequence only consists of two camera placements with exactly a 180 degree shift! It was obviously possible to successfully break the rule, and this discovery called for more of the same. In a later scene where Minus, looking for his now missing sister, climbs down the ladder to the hull of an old shipwreck, the same technique was applied. When we looked at the rushes, the ladder, which in the first shot went from upper right to lower left, had in the reverse one shifted place, now running along the opposite diagonal! We had overlooked the mirror effect, and in order to successfully apply our discovery, there *was* one restriction: the image could *only* contain horizontal and/or vertical elements. Any diagonal components triggered this unacceptable mirror image — unacceptable because it created total confusion.

If, in *Wild Strawberries*, Bergman had exorcised his mortal fright, in *Winter Light* the clergyman's son subjected his religion to a deep, searching scrutiny. The result was a film Bergman himself regarded as 'anti-Christian but not anti-religious.' 'When I started I did not clearly see how much of this whole, bizarre, external lot, which had stratified ever since my childhood, obscured the essential thing.'[5] The Swedish writer Pär Lagerkvist observed that Bergman let go of 'the holy rubbish' that in the church obscured the sacred. Bergman the script writer and Bergman the director also fought another battle. Was *Winter Light* a film the public would come to? *Through a Glass Darkly* had met with approval by the critics, but since their reviews appeared to march to the tune of one-up, one-down, we expected negative reactions to *Winter Light*. The trend was so obvious it turned into an editing room joke: 'Oh, isn't it great, now we are going to work on a masterpiece!' Next film and we would mockingly lament: 'Oh no, we have a flop on our hands.'

Hardly anybody is likely to regard it as a good idea to start a feature film with the entire length of the morning service, including holy communion, but Bergman initially thought it could work without making the film front-heavy. His religious respect also made it questionable not to start the service at its proper beginning, but once in the editing room the director in him saw that the earliest part had to go.

Winter Light was shot in fifty-seven days and had an unusual number of scenes re-shot — mostly for technical reasons. A Newall camera had replaced the Mitchell, but we did not have the American service, where the camera, during the whole shoot, would be attended by a factory engineer, and our Newall caused us technical problems resulting in re-shoots. A then new, highly light-sensitive negative, Double X, was used but the negative batch, reserved for the film, unfortunately had some problematic reels. All the same, it *was* a great negative for the light Bergman wanted for this film 'at the bottom of the vale of tears' — austere, grey, and lifeless as only a Swedish midwinter day can be. All aesthetically pleasing illumination from artificial light sources was banned and more and more lamps turned off until Sven Nykvist, the

Director of Photography, and the not very happy electrician mostly worked with candles. Finally Bergman had the compressed, realistic light he envisioned. The old, time-honoured clap,[6] which not only spread chalk dust but also did its best to fray actor's nerves, was no longer clapped in front of their faces. It had been replaced with an electronic signal from the Nagra,[7] but the device had been incorrectly hooked up, and the sound tapes did not sound as they ought to. When this mistake was discovered, two days worth of work had to be discarded. And yet another re-shoot followed.

As if all this technical devilry was not enough, Gunnar Björnstrand, although one of Bergman's favourite actors, struggled with his role as the doubt-stricken clergyman, wondering if there was *anything* in this character that the public would like? Most of the the technical mishaps caused irritation and slowed down the beginning of the shoot, but I believe they were not entirely unappreciated, in as far as they all gave the director another opportunity to work with the actor on his performance.

During various times, although in vastly different guises, film has always made use of 'sign language' of one sort or another. The most well known were probably the fade[8] and the superimposition[9] that were constantly used during the silent period to signal to the audience that time had passed — the 'fade' — or that the story had moved to another location — 'super' for short. As did most other directors, Bergman made use of these devices, but he also gave them a newness we had not seen before. I do not know where his inspiration came from; was it his keen interest in and considerable knowledge of cinematography that led him to it, or had he somewhere come across something similar and made it his own? Whatever the source, *Winter Light* has a number of unusual-looking superimpositions that were achieved by keeping, for a short moment, the middle part of the fades in unchanging light, before letting it all fade conventionally. A traditionally executed superimposition has a calm, floating feel to it, but when the middle frames of momentarily unchanged exposure hover above and beneath each other, it takes us to metaphysical spheres where the here-and-now-reality is being manipulated. The film becomes the instrument that pushes us beyond our daily realness into a dream world, where we are made to believe in experiences as yet unknown. Both the director and his editor took to the new manipulation and used it more than once, not least in *Persona*, where the technique really shows its versatility.

Multi-camera shoots were not on Bergman's menu when I was his editor, but as an exception, it was used once in *Winter Light*. The short duration of the desired low afternoon light when filming the fisherman's suicide, together with the time-consuming make-up and the need for perfect continuity, would have made a single camera shoot a nightmare. Not having done any multi-camera editing before, I did not know that it would be different, but it *was*. However I cut between the two cameras it did not *look* right, and before I finally understood that I should drop logic and only trust my eyes — if it *looks* right it *is* right – my trial-and-error 'editing' had left me with the most spliced-together piece of film that I have ever produced. Filmstrips resembling minced meat do not go smoothly through projectors, so I also had to eat humble pie and order a new work print that I then had to fashion accordingly.

The making of *Winter Light* was documented in a unique way. An old friend of Bergman — the journalist and writer Vilgot Sjöman — was preparing three TV programs about the director and his film. After having done interviews and sound recordings during the shoot, he later occasionally also turned up with his microphone in the editing room. 'L136' was Svensk Filmindustri's production number for *Winter Light*, and Sjöman would eventually publish *L 136, Dagbok with Ingmar Bergman*.[10]

When we edited *Winter Light*, Sjöman, who by then had also become a budding filmmaker, was also at the editing stage of his first feature film. In our editing room he not only got material for his TV programs but also, I think for the first time, had the opportunity to see Bergman exercise his unfailing detachment in front of his own footage. As a director, Sjöman was of course not as experienced as Bergman, but more to the point, Bergman's disciplined lack of attachment did not have concordance with Sjöman's less generous nature, and *that* prevented him from seeing that, for the overall balance of the film, the cutting of the scripted and subsequently filmed opening was a necessity.

'After all that hard work, after all that trouble!' Sjöman questioned, but Bergman was adamant, brandishing his favourite war cry: 'Kill your darlings!' Not just years of experience, but also an unusually critical eye, not least when trained on his own work, had taught Bergman what worked and what did not. And it did not stop in the editing room. Once his films were released, Bergman used to go to the cinema and sit in the dark, taking in how the spectators reacted to the film. Diminishing attention was a signpost worthy of attention! It probably does not boost your ego all the time, but it is undoubtedly one of the surest ways to clearly understand the nature of your mistakes.

Bergman had learned to always exercise a healthy mistrust in front of the images he cherished the most. In *Winter Light*, driving to the afternoon service, the pastor has to stop his car at a level crossing. Together with the red-nosed, cold-stricken school teacher, he sits waiting when a big smoke-billowing train passes. The images were stunningly beautiful, and we had plenty — but most of them fell in my trim bin! Sjöman was almost at a loss for words, but Bergman insisted: 'The novice loves every image he has created; only experience teaches him severity, distinction. The healthiest of all work maxims: Be suspicious of what you have fallen in love with. Kill your darlings!'

Later, editing one of Sjöman's feature films, I realised that, although he now had more experience, he was in some respects still what Bergman labelled 'the novice.' To my unspoken irritation, he would drag superfluous footage with him for what felt like an eternity. Sooner or later it had to be dropped, but in the meantime this habit had not only made the job harder but in one respect also riskier. Repetitive looking has a tendency to blur your initial vision. If I, with my habit of looking at images all the time, am struck by something special at that first viewing, there is a good chance that others will be struck too. Lengthy, repetitive viewing of similar takes has a fading effect on the perception, and that is why I wish to avoid it as much as possible. No wonder Bergman's usual habit to make his choice between duplicates at the daily screenings was such a help in keeping one's judgement sharp.

His attention to detail did not stop with the image. His love for the human voice was as great as his love for music, and as a musical 'instrument,' it was always treated with the care given to treasures. Bergman detested mumble, did not tolerate it, and insisted that if there was dialogue, it was meant to be heard. He also maintained the notion of sound perspective, and I can only recall one very notable exemption. It occurs at the end of *Through A Glass Darkly* where Minus, in a very wide shot, runs along the beach. The boy is a distant figure in the landscape, but his shouted 'Dad spoke to me' has the sound perspective of a close-up. Equally important was the atmospheric background sound; it had to be crystal clear and, like dialogue, void of any technical interference. His special bête noire was a very faint repetitive noise that from time to time could be heard from somewhere inside the camera. All efforts to eliminate it were in vain: even after the camera had been wrapped in the thickest of covers, you could pick it up. The technical sophistication on the sound side was not yet what it would later become, and post-synchronisation all too often lacked the vibration always present in natural sound. Even when mixed with atmospheric sound, it was not equal to original dialogue sound, and Bergman detested it. He only used post-syncro sparsely and for very short dialogue. When filming *Silence,* the problem was acute; any interference would disturb the desired sharp contrast between the rumbling sound of a tank driving through the deserted streets and the eerie silence in Ester's[11] hotel room. Bergman solved his problem by inventing the 'wild' sound.

All dialogue scenes were shot in two different ways. The first was in the usual manner with synchronised sound, but as long as the sound was clearly audible, the boom man, for once, did not have to worry about the quality of his recording. When Bergman was happy with the performance and the cinematographer was sure that his camera movements were all correct, the scene was repeated. Now with only the Nagra running and no longer restricted by the framing, the microphone was free to find its ultimate position. In the editing room, it was then up to me to format the 'wild' sound in such a way that it became congruous with the original take in every minute detail. The sound system in my editing table, originally not very sophisticated, was upgraded, and a set of earphones helped me to work undisturbed by external noise. The work had its surprises: some because of the nature of acting, some of a technical nature.

In the theatre there is a give and take between the good actor and a captive audience and this has an effect on the timing of the delivery — pauses are stretched to their maximum! While filming, the all observing, but inert camera lens has replaced the emotive reactions, and for some actors that impacts on their pacing. The practical effect showed immediately. Ninety-nine times out of a hundred the 'wild' sound takes were shorter than those recorded when camera and sound had been running together. Seldom a great deal, but there was a small difference that needed some adjustment.

Instinctively, I took the same piece of tape from a new transfer, but to my big surprise it did not work. I could not give a name to what had happened — all I knew was that it did not sound correct. After some experimenting it became clear that if I instead chose a pause from another place on the same tape, the correction was inaudible. The explanation is probably the actor's breathing, so light that the ear hardly picks up on it, but some days these pauses were driving me batty. The work *was* very interesting, but also totally exhausting. There were times when I ended up not trusting either my judgement or my ears any longer. The entire dialogue track in *Silence* is constructed this way; Bergman loved the results of my labour, but the success of the method had its price. From then on each time he heard irrelevant noises he called for wild sound. It certainly made the filming easier, but when continuity did not react to actors making dialogue changes between takes, the method became a nightmare at my end. I raved and ranted and eventually put a sign on my editing room door: 'In here the impossible is done every day, but please note that miracles demand more time.' Even with the help of time the 'miracles' could not always be performed, and wild sound became *my* bête noire.

My favourite Bergman film? Each time the question is asked I hesitate for a moment, for every new film meant renewed pleasure and satisfaction, but I seem to always end up choosing *Persona* — because of the film itself and also due to some newness in the editing routine. The beginning, the middle, and the end of the film were noted but not elaborated on in the script — nor filmed at the same time as the rest of the footage. These sequences were slowly built during the editing process, image by image with shots from earlier films, which Bergman already had in mind, and new ones — the old type of projector with its glowing coal bar among others — but the film itself, together with logic and emotion, also 'suggested' some images. Ideas were tossed around, 'shopping lists' given to Sven Nykvist, who went out and filmed. New images were incorporated, visuals changed place, some ended up in the trim bin. New orders were issued, and finally, one day, the three sequences felt right.

Once the film was released, we had a delightful and, at the same time, annoying surprise. The images of the coal bar burning the film were so realistic that the projectionists thought that the film was on fire and stopped the projection! The newer safety film does not burn, explode, or melt as the old acetate-based film had done, but that seemed to have been forgotten in the heat of the moment. Notices, warning the projectionists that this was only an effect, had to quickly be printed and pasted in each can containing the 'dangerous' reel.

These sequences have often raised the question, 'What does it mean?' I do not think they in themselves import something specific, but they are signposts telling us that we have left 'reality,' as in daily life, and gone through the looking glass. Different rules are at work, and consequently anything can happen, as it does in dreams. Logic, as we know it when awake, is no longer applicable, distance is not a problem, time not an issue, and so on. If we are willing to open up to such feelings, it becomes easily acceptable, and it is such a pity that the audience, to a large degree, has let itself believe the critics' dictum that Bergman films are 'difficult' films. That they are serious films and very emotional ones I think is beyond question, but that does not necessarily make them difficult to understand or relate to. But if you do not like the message, you can of course — although it is not very fair — shoot the messenger.

Initially *Persona* was not planned for 1965. It was not even written. On the table was a three-hour long sombre manuscript, but in spring when the preparations had just started, Bergman was taken ill and admitted to hospital. Everything was put on hold, and when he was on his feet again, there was not really enough time to set such a big film in motion. I think *Persona* was brought about by two things: by having revisited old territory from his childhood, and then, when he had just come home from the hospital, a chance meeting did the rest. The private hospital *Sophiahemmet* had its own chaplain, and Bergman's father had once filled the position. The family at the time lived in a house on the hospital grounds, and young Ingmar had played in the surrounding park with its morgue and a house for old retired nurses.

In 1964 Bibi Andersson played the leading role in a film in Norway and had then met Liv Ullmann, an already well-known stage actress. The two became friends, and in spring 1965 Liv had come to Stockholm to visit Bibi. Out walking one day, they met Bergman, and the three of them stood talking for a while. Bergman's film-trained eye immediately noted the sameness in the shape of their heads and details of resemblance in their faces, and in his mind it gelled with old memories, thoughts, and observations of human behaviour during his hospital stay. He went home and wrote *Persona* in a surprisingly short time, leaving the other script on a back burner. It was never realised, although parts of it have shown up in later Bergman films.

When reading the script of *Persona*, I had not detected anything out of the ordinary. In the early part there was a fairly elaborate sequence in which, after leaving her patient,[12] the nurse[13] goes back to her quarters in another wing of the hospital, and before she finally goes to bed, busies herself with a number of things. It was not until I actually saw the images that I started to wonder how Bergman intended to cut these scenes together. That was unusual, for I normally would have had a pretty good idea of his intentions from reading the script. When editing started, I usually only took notes or marked the film when he asked me to do something that varied from what I had expected, but this time it was different. When we went through the sequence for the first time, I marked and scribbled in an unusual way that made Bergman nervous. 'Is there anything wrong?' 'No, no! But you wish to start here?' — big in-mark on the film — 'and end here?' — big out-mark. This went on for most of a morning, and when lunchtime came, a rather unhappy Bergman left the editing room. An equally unhappy editor started to work and blindly followed marks and notes, but the cuts did not make any more sense now than when I had marked them. Once finished, I spooled the film to its beginning, sat back, and looked at what I had done. It not only made perfectly good sense, but even more to the point, it created an interesting contrast to the surrounding rhythm, and it finally dawned on me that Bergman, in the same film, successfully had brought together two differently styled narratives. My confusion did hurt for I thought I had reached a level of insight and workmanship that would allow me to detect whatever my director had intended. That's what vanity does for you, digging the potholes, so you can fall head first into them!

As long as you take some learning from a comedown, it *has* served some larger purpose, and in *Shame* it brought to bear. Bad acting by a normally very accomplished actor put us in trouble, especially as continuity dictated that at least part of the role had to be left in. We tried all sorts of cuts, but nothing worked. Spooling back and forth, I suddenly remembered the sequence that had been my nemesis in *Persona* and figured that the same principle could now be applied. I started to suggest cuts that made Bergman stare at me as if I had gone mad, but as he had no counter proposition, I was told to try it. He left tired and irritated, but not before letting off some steam: 'We can always order a new work print when you have destroyed this one,' and he was gone. Later that afternoon, when I was in the midst of my creative efforts, Bergman came back very quietly and without a word positioned himself behind my chair. For about fifteen minutes he stood there looking at what I was doing, and not a word was said. Then he left as silently as he had entered. Although initially suspicious, he was too intrigued to wait for the following day's screening. Curiosity was, among many other things, a substantial part of Bergman's makeup, and he had learned how all his different tools functioned. There was never any doubt as to who was the conductor of the orchestra, but Bergman also greatly appreciated his 'musicians' and once he had given his instructions left them to their tasks, and later often voiced his appreciation of their work.

My re-cutting had worked, and the following day Bergman was happy and complimentary but also very curious about where I had picked up the idea. Laughingly I told him *he* had taught me, with the opening sequence in *Persona*. Paying attention to *what* he did and *how* he did it — and in what context — taught me something new almost every day. It all had a natural logic that I found easy to understand and retain, but when he got into his pedagogic mode, which fortunately did not happen very often, I felt things became complicated. The re-cutting in *Shame* made me also, probably for the first time, become fully conscious that the forceful impact of the virginal first-time-view has more than one aspect to it. I have earlier mentioned how quickly the newness of the imprinting fades, but this latest re-editing made me also clearly understand that a successful outcome only is possible if and when you have arrived at a different pattern of thinking and can see your images through a 'new pair of eyes.' It is far from easy, and I do wonder over the strength with which nature seems to resist obliteration of that first look. Is there in this context a connection between us and birds, who might disappear if imprinting of their migration routes faded?

By 1965 film censorship had eased considerably in Sweden — at least compared to some countries outside Scandinavia — and more and more overtly erotic content appeared on the screens. Bergman, in *Persona*, not only went the other way, but he also avoided the pit-fall of flashbacks! I take my hat off. There is no sex, no nudity beyond bathing suits — and in *Persona* they are not even bikinis —but I think it is the most erotic of all Bergman's films. To make it all the more astonishing, the effect is created by the deadliest sin in filmmaking — exposition! The first rule — *show*, do not tell — is gloriously broken in an interior scene in a summer cottage where the actress and her nurse sit together late at night. A heavy summer rain is falling outside, an open fire gives warmth to the night, and the two women have had some wine. The actress, who with great willpower has not uttered a word for some considerable time, is still silent while the nurse, as usual, chats away. Out comes an event that took place a couple of years back when the nurse, already engaged to a young doctor, had spent some summer time on a small island. When her fiancé returned to his work during the week, she kept company with another girl, and thinking themselves alone on their island, the two went swimming in the nude. One day two young boys appeared, and the older one eventually had sex with both girls. The following weekend the fiancé was back, and she recalls that 'our sex had never before or later been as great as then.' Soon after, the nurse found herself pregnant, and her fiancé helped her to arrange for an abortion. 'We did not want any children, at least not then.'

She has never told her story to anyone, but this night it tumbles out. Her belief that she has found a good, elder sister in the actress and carried by warm, comfortable feelings of trust, and a glass too many, the bubble of guilt finally bursts open. All we *see* on the screen is the nurse in her white bathrobe slouched at the table, telling her story. The actress, dressed in an elegant night gown, is propped up on her bed listening and looking. And storing facts for later use. Ullman is performing in this scene the most eloquent intellectual cannibalism I can recall ever having seen on the screen. I have over the years also had unmitigated pleasure in listening to all the sex-scenes described to me; scenes *I* never edited, but all figments of sexual fantasies and, no doubt, a somewhat faulty memory of the film.

Editing *Persona*, we had, on more than one occasion, very good reasons to grumble about less than adequate continuity, and one day Bergman declared that, in the next film, I was going to do the job. Keeping the continuity going through a film shoot is immensely demanding, and it is also a very delicate job. An eye for detail is needed, constant attention, speed, diplomacy, presence of mind and that is probably only half of it. I had never been trained in this capacity, and I had absolutely no wish to try it. Being richly endowed with what the French so tellingly designate as *l'esprit d'escalier*[14] I need time to think before correcting what turns out to be a mistake. The editing room provides you that time, but the set hardly ever does. The cost of mistakes can be exorbitant, and they make life unnecessarily difficult for the actors, not to mention the director. I doubted I would be good at it, and although from an editor's point of view I would deeply appreciate improved continuity, I had no desire either to learn the job or to do it. I also feared that the script girl's intimate knowledge of the footage would rob myself as editor of one of my most valuable assets: the freshness of the eye seeing an image for the first time.

I felt experimentation had gone one step too far, but all my arguments were countered. When Bergman wanted something badly enough, his powers of persuasion were beyond belief. So, on *Hour of the Wolf* I reluctantly found myself occupying the script girl's chair. The first week was sheer hell, and I only survived thanks to help from a totally unexpected source. The chief electrician and the gaffers kept an eye on me and would pass me whispering, 'Have you noted this?' 'Don't forget to take a Polaroid of that' or whatever they thought I may not have remembered. They were all old hands, and I had by then been at the studio long enough to know them — sort of — but I had never worked with them. Their concern and helpfulness were deeply touching, and if I managed to get through the ordeal without too many scratches, it was purely thanks to their generosity.

Finally back on firmer ground in my editing room, I eventually discovered that the experience had actually given me some advantages. If I needed to look at a different take of a scene, my image and sound memory were so clear that a glance at my continuity notes immediately told me whether or not that take was even worth looking at. It also came as a big, but very pleasant, surprise to discover that the freshness in front of the images was still there. Both on the set and when looking at the rushes, I guess I had been far too occupied with the myriad of technical details to see anything else. Although I had been deeply involved with the film for months already, it was only in the editing room that I really perceived the artistic qualities in *Hour of the Wolf*.

The experience had been gruelling, and although the result was satisfactory, I was not going to repeat it — whatever Bergman said or did. Entering into the editing of the film, the memories faded, but my continuity script refused to let go of two particular days. It had been covered as carefully as possible and had gone through some extensive cleaning, but it still gave off a lingering, very unpleasant smell of bird droppings, courtesy of a flight of beautiful white pigeons scared witless. The film has a night scene where the birds unexpectedly appear in the dark, and a keeper of carrier pigeons had brought some fifteen birds to the studio. The scene was set up and rehearsed without disturbing the birds, and eventually we were ready for a take. The camera rolled, the cages were opened, the birds flapped their wings, exited their cages, and flew straight up to a cornice under the ceiling. There they sat! Nothing would make them lift until they were prodded with long fishing rods, and during that exercise they 'rained' on anything and everything. The following morning the cornice was gone, many more birds were waiting, as were stagehands all waving their fishing rods just out of the camera's lens field, with the hope of keeping the birds in it. As they now had nowhere to land, they flew around in a very agitated state, crapping on us even more badly than the day before. I had constructed a plastic tent for my script and dressed myself in my sailing gear, but the sound engineer was not tolerant of the 'plops' oilskin and plastic emitted when crapped on, and my camouflage had to come off. At the end of the day, I spent a long time in the makeup department's shower, sending thoughts of admiration to the people who had worked on Alfred Hitchcock's *The Birds*.

With *Now About All These Women*, Bergman, in 1963, took the big step into colour, but it was not done lightly. Looking at colour films, especially American ones, Bergman often voiced his aversion for their screaming brightness, and if *he* was going into colour it had to be something light and elegant. We looked at a great number of colour films from different countries, and eventually a meeting with all his technical personnel was held. Long discussions resulted in elaborate test shoot-ings that went on for months, and I can not think of anything at all that was not put under the lens before a choice was made. Raw stock, positive film, different kinds of makeup, dress material, wallpaper, upholstery, nature's different shades of green, you name it. Everything was tested with different light and in particular combinations, and every combination got its own identification number. The job to keep track of it all had become mine. It was an unusual job for an editor but also a rare opportunity. Normally I only saw results, now I could observe how they were obtained. The time and effort spent on all this certainly paid off as the final film has a very stylish tone.

I guess it might have given Bergman some measure of satisfaction to use his own medium in both mocking his adversaries — the critics — and give the audience *his* take on the idols and their idolaters, but *Now About All These Women* will never have a place among the great Bergman films. All the same, I have always felt that it was treated a bit unfairly; not because of what it was, but rather because of what it was not! Ever since the delightful *Smiles of a Summer Night* (1955), the public wanted Bergman to make another comedy, but he did not oblige. When *Now About All These Women* came out, it was regarded as a comedy but of lesser quality than *Smiles*, while in reality it is a satire. It is a very elegant, and sometimes very witty one, but also a rather jaundiced reflection on the ways present society treats their artists, and that criticism did not go down well. I had some fun working on it, but it is not a film that moves me, and I think it has to be attributed to the aloofness of Jarl Kulle — the comedian who plays the role of the Writer-Critic. He is, as always, very elegant and sometimes also funny with all his stupid manners, but he is ice-cold, and there is not even a scrap of affinity between him and the beautiful and attractive women who flutter through the film. Rumours had it that they all, at one time or another, had been the director's amours, and I do not think everybody looked forward to the location filming, where we all would stay in the same hotel. But we need not to have worried: everybody was on their best behaviour to an extent that was almost laughable.

Thanks to my involvement in the elaborate preparations, I spent much more time on *Now About All These Women* than any other Bergman film, and my last glimpses of it somehow *fitted* the film. When finally one could be sure that the sets and props would not be needed anymore, the cleanup started. We were already well into autumn. One day I happened to pass the painters' building on the studio grounds, and outside, surrounded by a number of potted palm trees that looked strangely familiar, stood a young apprentice wiping each and every thin leaf with some foul-smelling paint remover. The exotic plants had been rented, but as their natural colour in Bergman's eyes looked too similar to spinach-green — and that was a no-no — they had been treated with a greyish spray. Convinced that the nursery would prefer to get them back in their natural splendour, the props master had ordered the rub off. I suspect the future life spans of the trees and that of the film might in the long run have matched each other. The following year we were back to black and white. Can you imagine *Persona* in colour?

OTHER STARS

When the yearly Bergman film was finished, I worked with other directors, and as I was on contract with Svensk Filmindustri for near-ly a decade, I encountered quite a few, not least in 1967-1968 when the management came up with the idea for *Stimulantia*. Presented as a full evening program, it was a collection of short films written or co-writ-ten by the directors, who in years represented all ages. The idea in itself was interesting, but *Stimulantia* had problems. It lacked a unifying framework that would have given it the feel of a feature-length film, and it was also too much of an art-cinema idea to have any hope of great acceptance outside the limited Swedish film sector. If truth be told, it probably also lacked enough 'naughty bits' to excite a larger public. What such content can do was, with all desirability, proved by *The Silence*, the only Bergman film that made its money back in Sweden before it was even exported. Not that it was not worth the attention, far from it, but I think one has to be very slow on the uptake not to realise that it was the fornication scene in the cinema that brought forth such an economic achievement. In *Stimulantia* the only director walking down the 'naughty' path was Vilgot Sjöman who trained his camera on a man keeping a beautiful black woman ensconced in his apartment. She emerges from her hiding place in a wardrobe when his wife has left for work, and he starts their day by giving her a morning bath in a glass-fronted tub. *Negressen I Skåpet*[15] was both elegant and very amus-ing, and for a change, the director had no trouble with the film censor.

On a personal satisfaction level, *Stimulantia* brought to my editing room directors I had not met before. Gustaf Molander was by far the most interesting one. He not only belonged to another generation, of which I had no working knowledge, but also represented such an important part of Swedish film history. He had been a very respected director, although he often suffered critical comparison with his younger brother Olof, also a director but in the theatre. Gustaf had

started work at Svensk Filmindustri in 1923, and in his filmography are
Kvinna utan ansikte[16] (1947) and *Eva* (1948), both written by a young
Ingmar Bergman. At the age of seventy-nine, he was now lured out of
retirement to direct Ingrid Bergman and Gunnar Björnstrand in
Smycket,[17] based on a short story by Guy de Maupassant. The script
was co-written by the director himself and the very witty writer and
actor Erland Josephson. This was, however, not the first meeting
between the actress and Gustaf Molander, who had, in 1936, directed
Ingrid Bergman in *Intermezzo*. Three years later, now in Hollywood and
directed by Gregory Ratoff, she made her English-speaking debut —
in a film with the same name as well as based on the same story. Since
her departure for Hollywood, *Smycket* was her first — and so far only
— return to Swedish film.

From my years as an aspiring actress, I still had some lingering,
painful memories of the name Molander, but that was owing to Olof.
The students in my acting school had permission to observe rehearsals
at Dramatiska Teatern, and I was a frequent visitor at Olof's rehearsals.
Sitting quiet as a mouse high up in the theatre, I had seen some of his
fabulous *mise-en-scène* take shape, but etched in my memory was unfortunately the sad day I saw him exercise, with a lot of determination,
what seemed deliberate, mental cruelty. Molander was in the early
preparations of a Shakespeare play, and he had started the day with
nine or ten actresses on the naked stage. It did not take long however,
before the first one fled weeping into the wings, not to be seen again.
By eleven o'clock he had driven them all, the most experienced to the
youngest, off the stage in various states of despair. The last one to walk
out was the director's leading lady, Inga Tidblad, who was a remarkable
actress and no longer a fledgeling. She was the only one who did not
cry, but she was spitting mad, and the two of them, alone on that naked
stage, staring each other down, was in itself a mini-drama. It could
probably also have been quite delightful had the whole experience not
been so devastatingly cruel. I refused to believe that this was 'creativity,' and that handling your 'instruments' in such a way would add anything positive to the process. How can you expect to play on a violin

that you have just destroyed?

My worries were unfounded. Gustaf Molander was a kind man and a director with all the knowledge in the world, but his world was a world gone by. I doubted that he knew much about the French New Wave and how it had so radically altered our film language. To find myself in 'the old school' for the first time was interesting, but there was a serious problem: Molander's film was heavy, and its tempo slow, while the rest of the participants in *Stimulantia* were all of a younger generation with a modern, much lighter film language. I feared *Smycket* risked sinking like a stone. Something had to be done, and I asked myself what would happen if I just cut out the many time-denoting fades? Snip, snip, snip! Most of the heaviness was gone, and it looked great! The editing did not alter the story, only the fashion in which it was told. I spliced the bits back and the following day breached the subject as delicately as I could. Gustaf Molander listened without interrupting, head bowed. After a long silence he lifted his head, looked at me, and said with intense astonishment: 'Can one do that?' I said I thought so and added 'Do you wish to try it?' He nodded with smiling eyes, and cut by cut the manifestations of the past fell into my trim bin. It must have felt great to realise that even at the age of seventy-nine one's profession could still offer some surprises! I do not think The New Wave was terribly new anyway, for the silent cinema provided more than one example of a striking film language, and those who survived the Wave's first euphoria and numerous fatalities had certainly done their classics.

A film named *491*, scripted by Lars Görling, a writer in his early thirties, was directed by Vilgot Sjöman in 1964. This sexually bold film was banned in Sweden and temporarily barred in the USA, thereby no doubt helping to give Sjöman a reputation as notoriously risqué. I can not remember Görling getting tarnished, and he went on writing *Tillsammans med Gunilla måndag kväll och tisdag morgon*,[18] but this time he would make his debut as a director as well. I had been told that I was going to be his editor, and the news was not very welcome. At the time, I was working on a real 'turkey' with a rather stroppy first-timer who

had provided me with miles of insignificant takes but not enough cov-
erage of essential scenes. Two debutantes in a row was more than I
needed, but as I was the only full-time editor at the studio, I also knew
that I would not be able to get out of it. Was there any way I could
mitigate a second disaster?

There is no denying that if you have any analytical skills, other
people's mistakes are the most excellent low-cost learning material you
can come by, but would my present novice director allow Lars Görling
to visit the editing room? To my surprise he consented. Görling and I
had hardly ever spoken, only from time to time seen each other when
491 was made, and I had heard that he had been present, if only very
sporadically, during the filming. One day I found him sitting alone in
the cafeteria and walked over and asked if I could sit down. We started to talk about his new film, and I mentioned that if he felt it would be
useful to observe a bit of editing work before he started out, he was
welcome to the editing room when I worked alone. It turned out to
have been a good opening. Some days later Görling came for a visit, sat
down, and looked at what I was doing. We barely talked and I doubt
he stayed even one hour, but he continued to come back on other short
visits. One day when I was desperately rolling back and forth over
some barely rescuable material, Görling said: 'Why did he shoot it that
way?' Good question, but mindful that you do not criticise other director's material with a third party I asked: 'How would you have done it?'
He thought for a while and then suggested a sequence of shots that
sounded far superior to what I presently had on my hands. Then he disappeared and only paid me one or two more flying visits, but by then I
was convinced that my future editing assignment would be much less
painful than the present one. In some ways it was, but I had also counted my chickens before they had hatched.

Anything connected with cars and car racing made Görling tick, so
it was no surprise to find his film located in that world, but I felt he had
gone overboard with driving sequences. Already when synchronising
the material, I had no doubt about the tug-of-war that lay ahead:
Görling wanting to keep every frame of a sports car speeding through

a landscape, and I trying to establish some equilibrium between the core story and all this driving!

It had always been normal procedure to have an uninterrupted look at all the footage before any editing started, but that was not possible with Görling. He lived in such an intense fear, doubting the worth of what he had shot, and none of my reassurance or encouragements made the slightest difference. The first day, after having looked at only a couple of 300-metre reels, he began to perspire profusely, the blood had drained from his face, and he got up and left without a word. He did not turn up the following morning, but a long telephone conversation later in the day, and my suggestion that we should proceed in smaller steps, finally lured him back. All went well for a while although we, of course, progressed very slowly. When unexpectedly management inquired, I reported that all was well, but that the editing was going to take a bit longer than usual. A few days later the studio head Allan Ekelund called, telling me that the date for the premiere was set. It did not take much to figure out that with such a deadline the editing work had to be sped up considerably, and I told Allan that he had better let Görling know. He gave me some bull about me having such a good hand with the director and how much better it would be if the news came from me. I had already seen examples of Allan's cowardice and could not even be bothered to argue for very long. I was angry but hardly surprised. Ironically, the following day turned out to be the one when Görling held out for longer than he usually did. Knowing what I had to do, I toyed for a second with the idea of sending him down to Allan Ekelund's office, but in the end I cared too much for my director, and finally told him our news. Görling stared at me, started to shake, got up from his chair, grabbed his jacket and was gone. It was several weeks before I was going to see him again. I busied myself for a couple of days with the footage we had already looked at, but then called Allan Ekelund and told him where we were. His response was: 'Cut it yourself. It can always be changed later.' If that was a studio executive's appreciation of an editor and his understanding of the work in an editing room, what was the use of arguing? This time I just hung up on him.

The ethics that once guided me as a journalist had been clearly defined, but when I came to the film business, the water seemed murkier, and I had searched for a clear-cut definition of my place and that of my work. My conclusion: I was the midwife, but it was not my baby. It had to be my professional pride that the 'baby' came out in one piece and with no visible marks even if forceps had been used, but it was *not* my child! A child which was always attentively, and sometimes also lovingly, cared for but in the long run not even an adopted child. Today I still see the director as the parent and the editor as the dedicated nurse. Consequently I would argue, as long as I saw fit, for what I thought best for the film, but if the director was of another opinion, he or she had to stay in the editing room and tell me *exactly* what they wanted. I would execute their wishes, but I also reserved the right to take my name off the film if I felt that their instructions led to a disaster.

I lived through a terribly uncomfortable and very unproductive week. Görling refused to come to the editing room, there was a deadline looming, and I knew exactly where his and my judgement differed. I finally had to make up my mind and look at the material through my own glasses and treat it accordingly. There was a good plot, and it was well filmed; my only real problem was with what I saw as an overload of driving sequences. Görling's passion for cars and racing had gone into overdrive. When I had a 'fine-cut' I called Görling and suggested a screening. Fear immediately raised its ugly head, and he refused, but curiosity must have won the battle for the following morning he *was* back at the studio. We screened the film in the theatre and then went back to the editing room. After lengthy discussions, I, against my better judgement, reluctantly had to start to lengthen the driving sequences. The film passed the studio screening without any more changes and had its premiere on the chosen date. Several weeks after the premiere, Görling turned up unannounced in my editing room with a bouquet of flowers saying: 'I should have listened to you, the driving sequences are too long.' He had spent a number of evenings in the cinema, sneaking in when the film had started and observed, from a seat in the back, how the theatregoers reacted. It must have hurt to notice their diminishing concentration while his beloved cars raced and raced. He not only saw the truth, but had also taken the trouble to drive all the way out to the studio with the sole purpose of telling me.

It had been a very unusual and partly difficult experience, but there had also been a great deal of pleasure. Görling could be good company, he was a generous person, and his talent and willingness to learn made him truly loveable, and it made the work easy. His insecurities and his depth of despair had an intensity that was very frightening, but at the same time Görling's intellectual capacity and his unusually quick comprehension were a sheer delight. Evidently he had a great talent for cinema; the studio planned a new film, and I was looking forward to it. He had told me he had something on his work table.

In 1966, Görling — most likely by a sheer foolish mistake — died of an overdose. Swedish film lost a very promising director, and I lost a dear friend.

WEARING TWO HATS

When it opened in the early 60s, the Swedish Film School offered me a full-time teaching job. That I had no formal teaching qualifications did not seem to worry my future employers, but what I found alarming were the proposed arrangements. The school year was divided into two terms, with a short break for Christmas, and a three-month break during summer, when the students were supposed to gain job experience. It was surmised that the teachers were to both have a break and be able to reconnect with the industry; 'Not to lose touch' as it were. When it came to the teachers, I found the plan absurd. Summertime in Sweden was also preferred shooting time for most films; the theatres were closed, actors were more easily available, and in this frozen country a disproportionate number of scripts, with unrealistic hopes, called for sunny, summery exteriors. Editing would consequently only start in autumn — as did the school! So much for 'reconnecting.' Not all feature films, or even the majority of them, were cut in the same short time and orderly fashion as a Bergman film, so even if, by chance, a chain of fortunate circumstances begot a 'reconnect,' it also made any rest an illusion. I am sure the idea looked very good on paper, but in reality it was tenuous at best.

I thought there was a solution and suggested that they might be better off with two part-time jobs as that would allow for much more flexibility to go between the school and the industry. They listened patiently and then shook their heads. Two pay cheques, two pension forms, etc., etc. Oh no, all that was far too complicated. We parted ways, and I continued at Svensk Filmindustri.

The following year three film students spent their summer at the studio, and after a short while, they started to regularly seek my company in the cafeteria. They were pleasant lunch company and it did not take them long before asking if they could come to my editing room. My explanation that it could not happen, unless the director I presently worked with, had given his permission, obviously came as a surprise.

Unless there is some riveting acting to watch, it quickly becomes enormously tedious to be an observer on a film set where the process is endlessly repetitive. Since everybody is pressed for time and has to concentrate on the job at hand, nobody is likely to have time to answer questions from an outsider. We all need role models, especially in the beginning, but students also need explanations for *why* things are made to happen the way they do. Without it they seldom process what they observe, and they risk simply becoming clones — which is not very good and also utterly useless. To sit in the background in an editing room and observe the work of an editor and a director would not be much more enlightening because, when the two know each other, I find that there is usually not a whole lot of discussion going on — at least not as long as things run smoothly. You might debate *why,* but the *how* is hardly ever brought up, and if it is, it is not on a level that the beginner normally is ready for. Given permission to visit when I worked alone, the three film students showed both interest and intelligence. They were very attentive and it only took them one morning to learn that my editing room was not a place for chatter; the concentration on the rhythm of my work excludes any such thing and they disciplined themselves to patiently wait for the appropriate moment before voicing their questions. Through our lunch conversations I had gleaned that the school was not living up to their expectations, but it was not clear to me if this was a result of the students' exaggerated anticipations or because the school was malfunctioning.

I know that when recruiting teachers, the pool to fish in had been neither wide nor deep. As happens everywhere, the very best people are usually already employed and happy where they are, and inflexible employment conditions are not going to help to lure them away. Others, often freelancers, can be outstanding performers in their chosen field, but do not necessarily have a flair for teaching. By the same token, art students seem to have some common traits: overlooking that doing well takes more than 'inspiration,' and their sense of entitlement is seldom modest. Very soon I was taken to task. 'Why are you not teaching at the Film school?' I explained the reasons and thought no more of it until the studies rector, Bertil Lauritzen, called, telling me that a student delegation had come to see him, *demanding* that I be employed. That their action was a cry for help was easy to understand, and as my resisting-powers in such instances are not very good, I did understand them. All the same I felt — and also let them know — that they ought to have talked to me before marching off to the higher echelons; not just assuming that teaching them and their comrades would make my day. To their good luck, I had not forgotten that my own employment at Svensk Filmindustri had only come about by sheer chance, and what had ensued had left me with a sense of moral duty to pass on all this tremendous knowledge effusing from Bergman's editing room. I promised to think about the school's offer.

It was slightly more complicated than just thinking about it, for I had a full-time contract with the studio. There were, however, two facts in my favour. The political powers that had created the Swedish Film Institute and the Film School had, while to some extent easing their economic burdens, also put certain responsibilities on the industry, and Bergman had accepted to act as the school's inspector. Were my employers really in the position to say no? On the condition that my work at the studio would not suffer, they and Bergman gave their somewhat lukewarm blessings. The school acknowledged that the studio had first call and agreed to a contract on an hourly basis. If I already was a workaholic, I now ended up in good company: the film school students seemed to work 24/7. Their demands on my evenings and weekends were both insistent and never-ending; there was no longer any space for my own interests outside work. To teach was interesting, however, and to my delight I very soon became aware that my own way of thinking started to become influenced by it. The process of explaining the same rules over and over again led me to ask: 'Is this really the only way? Can it not be done differently, and if so, what will happen?' It did not change the basic rules, but it opened up new ways of looking at their applications. As long as things run smoothly, there is little or no incentive for such mental processes.

Although I had gained knowledge and experience in Bergman's editing room, it was through my teaching that the knowledge finally gelled and gave new depth to my own aptitude.

With no formal training, I knew nothing of accepted teaching methods, and that was probably just as well. Film school students, at least if they are aspiring directors, seem to have a creative drive on a higher level than most other students. With few exceptions, the ones I met came to the school intent on making 'a *new* cinema' but without much knowledge of how to even make the old one. To leave them enough individual creative freedom, and at the same time hold them to learn the basic rules, was more easily said than done. There was of course some opposition, but on the whole they not only understood but also accepted, although sometimes grudgingly, that my few rules had some basis, and for the most part, we had quite a good relationship. Like all new institutions, the school had yet to find its form. It *was* truly chaotic, and the students *were* unhappy and as a result unruly. The first year's group had been put to work on a small film of their own as soon as they arrived. In theory it might have appeared to be a good idea to give them some hands-on experience. In practice it turned into a disaster. They did not have enough background knowledge, and a first-year camera student filming for a first-year directing student was in reality the blind leading the deaf. Their material was so lacking in most respects that no learning was involved, and their efforts to make any sense of it in the editing room only led to despair. The school was indeed a very sorry place, and although the reasons for it no doubt were numerous, the main one was of the school's own making.

In order to select the most gifted students, the school had requested a psychologist to construct a test that would detect the most gifted candidates. What they had not understood — and certainly not bargained for — was that this would also land them with the most stubborn, the most opinionated, and most individualistic students! Realising they needed some help they had, shortly after my arrival, asked the psychologist to come in and give advice. His first act was to have an individual talk with everybody: management, staff and students. For me his presence brought back some old memories from my time as a journalist.

I had written a four-part series about the Swedish national defence and it had involved going down in a submarine, flying in the two-seater training version of our latest attack plane, and going on manoeuvre with the army. Talk about 'embedded!' At the time the word had not yet moved from the dictionaries into everyday parlance, neither had feminine military field personnel found any place in the general's thinking. Presuming that it was a secretary at the paper who had made the request, there was always the same consternation when I first turned up. Everybody, without question, had expected a male journalist, but once over the fence, I never had any difficulties; it was the jump that sometimes asked for inventiveness. When I made the initial telephone call I would give the name of the paper I was writing the article for but not volunteer my own. Once the deal was done, and they asked who the paper was going to send, I truthfully answered 'Redaktör Ryghe,' mightily pleased that the Swedish word for editor is genderless.

The topic for the fourth article involved an interview with a psychologist mandated to develop a test that would prevent the defence from wasting time and money in training people who further down the road turned out to be less than desirable soldier material. To this end he had also written a new training manual, which I needed to read before setting off to interview him. A polite request to borrow the book from the military was turned down with the explanation that it was classified material and could not be taken out of the Headquarters! Could I come to the Headquarters and read it there? After much hesitation, I got the permission and endured, under ultimate politeness, the most ridiculous Sunday of my whole life. I was let into the locked building in the morning and escorted to a room where the manual, a notepad, and several pens were all laid out in neat formation. My handbag was given an inspection, but my briefcase was taken into temporary custody.

My gaoler, a very nice officer, offered to fetch me coffee and then left, locking the door behind him. He brought me coffee, returned midmorning to inquire if I wished to make a visit to the washroom, later brought me lunch, offered afternoon tea and another washroom visit.

Each calling ended with the sound of the door being locked. Finally, at five o'clock, he let me out, but not before having read my notes and checked that all the pages in the manual were intact! The 'master-spy' got her briefcase back and was free to go home and prepare for an interview with the author of this remarkably secret document.

Meeting the author was not fraught with the same rigmarole, but I had a nagging fearfulness that all my questions would go through his psychological value system before he answered them. Paranoid? Possibly, but who would not be after having been in the lock-up? I could have spared myself all this angst because the eventual article met with approval and compliments. It had been years since that first and only meeting, but he still remembered it. However, this time, he was the one asking the questions: 'What do you think is wrong?' It took some effort not to laugh. 'Is it not obvious? You tested the students, but you did not test the teachers!' I honestly did not try to be uppity, but to me it seemed all too evident. The good doctor smiled and let me go.

My teaching debut had been a baptism by fire. The day I arrived I was asked to make contact with what the school considered its most problematic student. He had arrived with only rudimentary knowledge of filmmaking and a burning desire to make *the* film about boxing, his all-encompassing passion, and into the bargain he also brought a considerable distrust of all authority. After the shoot he had locked himself in the editing room, refusing to let teachers or co-students in. The fact that I came from outside and thus was unencumbered by his earlier run-ins with the staff might have acted in my favour, unless it was simply that he finally had come to the end of his tether. Whichever, the door opened a crack, and I met Chaos. There was no story unfolding on the screen, his work print was in bits and pieces with trims all over the place. He could not find anything he was looking for, and to add insult to injury, the poor guy had no hand at all with his editing table. It would have taken ages to put some order to this muddle, and as I suspected the end result to be more humiliation than learning, I suggested a new work print — if I could obtain one. The offer was accepted, and the school obliged. We started anew by screening all the footage and then had a long conversation, telling each other what we thought we had experienced. The director was still totally absorbed by his initial idea and imagined that all of it was up there on his screen. It was clearly not the moment to tell him otherwise, so I fell back on theory and recounted some of the things Bergman used to tell Vilgot Sjöman about the damage you will inflict on your story if you try to 'bend' your footage, try to make it conform to the intentions you once had. What unfolds on the screen is the *only* story you have, the script is no longer relevant, and if there has been any straight thinking at all, the footage is telling *something*, and it is *this* you have to work with. As a morale booster, I also mentioned that not even Bergman films left the editing room in a shape and form identical to their scripts.[19] I also talked about the concept of unhurried, methodical editing from beginning to end, repeated as long as necessary, and promised him that, if he kept to this order, he would effortlessly also detect the rhythm inherent in his footage. To my great relief, this seemed to make sense to the now much calmer student, and it was time to show him that his editing table was his tool and not his nemesis.

His mental dexterity was, at least in the beginning, superior to that of his hands, but he was far from clumsy, and best of all, he was determined to learn. The orderliness quelled the earlier panic and my avoidance of authority made him a different person altogether. He mastered the basic rules very quickly and — best of all — the way he looked at his images started to change. I spent a couple of evening hours with him every day for about a week, but never offered any value-based comments, only intervening when he was on his way into a technical error. Then came the day when he politely declared that he now wanted to work on his own. Fine! After some time, I was invited back to look at his efforts and was shown a well-working little documentary on a boxer's daily workout. He had eventually come to the probably painful but necessary realisation that he had not brought in the imagery needed for the big boxing film he had been dreaming of. Once he had come to terms with the facts, he had been free to see that his images intimated a related story that only waited to be told. And he had told it! I was very proud of my student.

Contracted to a studio where other editors were only seldom brought in, I knew my colleagues' work from the cinemas, but I did not meet them in person. One in this group was Margit Nordqvist who, when she came to the school, had for years worked in both the film industry and TV. She was experienced, did not take any bull, and was humorous and warm; we worked well together. With time we also developed a long-lasting friendship that we kept alive even after I left Sweden, and until an undetected stomach cancer in 1994 caused Margit's deplorable death.

When I started, Margit had already worked at the school for some time and it did not take us long to understand that our readings of the school's problems were identical. Both believed that the right teaching approach was *theory through practice,* but we also knew all too well that it was not a good idea to start by throwing the students in at the deep end. Something had to be done, and we spent considerable time trying to find a method where the theory was learned by doing, giving the students their hotly longed for hands-on-experiences and, last but not least, showed immediate results. It was quite a tall order, but the idea we finally came up with was good because it was simple, not very expensive, and it would allow us to teach what basic mistakes look like and what they lead to. Bertil Lauritzen gave his okay, and we started by writing a simple script with about fifteen dialogue-free scenes for two actors. At the beginning of the summer recess, the head of the camera department kindly helped us with the filming. He was quietly amused by our 'invention,' which amounted to each scene being filmed a number of times but with only one take that was correct in all technical aspects. In the others, we smuggled in an assortment of all the common mistakes we could think of: looking in the wrong direction in relation to the preceding scene, entering from the left side of the frame when it should have been from the right, letting an object suddenly appear from nowhere in the middle of the story, framing so that you could see objects beyond the limits of the set, etc., etc. Between the two of us, Margit and I playfully made use of our past negative experiences in our respective editing rooms, and we did not lack material.

In autumn, the new intake was started off by learning how to use an editing table and some basic editing skills. Once that was mastered, they were each given a work print of our footage and a list of the rules: a prescribed editing time, the minimum of scenes that *had* to be used, and a set length for the final edit. We arranged our working schedules in such a way that one of us always was at the school during their editing time, and we did help out in technical emergencies but steadfastly refused any 'creative' help or advice. Our standard answer to, 'Will it be better if I do it this way or that way?' was, 'Try it both ways and see for yourself!' When time was up, we arranged the big 'gala premiere' and together looked at all the films. Their realisation that every student was showing a different film, although they all started out with the same footage, became a valuable base for reflections on the editing process. Was the mandate to produce the best possible film in a reasonable time frame, or was it to see in how many varying ways you could cut your footage? The students differed in their approach, and that was fine with both Margit and me, as long as they understood and respected that the trial-and error situation they were allowed at the school would not exist in the film and/or TV-industries where expectations and rules were very different.

By depriving our students of dialogue, we hoped to draw their attention to the concept of visual language. Except for the hearing impaired, spoken language is the normal tool for communication in all Western cultures, and more often than not, the information emitting from an image is not conceived as 'language.' As we expected, they all complained about the fact that our little film had been mute, but looking at their films and discussing the image content, they started to see that what they had been given was explicit enough to *show* the story. Depriving them of dialogue had been our way of introducing the retraining from ears to eyes, but to effect change from *telling* towards *showing* takes constant awareness and frequent pushing. I had for years been dealing with this concept in my editing room, but without the need to either verbalise or teach it. It now became an amusing challenge to find the right tools to take it from theory to practice. I saw it as an analogue to learning Chinese; initially you have to understand how a sign language works. To then master it, your way of thinking has to change, otherwise the new grammar does not make sense.

Another eye-opener was to experience the strength of peer pressure. Neither Margit nor I sat on a pedestal, and in most cases we were approached more as friends than as teachers, and our technical teaching was seldom questioned. When we felt that we had to be 'content critical,' the majority of the students normally listened and accepted what we had to say, but when it came to films that were so 'artful' that the story was lost on the viewer, the culprits always tried to save their skin by pretending that 'we were another generation, and we did not understand.' When some of their fellow students also voiced their confusion, the argument did not wash, and I learned that teaching in groups, if they were small enough, often worked better than individual tutoring.

Wearing two hats meant both fun and frustration. The frustration lay mostly in the fact that I never felt that I had enough time for the students, while the fun part was in the interaction with them, together with my own need to think through and find accurate words for what until now had been habit and intuition. Repeated mistakes I abhor, and I wished to be able to make my students understand how best to avoid them. In my experience it starts with taking a long, hard look at what you have done once the toil is over. When something does not work on the screen, most of the time it is not very complicated to find out where the fault line goes, but to dissect the fine details of the good, or even great, is much more difficult. The exercise is often painful, but the real learning is only arrived at when one can explain why something is successful or faulty. Whether as editor or director, the process of stacking the 'shelves' in your brain with a reference library of what had or had not worked is the only available insurance against mindless repetition of old mistakes. Why continue to parade them, when there are so many new ones lying in wait for you?

IN THE COMPANY OF STRANGERS:
Russia beckons, but the ship sails to Montreal

Still living in Sweden, my understanding of how the rest of the world saw us as a country was probably inadequate, but it also worked two ways. Because I was born there, grew up there, everything was familiar and more or less acceptable. When people abroad asked me where I came from, Sweden ever so often was confounded with Switzerland, and I slowly realised that being a small, northern country, its name and geographical position, its culture, and the rest of its characteristics were, to most people, beyond the frontiers of general knowledge. At the time — the mid-60s — Sweden was the ultimate welfare state, and that seemed to be known far and wide. Statistical claims made it *the place* where the grass was greener, but for me it had started to become too green. Social security that I did not think I needed or wanted was forced upon me in the holy name of equality. Even if it took a hefty chunk out of my pay packet, I was fully prepared to carry my part of the obligation to provide every citizen with basic needs, but beyond that I felt, and still feel, that everybody should be allowed to make their own choices.

I also unexpectedly met with something that both frightened and saddened me. One of my colleagues at the studio — an exquisite craftsman — suddenly, almost from one day to the next, had lost his quest for flawlessness. The very high quality of his work was no longer in evidence, and he even saw it himself, but offered utterly embarrassing excuses and reasons why it could still pass. His health seemed as good as ever so *why* did this happen? The logical, deeply disturbing question was not far away: what guaranteed that I was not going to end up in the same corner sooner or later? I was happy in my work and had no reason to doubt that the contentment would not last as long as I wished it to. The editing of Bergman's yearly film was something I still looked forward to. However, I also found that this work had had an unexpected and wholly unwanted consequence: I had become pigeon-holed as 'Bergman's editor.' I found it not only uncomfortable, but also misdirected; I did a lot of other editing as well. The irony was that the director himself had never tried to shape me in such a way, but the more his international reputation grew, the more adhesive the label became. Spending my holidays abroad had not only started to widen my horizon, but also given me a taste for something beyond the Swedish smug contentment, which started to become more serious than slightly irritating. I figured that if I left not only Sweden, but also all the security and comfort my life there afforded me, I might have an opportunity to avoid the sort of decline that had befallen my studio colleague. Never one to come to important personal decisions quickly, it took two years before I was sure of the next step. My friends said I was courageous, but I am not so sure about that. It might be common sense to take to your heels, but I do not know if it is a sign of courage. What I do know is that I have never regretted having left, and any desire to return has not ever upset my sleep.

I had already for some time had a wish to go to The National Film Board of Canada, but that my first destination became Montreal was a mere coincidence. Svensk Filmindustri had generously sent me to Russia on a study tour. Moscow had been the first stop, but both the city and the rather pompous Mosfilm left me cold. The studio was large, old, and in my eyes as outmoded as many of the films I was shown. All the same there were some interesting things, such as a meeting with the young Andrei Tharkovsky. I had already seen his second feature film, *Ivan's Childhood*, and had admired both its humanity and the director's skills. Like many of the films produced in Russia during the 60s, *Ivan's Childhood* was inspired by events from the Second World War and the artistic fermentation had only taken some twenty odd years. It made me conscious that the events from the First War, which had inspired films like Joseph Losey's *King and Country* (1964), had needed double that time before horror had nurtured inspiration. The high speed of the information age suddenly became tangible. Tharkovsky had made *Ivan's Childhood* in 1962 and a year later had his script for *Andrei Roublev* ready. When I met him, he was still waiting for the green light and, as it turned out, would have to do so until 1967. After he heard that I had not seen *And Quiet Flows the Don*, Sergei Gerasimov's fascinating rendering of Mikhail Sholohov's novel about the impact of revolution and war on a village family at the time of the First World War, he arranged for a screening. I greatly enjoyed the film and was awed by its ability to progress so slowly without being tedious. At the time it was only, at least to my knowledge, the Japanese and the Russians who successfully mastered this form of storytelling: slow, majestic, detail conscious, but never leaden.

An entire morning spent in the editing room with Eisenstein's old editor turned out to be good fun. I was taken to a fairly large room where a fine-boned, white-haired elderly lady dressed in a white smock worked at a big, clumsy editing table. My guide introduced us, and Esphier Tobak's first words were: 'Do you not think it is a shame that somebody my age still has to work?' As one could clearly sense that even wild horses could not drag her away from her beloved table, I could not keep myself from laughing and told her that I did not think it was such a terrible thing. She in turn started to laugh, and what, at the outset, was only meant to be a courtesy call turned into a couple of animated hours between two colleagues. She was working on a documentary about Lenin in Switzerland, and with much pride pointed out that she was the only editor at Mosfilm allowed to work on her own without the director present! She showed me how she worked and demonstrated her Russian-built table. Big and clumsy it might have been, but it had one excellent feature that my elegant, German-made table in Stockholm lacked: a small prism at the top of the table that allowed you to screen a small roll of film without removing the big one you were working on. Western Europe had not yet started to build the double-screen tables, but when they arrived I never took to them. Not only did I find them complicated but the convenience of two screens spelled danger for the useful practice of memorising all your footage. That little Russian device was, however, in all its simplicity, a desirable, excellent helper and time saver.

I stayed in a hotel that startlingly resembled the one I had visited on my screen when working on *The Silence*. It had the same imposing, sparsely lit, endless corridors, where ten-year-old Johan had roamed, while his mother Anna was out and his aunt Ester lay dying in her room. My Moscow hotel had beautiful parquetry floors that had not seen any beeswax in a very long time and perfectly starched linen frayed along the edges.

The more than one million daily visitors to Moscow seemed, by their clothing and their features, to come mostly from the eastern Russia that lay beyond the Ural mountain range. Visiting a dubbing studio housed in a former church, I was told that Russian films were dubbed into twenty-three different languages — languages not dialects — for distribution in Russia alone! The visitors livened up the street scene, but I all the same found Moscow a very drab and austere city. The first snow of the year fell on my last night there, and the following morning, all the way to the airport I saw brigades of bundled-up elderly women sweeping the streets with brooms. An old transport machine from the war, with metal seats devoid of any upholstery, and a not-too-well-working air pressure system, took me on a bumpy ride to my next destination.

Saint Petersburg, or Leningrad, as it was then called, was very different. It had a lighter atmosphere, people seemed more approachable, and the city itself, built on several islands in the Neva River, was beautiful. Arriving on a Wednesday morning, before doing anything else, I asked my guide if she by any chance could get me a ticket to the Saint Petersburg Symphony Orchestra's weekly Wednesday evening concert. I did not have high hopes, for in Moscow I had already learned that tickets had to be bought well in advance, and for some unexplained bureaucratic reason you were not allowed to buy more than one ticket at a time. Consequently, every day started in a lineup in front of the ticket seller. I do not know if it was a cultural habit, the overcrowded living conditions, or some other factor, but every cultural venue — whether theatre, concerts, circus, or ballet — was sold out to the last seat all the time. Sure enough, there was not a seat to be had, but my guide had obviously great powers of persuasion, and the person at the box office finally gave in and told her that if I came down there fifteen minutes before the start of the concert, they would see what could be done. I turned up as summoned, gave my name, and waited. Shortly a man came out, greeted me, and took me inside to a harmoniously shaped, long rectangular hall with high-backed chairs on the floor and a raised podium at one end, but with no balconies or upper levels. Behind a couple of low, wide steps, leading to the side areas, were more seats. Some empty tabourets were placed on the first of the steps, and I was directed to one of them.

On the program was one of Dimitri Shostakovich's symphonies, and although he no longer lived in Saint Petersburg, the composer himself was present and conducted it. The orchestra was at its best, and the audience electrified. The applause did not stop. In Moscow I had gone to a couple of Chekhov plays, and each performance had been a revelation. I thought I knew my Chekhov but oh no! What I experienced here was not only masterful performances, but the bearing of a soul where tears and laughter, joy and sorrow, melancholy and energy were inseparable parts of the whole. A volatile mixture of feelings that in the West always seem to be compartmentalised. In this concert hall I met the same kind of dramatic intensity, where the audience members were not mere listeners but — still on their chairs — true participants. In the intermission I was taken to the green room and introduced to the composer and others, served champagne and caviar-filled canapés. Who had my guide made me out to be in order to swing all this and a ticket that I had not even been allowed to pay for? The intermission over, I was escorted back to my seat. When the concert ended, I was again fetched and asked if I would like a cup of tea. This graceful person, with enough English and German to make a conversation possible, took me to a place where you got tea and baked goods. Everybody was eating and drinking standing up, and there was a constant coming and going of people who either had just finished a late day shift or were going off to a night shift. Finally I was accompanied back to my hotel.

The city, which during the war had suffered a two-year deadly strangulation by German forces, had in the intervening years risen from its ashes. Before the war, I was told, the centre had been overbuilt with a mixture of original baroque buildings and later copies. At the end of the war, with nearly every building in Saint Petersburg more or less severely destroyed, the city had been divided up into what they called 'architect zones.' Each of them were closely looked at; original baroque buildings were kept, restored and made into government offices — the copies bulldozed. There was a huge homeless population with immediate needs, and big colourless housing complexes had been erected further out from the centre where the pastel-coloured little palaces now formed a very graceful nave. Lenfilm's studio had before the war been in the central city, but they had at the time almost out-grown its space. Now they were located some twenty kilometres out of town where they had built new studios. With mobile walls, the size of the shooting stages were made flexible, the equipment was modern and light and the whole atmosphere very different from the one at Mosfilm. I had already seen some recent feature films made by Lenfilm and had been impressed both by artistic values and by technique. Now I also got the impression that this was a place where it might be very inter-esting to work for some time.

Once back home in Stockholm, I talked to the person who had arranged the trip. He imported Russian films, seemed to have excellent contacts, and was, as always, more than willing to help. It did not go quickly, but the word from the Russian side was positive, and I started to learn the language. Then, after a considerable wait, the Russians demanded that my request should go through official channels, and I turned to The Swedish Institute for cultural exchange with foreign countries. As I did not intend to do research, but wished to go to Lenfilm and work as any other editor, my request was a bit out of the ordinary. The difference was evidently appreciated by my contact per-son who turned out to have been a senior lecturer at the university in Lund when I was a student. He did, of course, not recognise me but was always interested, helpful, and personable. There was another long wait while The Institute tried come to an arrangement with Lenfilm, and from time to time, I was assured that things were on the right track. Initially they might have been, but eventually they became derailed, and we were told that I could only come to Russia as part of a Russian-Swedish co-production. Nice try, but no thank you! To make up for the disappointment, I was asked if there was anything else The Institute could do for me? Yes, if they could find a way to send me to the National Film Board of Canada, as well as to Redwood City in the States, where I wanted to learn videotape editing, I would be grateful. Little did I know that The Institute, only days before, had entered into discussions about a co-production between themselves and NFB. It was the first time The Swedish Institute ventured into film; so far they had only been involved in the print medium.

The following week I was called to a meeting and introduced to John Kemeny, a National Film Board producer with the Challenge for Change program. It had started in 1967 when the Canadian director Colin Low made a film on Fogo Island in Newfoundland where a small fishing village seemed doomed to be depopulated. Sweden had seen radical changes when, after the Second World War, the economy impacted on the labour market. Among those hardest hit were the forestry and fishing industries. Canada had similar problems, and as Sweden was known to have found what seemed workable solutions to many of its troubles, the Challenge for Change program was interested in looking at the Swedish methods. They had a co-production in mind and wished to send a director, Mort Ransen, and a cameraman, Martin Duckworth, to Sweden. I was asked to become part of the project, employed as the Swedish production manager and then the future editor in Montreal. The films were going to be shot during the summer and autumn of 1968. I had once again been in the right place at the right time!

Well aware that my decision to leave would not be popular, and could also create a problem that might be difficult to solve, I wished to give Svensk Filmindustri an early notice. When, at the end of 1966, I signed the contract for the coming year, I accordingly advised the studio that it would be the last one. Nobody believed me. Although I insisted that I was serious, they seemed very sure that there was nothing a good salary increase could not fix. Workloads and contract dates had no understanding of alignment, and at the end of 1967, I still had unfinished business in my editing room. We agreed on a short-term contract running until I had finished the work already started, and in this way *Shame* became my last film with Bergman.

In early spring I established an NFB office at The Swedish Institute, did research for the Canadians, learned the 'ins and outs' of customs regulations, and scampered around to find an assistant camera person and a sound engineer who could both speak English. Today it would not be a headache to find such people, but back then it was. An American who lived in Sweden finally became the assistant cameraman, and the sound technician was a Swede with some very basic English when he started the job. The choice of Mort Ransen as the series director had not been a happy one, and I did not understood why he had been chosen — I was later told he had been the only one available — nor why he had accepted the assignment. Mort on principle disliked Sweden because it was a capitalistic country, albeit with social-democratic policies. Once in the country, he did nothing to verify whether or not it was, as he liked to think, a place of capitalist decadence and bourgeois degeneracy. It started badly. When I brought him and his girlfriend to the hotel, the receptionist first insisted on changing the double room I had booked to two single rooms. In 1968, two unmarried people in a double room was not a reputable Swedish hotel's idea of decorum. The touted Swedish sexual freedom got its first chip. Because Mort made a point not to show the slightest understanding and/or respect for any Swedish customs or feelings, it was not a very easy nor a very happy shoot.

Martin Duckworth was very different, not always that well organised but enthusiastic, open, and warm. When I asked him about his impressions of Sweden, he sent me the following:

1968 was the year when the dream of a world of peace and justice seemed within reach to my generation. Sweden was a model. What impressed me most was that the country reminded me strangely of my adolescent years in Nova Scotia — the rocky coast, the school gymnastics, the afternoon coffee breaks, the suburban malls, the church sermons, the military displays, the loneliness of the city (Stockholm) at night. Ulla helped me get images of all these things that then haunted me. When back in Montreal, she taught me how editing can make poetry out of disconnected images. The result was my first (own) film, *Passing Through Sweden*.

Reading Martin's note I was somewhat perplexed as I would have done exactly the opposite: gone for the new and unknown. I do, however, think that it is a film we both can be proud of. Not only has it stood up surprisingly well against the ravages of time but it also has had an insistency in following me. Thirteen years after its birth, I met it in, of all places, the film library at the Australian Film School. Less of a surprise — at least from a geographical point of view — was that after my return to Montreal in 1992, Martin asked me to be present when he showed it to his Concordia University students. A week earlier these same students had been seduced by the magnitude of IMAX, and although they still talked about it with awe, *Passing Through Sweden* succeeded in holding their interest. I was pleasantly surprised by how fresh the film felt, and Martin got so emotional watching his own first film that he had to leave the room for a while.

In the beginning of November 1968, I closed down the Swedish production office and packed my bags. Because I was exhausted, and in the hope of taking my soul with me, I had decided to travel more slowly than by plane. On my way over by ship, I was also going to spend some days in England where I had an invitation to give a talk to The Editors Guild in London, and then before leaving from Liverpool, I had to make a short visit to Dublin. It was to be my first experience giving a speech to a gathering of my peers, and on my first morning in London I deeply regretted that I had allowed myself to get into something like this. In the end, however, it turned out to be a very nicely organised low-key evening beginning with some drinks before the screening of *Persona*. I then said a few words, invited questions, and before long it became a very animated exchange among editors, eventually continuing over supper. The following days were filled with studio visits, impromptu invitations to screenings, and small, informal gatherings with people who had a genuine interest in our mutual work. I had always liked London, and this visit became memorable as it made my first timid steps on the world stage easier and much more pleasurable than I had ever anticipated.

After five hectic days, I turned north and drove to Liverpool in the worst 'pea soup' one could imagine. Normally I like driving and had been looking forward to seeing a part of England that was unknown to me, but this drive was unnerving — until I encountered some British civility that took away some of the strain. At a constant speed I drove behind another car and its tail lights, faint as they were in that grey bubble, were a big help in keeping me on the road. After some time, the driver slowed down, and as I did not dare to pass him on the single lane road, I had to do the same. He sped up, he slowed down, and I could not figure out what he was up to until it finally dawned on me that it might be a signal for me to pass him. We were in a pocket where the fog was slightly less thick, and you could just make out that there was no oncoming traffic. For the rest of the long drive to Liverpool, we took turns guiding each other. Just outside the city, the fog started to lift, and I could for the first time clearly see the other car, and in the late afternoon we honked our horns, waved to each other, and this total stranger took a roundabout while I drove on down to the harbour and left my car with the boat people before boarding my plane to Ireland.

The Dublin visit was also work related, as John Houston, who was filming there, wished to talk to me. At the time, he was toying with the idea of establishing a film school in Ireland, and wanted to know if I would be interested in working there. His plans were still vague, but I was not averse to the idea; from what I had heard and read about Ireland and the Irish, it seemed to be an unusual and very interesting place. My Dublin host was Patrick (Paddy) Carey, an Irish filmmaker and cameraman who had worked on, among many other films, *A Man For All Seasons*, Fred Zinnemann's remarkable film from 1966. Paddy had for some time kindly acted as my 'agent,' and thanks to him in London I had already been able to meet with some directors who had manifested their interest in future collaborations. In Dublin Paddy introduced me to film people, showed me the city, and took me to friends who lived in the countryside. I had left Sweden in the first days of snow and winter frost, and England, although much milder, had showed me fog at its worst. After that, Ireland was almost unreal: sunny and warm with azaleas and rhododendrons in bloom, it certainly lived up to its name as the 'Emerald Island,' but at that time of the year Dublin could also be fogged in, almost without any notice. Each evening Paddy called the weather forecaster to learn if another 24 hours could be safely added to my stay, and then made more plans for another well-filled day. I finally flew from Dublin to Liverpool on the date my boat was going to sail, and was on board at four o'clock. An hour later we weighed anchor, and I was on my way to Montreal.

Three hurricanes made for a bumpy ride, nearly four days longer than expected. Fewer and fewer passengers appeared in the dining room, and the ship's doctor was a busy man. The honour to have been placed at the captain's table did not count for much, as our captain spent most of his time on the bridge. The second evening he was called up halfway through his dinner, and after that his chair stood empty for the rest of the journey. A couple of times, however, I was to my surprise invited to share his afternoon tea. His personal purser would come and find me somewhere on the wet and blustery deck, extend the invitation, accompany me to my cabin so I could shed my wet attire, and finally lead me to his master's living room, serving a very nice tea. The captain looked more and more sleep-deprived as the days went by, and yet another hurricane battered his ship, but he was easy company. To my great surprise, I found out that this tall and sturdy man relaxed by doing beautiful, delicate needlepoint.

In the dining room we were four people around his table: an American couple returning home from their yearly golf season in Spain, and an extremely quiet man in his late twenties — as far as I could guess. He only spoke when ordering his food, but the Americans did not seem to notice. They had already made several crossings, and finding out that this was my first one, they showered me with all sorts of advice — among other rhubarb I got to know when to book the beauty salon if I wished to disembark with my vanished curls in perfect order. They were undoubtedly well-intended, but also utterly boring in their endless retelling of their own carefree existence and with no telescope focused outside its perimeter.

After a day or two, I noticed something strange. The quiet man at my side, at every meal without exception chose the same courses as I had ordered from the extensive menu. Unaware, the American couple prattled on over their own clever choices, but I started to become intrigued. I never saw him on deck; we only met in the dining room, but then one night I spotted him in the bar and went in and sat down. I was politely offered a drink, but otherwise nothing much was said, and I eventually went back to my cabin none the wiser. Assuming that a couple more drinks might annihilate his shyness, the next evening I waited a while longer before turning up. The hunch panned out, and over the following nights I listened to an intriguing tale. As I had guessed from his accent, Jack was American and after having spent a number of years on an American oil field in Saudi Arabia was now reluctantly on his way back to the States. He had come out as a youngster, and as it had been his first time away from home, his new freedom in this little American compound had seemed very attractive. But as he slowly worked his way up to a supervisor position, unusual for his age, the mess life, the alcohol, the girls, the cinema began to bore him, and he had started to venture outside the gates. This way he got to know some Arabs, eventually made friends among them, and spent more and more of his time off in their company. He got invited to their tents, shared their meals, and went hunting with them in the desert. This lifestyle excited him more than anything he so far had known, but even if he felt less and less American, Jack was clearheaded enough to realise that he would never become one of them. I was not sipping my drink in the company of a new Lawrence of Arabia, but had the thrill to see passion conquer all feelings of inadequacy. The Western formality around the dining room table made him feel totally out of place, and he was unsure of how to behave. Jack's copycat ordering got its explanation. He had figured that the surest way of avoiding any faux pas was to do as I did! Unfortunately for him, our tastes were not 100% similar, and the poor chap had, without letting on, chewed on *Homard à l'Armoricaine* with the same reluctance as he had once, in an Arab tent, eaten his first grilled sheep's head. He had eventually taken to the sheep's head but doubted he would try the lobster again. He was quietly amused when I told him that the dish most often wrongly appears on menus as *'à l'américane'* although it hails from France, where the old Celtic name for Bretagne was Armor.

Montreal had been our original destination, but as the St. Lawrence river was frozen solid beyond Quebec City, the voyage finally stopped there late one evening. Early next morning we were to disembark and drive our different ways. Jack had never been to Canada, and when he realised that I hadn't either, he suggested that we should drive in company and over the weekend discover the city together. It sounded like a good idea, but in the grey light of early morning, Jack's shyness again seemed to have got the better of him. He and his car were gone. I, of course, never saw him again but have once in a blue mooon wondered what became of him. Did he ever adjust, did he return to the Arab world, did he drown in alcohol? Did he ever see Montreal? When the customs officer saw that I did not have winter tires on my car, he told me to forget the old, much more beautiful route from Quebec City to Montreal that Martin Duckworth had talked affectionately about. I was shown the way to the autoroute. The sun had come up, and driving through a white, icy landscape that had already been snow covered for more than a month, it struck me how it resembled Dalarna, north of Stockholm. After such a distance, had I by some wicked machination already come full circle, and was back where I had started?

Of course I was used to snow, but the ferocity of the Montreal winter was a surprise; after all, its latitude was considerably to the south of

Stockholm's. The good news was much more sunlight and longer day-light hours than I had been used to during the winter. On my first day, there had been a snowstorm warning in the morning, and by noon the Board closed down. Somebody helpfully took me to the nearest garage where I got winter tires on the car. Foolishly, in the beginning I thought that these on-and-off repeated snowstorm warnings were a bit ridicu-lous and that sending people home early catered more to laziness than to safety, but that was only until I myself got caught in a blinding snow-storm. I finally understood how suddenly and with what force it could come down on you; it was terrifying and something I had only known in the very north of Sweden, never in Stockholm. I also learned that weather forecasts were to be taken seriously, for even if the freezing rain or a snowstorm did not, as forecasted, materialise the following morning, there was no reason for jubilation. Sooner or later it would bear down on you in all its fury. I was familiar with icy roads but not with freezing rain that in a very short time transformed the whole city into a glassy, unbelievably dangerous ice rink.

The climate was not the only thing that was different. I had read about the strained relationship between the anglophones and the fran-cophones, and when working with Martin on the shoot of his own film, I had gleaned a few details about the political reality of Quebec but still knew next to nothing about the 'Two Solitudes,' this almost total divi-sion that existed at the Board and elsewhere. It took only one week before I ignorantly breached the etiquette and also, as never before, understood the discrepancy between the living reality and the account-ing for it. On Friday afternoons there were screenings of the films the laboratory had just completed, and the marching order dictated that anglophone films were shown first every second week and on alterna-tive weeks the francophones started. The two groups never looked at each other's work. I did not know this and on my first Friday at the Board, it so happened that the anglophones started. Once they had seen their films they left the cinema, but as more films had been announced I stayed in my seat. After a little while the francophones entered. They nodded in a friendly way, and the screening began.

When finished, we all left and went our separate ways. On Monday morning I was called into Kemeny's office and told that one did *not* go to the French film screenings!

Sweden was not free from racism — Gypsies and the Same, at the time still called Lapps, were among those who felt it — but this form of segregation was new to me, and I had no intention of embracing it. Once out of Kemeny's office, I went straight up to the francophone floor, offering excuses for my unintentional breach of etiquette. My French, which had not been exercised for many years, was by now almost forgotten; at the time of my employment, nobody had even cared to ask if I spoke both languages. Among the anglophones very few were biligual, while all the francophones spoke English fluently, and it did not seem to bother them that I could not express my excuses in their lingua franca. I was assured that nobody was huffed and that I was most welcome to all their screenings. I did go, and this in time helped me to come to two important realisations: firstly, that I had much more affinity with the francophone films than with what was produced by the anglophones in Montreal, and secondly, that I needed to learn French properly. Most of what the francophones created was clearly distinguishable as something of its own, unmistakably French-Canadian and thereby of special interest. With my European background, I had no difficulty in sensing where the francophones came from, but I have never felt that I had a grip on the Canadianness of the anglophone films — or the anglophones themselves. Even then their feature filmmaking was noticeably influenced by what the Americans did, and time has only aggravated that. The anglophones, as I have got to know them, have continued to be nothing more clearly identifiable than tempered North Americans.

In my Swedish experience feature films were much weightier than documentaries, but it did not take long before my interest started to shift in favour of the documentary side. The anglophone feature film industry was concentrated in Toronto, while thanks to the Board, documentary production in both languages was focused in Montreal. For me that was another very compelling reason for wishing to stay. The city, with its easy manners, its animated street life — the quirks of the weather permitting — its good food and international flair had quickly charmed me. Montreal represented the best of both Europe and North America, and the foreigner was generously left the space to belong.

When discussing my contract with John Kemeny, I had insisted on being provided with the kind of editing table — a flatbed — that I was used to. North America still used the vertical Moviola, and I had no desire to find myself forced to work on one. When I first came to Svensk Filmindustri, I had one day ventured up into the attic to have a look at what still remained of an old shooting stage built in 1919 at Råsunda by Svenska Bio, the forerunner to Svensk Filmindustri. There had been some genius to the construction. The floor worked as a turntable, and the ceiling and some walls were made of glass. This way the set got continuous natural light when the turning stage followed the sun's movement. The nave could still be seen, surrounded by all the flotsam and jetsam that had accumulated over the years. An odd-looking, dust-covered small machine had caught my eye. It was a Moviola, bought when a visiting American production had requested one. It was the only machine then used in the States. Once they had left, the oddity had been moved to the attic, never to be used again. I had taken a long look at it, but it seemed very impractical.

My gripe with the Moviola is that the film is positioned vertically, and the machine can only hold smaller film rolls. A flatbed easily holds at least three hundred meters of 35 mm film, and to me that is the gateway to be able to always feel the rhythm I am working toward. I guess it also is a question of habit. Once in Montreal, I saw that some editors created flawless work, but observing the work methods the machine imposed, I still found it awkward and very time-consuming. It did however occur to me that I could use a Moviola in the same way as the Russian editor at Mosfilm had used the small prism at the top of her table, and I had one brought to my editing room. My Steenbeck had come from Germany well before I arrived on December 1st, but it still stood crated in the basement, and it took some coaxing before I could get it up. Christmas was approaching, and it was party time! What was the great rush? The 'no-great-rush-mentality' was something I was going to meet more often than I cared for, but there was also a great deal of curiosity about this new editing machine and a trail of anglophone editors came to look at it. A francophone delegation spent several hours observing and asking pertinent questions before they returned to their own floor and ordered three tables! Eventually the rest of the Board bought several flatbeds, but there were editors who, like me, did not want to change and who stuck to their Moviolas.

I started to work on Mort Ransen's films, but it did not take very long before Mort lost all interest in the project and left it. I can not honestly say that I personally missed him, but I was deeply shocked to find that such manners were accepted. It has to be noted that the Board was not run as a very tight ship. Its glory days lay in the past, and it had started to slide down the slippery slope, but I did not discover this until I was already in Montreal. Watching how its state of creative and financial decline only worsened with every passing year made me both sad and angry. John Kemeny, shortly after my arrival, moved on to greener pastures south of the border, and the Swedish project was taken over by a producer who already had his plate full, and that undoubtedly contributed to the mess.

While Mort's footage was sitting in the cans, I went on to work with Martin Duckworth on his film, and that went much better. Martin had been critical of certain things in Sweden, and his material, and the final film, was informed by those sentiments but, as I saw it, in a very gentle way. Even so, this was not appreciated by some of the senior producers at the Board who felt that you could not, or should not, be critical of another country. I wisely kept my big mouth shut during the discussions that followed screenings, but alone with Martin, I voiced my firm conviction that this was bull. His film was not an official view of Sweden, but Martin Duckworth's personal rendering of his sentiments. He was the director, he signed the film with his name, and I could not see it being anybody's business to whitewash his feelings. I am afraid Martin had to endure quite a bit of 'indoctrination,' but in the end, the film stayed as he and I wished to leave it. I never heard of the Swedish Institute being unhappy. At the time I did not know it, but as I have become more familiar with Canada, I realise that what I had come up against was something very typical: Canadian politeness.

The Challenge for Change program was innovative, had stayed on track, and was at the end of the 60s one of the few vital aspects of the Board's anglophone production. Another of its producers, the American George Stoney, had inquired about my interest to edit one of the films he had just produced, so when Martin's film was finished, I continued with that project. George was an inspirational producer to work with. He offered some very fresh ideas, and his attitudes were much less cloistered than those of many of the anglophones at the Board. By the time I had finished work on Stoney's film, it had dawned on the Board that they had a Swedish co-producer who was waiting to see some results of their financial co-operation. I was then offered the job as director-editor of the Swedish material that was supposed to make four or five documentaries. However, I could only see the possibility of three, and as by then I had learned one or two things about the Board, I thought it unwise to sign a contract for this work before we had checked out that our opinions were at least reasonably aligned. We agreed that I should fashion one film, and then we should take it from there. It was, as time would tell, a very wise decision.

There was quite an amount of footage showing the building of a new suburb outside Stockholm that I saw fit for one documentary, and as it was all mute footage, I had the idea to cut it to Pete Seger's very popular song 'Little Boxes'. Thinking it wise to first see if I could get the rights and unaware that the lyrics were not his, I called Seger, explained what I was doing and what I wanted. He gave his permission and did not even mention any costs! The time of innocence? The finished film had the Board in an uproar. The younger people liked it very much, the older producers were horrified. If they had found Martin Duckworth's film critical, they were now in for far worse. The images, coupled with the song, made for a strongly critical documentary, but the footage was not in any way manipulated, and I felt that the stupidity of building yet another copy of already existing, not very successful commuter suburbs rightly deserved to be criticised. The producer in charge refused to even show it to the Swedish Institute, and my time at the Board came to an end.

In the meantime something that would have long-ranging consequences had come to pass: I had met John Grierson, the founder of the National Film Board. Invited by McGill University, he had come back to Montreal in 1969 and was giving a lecture series in the English department. His name was legendary in documentary circles, and I had already heard much about him in England where, before coming to Canada in 1949, the dynamic Scot had been the director of the General Post Office Film Unit. I had seen some of his films and found them interesting but also somewhat romantic, at least in form. To my knowledge, Grierson had always been a strong radical, and this unlikely combination fascinated me. I was intrigued and longed to meet the man who had coined the expression 'documentary,' but Grierson — who had a long memory — had made it known that he did not wish to see Board people at his lectures. He was still smarting from the treatment he had been given during the Canadian phase of the McCarthy period and, working at the Board, I doubted that I would be welcome.

A couple of months after my arrival, a McGill student who wished to interview me about Swedish politics had sought me out. I tried to make him understand that, although I might have some personal political convictions, my field was film and not politics. All that seemed to matter to him was my nationality, and as he refused to take no for an answer, I finally agreed to see him. We met perhaps three times for an hour or two, and he appeared to have got something out of our conversations, for he eventually invited me out for a thank-you dinner. It was an enjoyable evening, and among other things I learned that he belonged to Grierson's senior seminar. When I mentioned my disappointment in not being able to go to his lectures, my host did not see any problem and offered to arrange it. I was of course enchanted but insisted that he first ask Grierson's permission, which he promised to do. A week later he called and told me where to meet him. We were late and very quietly sneaked in and sat at the back of the lecture theatre. This was the first time I saw Grierson in the flesh, and he still resembled the younger man in pictures I had seen: a rather short, svelte man with a neat grey moustache. His outer persona reflected none of his inner passion, and I found his oral presentation a bit dry. The cinematographic footage he had chosen to show us was on the other hand impressively vivacious. Behind it I sensed a very experienced eye and a mind with a profound understanding of how an image can be used to both emphasise and expand a message. After the lecture I was introduced in the usual infuriating way as 'Bergman's editor.' Grierson looked at me and said, 'I don't like Bergman,' to which I countered, 'No, why should you?' I have always found it ridiculous that, because Bergman is a great director, you ought to like his films. If you do not understand that he is an unusually accomplished and knowledgeable filmmaker, I reserve the right to think you stupid, or at least short-sighted, but I can not see why you should not have the freedom to like or dislike his films. The answer seemed to please Grierson, who extended an invitation to join his seminar for supper. He lived in a downtown apartment hotel on Crescent Street and regularly invited his seminar, and often one or two outside guests, for a supper that he himself cooked. He was a good cook, and he liked good food.

Over the next six months, such invitations came regularly, but in addition Grierson also often invited me to dinner and always made a point in choosing restaurants where he doubted that I had ever been before. His pleasure in being correct was obvious when he inquired if this was the first time and I nodded assent. 'No,' he would say, 'I did not think they would have thought of that!' — 'they' meaning the Canadians. But you would, on the other hand, bring his wrath down on your head if you criticised something he held in respect. I sometimes reflected on how lucky I was that Grierson was my friend and not my enemy. He could be spiteful. When I met him, he was seventy-one years-old but had a vitality that many twenty-year-olds would envy him. He had very firm convictions and was utterly realistic but also showed a remarkable openness and a great curiosity. After I got to know him a bit better, I finally understood the romanticism that once had seemed so strange to me in his early films and that his outer persona certainly did not advertise.

We shared similar ideas about teaching, and we also had in common the conviction that all cinema ought to be informed by the geographic location where it originated. Accordingly, he firmly believed in the necessity for Canadian films to carry this subliminal message, and that was a sentiment I understood and agreed with. Thanks to all the questioning about Sweden I had gone through since leaving my native country, I had finally understood what it was to be 'home-blind.' I had naturally seen Sweden through the glasses of familiarity — so customary that it was blinding — and all this questioning had slowly started to lift the superimposition of the unseeing fixed ways. I had come to realise that if I ever went back and made a documentary about Sweden, it would look very different, and probably much more 'Swedish,' than what I would have made while still living there.

Grierson's company was not only pleasant but also very educational. I lacked his solid knowledge of early filmmaking, as I am sure he had discovered. Although he never let on, he took my 'education' in hand in a very unobtrusive and charming way and continued to do so even after we both left Montreal. He maintained that he did not know much about my domain, the modern cinema like the French 'New Wave,' and what had followed it. Grierson's familiarity with more recent trends might not have had the same profound depths as his knowledge and understanding of older ones, but his sensitivity to images was such that he 'knew' quite a lot all the same.

The big, delightful surprise was served up at the same time as some delicious lobsters at Montreal's best seafood restaurant. Grierson invited me to work with him! He flattered me by saying that if I did not come on board, he would not accept an offer co-sponsored by McGill University and the National Film Board. The Board had finally decided to come forward with the big peace offering, and Grierson, who in spite of everything he said, loved that institution with every fibre in his body, evidently had resolved to finally bury the hatchet.

The project, centred on contemporary cinema, was still in an embry-
onic state and lay at least one year ahead. Grierson still had engagements to fulfil in Great Britain, and I had, even before leaving
Sweden, signed a contract with Cyprus Broadcasting Corporation.
My prolonged stay in Canada had meant that I twice had asked to
delay my arrival in Nicosia, but that had not caused any problem.
Thus we agreed that I should work in Cyprus for a year or so and
then, when Grierson was ready to return, come back to Montreal to
start our collaboration.

My ideas about the National Film Board of Canada had initially
been based on hearsay and by viewing some of their masterpieces, most
of them a couple of years old. The institution I came to was no longer
what it had once been, although at the time this had not yet had any
noticeable impact on its reputation at large. If there were things to criticise and dislike, there were also still people and creativity to admire,
friendships and generosity to relish. The Board had always been a
training ground for new talent, and that notion still lingered. Through
Martin Duckworth, I had become aware that people in the camera
department, if they wished to experiment, had access to the costless use
of ends of negative film. I could not see why the privilege should not be
extended to other groups too and talked to the head of the camera
department. The question was new to him, but I was granted the use of
a camera and odds and ends of raw stock on the condition that I had a
cameraman watch over the equipment. Martin let himself be talked
into the role of chaperone, and on Sunday mornings we spent considerable time under the viaducts that carried the recently built express-
ways that criss-crossed Montreal. My car had once stalled in one of
these concrete caverns, and before the tow truck finally arrived, I had
had ample time to contemplate and become fascinated with their architecture. Martin patiently taught me the basics of the camera, and I then
played around with framing and light. The department head had laid
down a second rule: I had to show him what I had filmed. So when the
film came back from the laboratory, I had to endure a screening where
I, of course, got some critique but also, to my immense astonishment,

an offer to start an apprenticeship in the camera department! The offer was most flattering, but it did not really have enough attraction to derail my future plans. John Grierson had seen to that.

The Montreal I first got to know was a Montreal still basking in the golden glow and the great optimism that Expo 67 had given it. At the time there was nothing indicating that it would ever change, but unfortunately, time would tell otherwise. All the same, even today, from time to time, little specks of that unique Montreal charm still glimmer. The National Film Board might not have lived up to its great reputation, but I had gained some insight into a different culture, and most of all, my stay had allowed me to encounter John Grierson and become his friend. He and Bergman — otherwise as different as chalk and cheese — had one thing in common: they could, and did, inspire. The prospect of working with Grierson gave my future a silver lining. Strangely enough we happened to leave Montreal on the same day in late August and said our good-byes at the airport. Neither of us knew that it was to be the last time we were to shake hands. As we had agreed, we kept in contact by letters that were not only entertaining but also often taught me something new. If he had not generously sent me Kevin Brownlow's then recently published *The Parade's Gone By*, I would in all likelihood had missed it. Suddenly, after a little more than a year, Grierson's letters stopped coming. Much later, a friend from Montreal wrote and told me that he had died in Scotland.

I HAVE HEARD THE MERMAIDS SINGING

'I have heard the mermaids singing, each to each.
I do not think that they will sing to me.'[20]

In the 60s Svensk Filmindustri and I had come to an agreement that
suited us both. My overtime, and I had quite a bit of it, did not increase
my paycheque, but I got time off in lieu. My yearly vacation, together
with this additional time, allowed me to leave Sweden for about three
months during the winter, and I started to explore islands around the
Mediterranean Sea. First came Tenerife and the smaller adjacent
islands, then Malta, and after visiting Rhodes I was ready for Crete. I
had learned that there was fairly regular fishing boat traffic between the
two islands and my plan for 1961 was to come back to Rhodes and then
make my way to Crete. Through some very helpful contacts at
Stockholm's biggest travel agency I was able to get low charter-flight
fares and very flexible flying arrangements, but all my good planning
came to naught when the agency stopped their winter flights to Rhodes.
Hotels without central heating had made the warmth and sun seekers
from Northern Europe favour other places. Crete was not yet among
the chartered destinations, and the travel agents in Stockholm, by then
familiar with my tastes, suggested Cyprus. After lengthy birth-throes
the island had, in 1960, become a republic, the armed EOKA struggle
had stopped, at least officially, and the tourist traffic had not yet really
started. As archaeology had been one of my subjects at university, I
knew that Cyprus had a rich and varied culture. I took the suggestion
and landed in the port town of Famagusta.

The mosque of Lala Mustafa Pasha and the port with its old fortifi-
cations were beautiful and full of interest, but I did not find the rest of
the city very attractive. The mosque had originally been a 14th century
Gothic-style Latin Cathedral, named for St. Nicholas, and it was there
the Lusignans had crowned their kings as 'Kings of Jerusalem.' The

Turks, who now regarded it as their principal mosque, had, in accordance with the rules of their faith, whitewashed the whole interior to obliterate the medieval artwork so rich on figurative forms. This had given the Gothic stonemason's outstanding sculpture work a new, although originally not intended, shadowy quality that was very interesting. The many different rulers of Cyprus had all left their marks as they altered or built on to what already existed of the ramparts. On one façade I found, still preserved, the imposing, winged Lion of the Republic of Venice, together with the name and arms of Nicololo Foscarini, a Venetian Captain who remodelled the castle in 1492. Closer to our time, Shakespeare located the action in *Othello* to 'a sea port in Cyprus,' and it is generally assumed that it was Famagusta he had in mind. Over the entrance to the so-called Othello's Tower sits the coat of arms of Cristoforo Moro, in the early 1500s the Venetian Lieutenant-Governor on the island. It carries three mulberry pods, and the Greek word 'Moro' denotes both mulberry and Moor, but chances are Shakespeare did not know this double sense when he made Othello a Moor. No black-skinned Moor, with their inferior status, would have been even a commissioned officer in the Venetian fleet — let alone 'Captain of Cyprus.'

Famagusta had a long, sandy beach, and even in winter the water was warm enough to swim in; although I guess it was a question of interpretation. Cypriot men, dressed in overcoats, used to walk the beach, ogling the tanning flesh at the water's edge. The first high-rise hotel had already gone up, and it was all too clear what lay ahead. When I visited Famagusta a couple of years later, the whole beach was built up, and from this side of the city you could no longer see the sea. The island is not very big, and nearly a century of British rule had left Cyprus with a functional infrastructure that made travel easy. In the morning I could hop on a bus, get off at any place that seemed interesting, and then walk around taking in my first sights of the Near East. I was looked at with some mild curiosity because an unaccompanied woman was not a daily sight. After stopping for refreshment at some small coffee shop, I would wander around some more before finally taking another bus back to Famagusta.

Then an impromptu introduction to Panos Kyriacou changed my routine. The Cypriots are generally very welcoming, and Panos was indeed a walking poster for generous reception. He owned an import business, and as his own sales representative, he travelled all over the island, which he knew intimately. As a bachelor he also could, without any complications, invite me on his trips, and thanks to Panos I not only saw much more than I would otherwise have done but in his knowledgeable company Cyprus became brimming with specificity that made it uniquely pleasurable and colourful. When he insisted on inviting me for a skiing weekend up in the Troodos mountains and I told him that I had no appropriate clothing for such a trip, it did not deter him. Boots and skis you hired on the mountain anyway, and then he bravely took me on a round trip to his girlfriends' houses to borrow an outfit. The expedition was hilarious, for Panos's taste turned out to be for very shapely, slim girls, and since I was too robust for most of what they could offer, I came away with a very odd-looking outfit, ready to burst at the seams. That their beau was taking me away for the weekend did not seem to faze them in the least, but Panos was unusual in that he had a great faculty for friendship. He was one of the few Cypriot men I ever met who did not have the need to demonstrate what they assumed was their taken-for-granted sexual desirability, something I found very tiring. The girls were easy company, and once introduced, I then met them frequently, and there was never any tension. For both pride and pleasure of showing his native island, Panos sometimes even went to places other than where he had business, and it was one such trip that took us to Bellapais on the mountainous north side of the island. The small village, nestled between two deep ravines filled with almond trees in bloom, was dazzling. The flowers' silvery irradiation was a perfect, unforgettable framework to the fan-shaped formation of whitewashed houses, dotted with doors and window shutters of a very intense blue. The sight had a charm and a beauty all its own, and when later, as a farewell treat, Panos asked how I wished to spend my last day before returning home, a second visit to Bellapais was the obvious choice.

Another village visit has also stayed in my mind; Panos had taken me to Larnaca on the southeast coast, and while he attended to business, I first went to the museum and then explored the city. Later we drove west to look at a neolithic settlement where, once upon a time, nothing but perfectly round black stones had been the building material. Strange and dramatic, these dwellings looked like enormous, perfectly round anthills dotted on the landscape. We went further north to the twin villages of Pano and Kato Lefkara where we had coffee and *Lokoum*, the local name for the Turkish Delight the villages are famous for, as well as their internationally known lacemaking. Year after year, the men from these villages have travelled the world selling the lace their sisters, wives, and daughters have made, an industry that has turned both places into the richest on the island. As many as six churches already signposted this wealth. A couple of old men sat at the coffee shop, but when we walked through the lower village and to the upper one, we only saw women and children — not one single man — and all the women and all the girls, whether standing, sitting in a doorway or walking on the narrow, steep streets, kept their hands busy. The place was beautiful but unreal and in some strange way immensely sad. Seventeen years later in Canada, I one evening opened my apartment door in a Toronto high-rise and outside stood a man offering to sell me some lace from Lefkara!

Around 1960, the British author Lawrence Durrell had appeared on my literary map, and on my first trip to Cyprus I had brought with me *The Alexandria Quartet*. At the time this series of books seemed to have catapulted Durrell to instant literary sainthood, and although they were remarkable reading, I was not totally convinced that he deserved *that* status just yet. It was a literary judgement and not sour grapes as I in no way blamed Durrell for it, but the reading of the fourth volume, *Clea*, did, in the long run, cost me a very special relationship. My lover back in Stockholm frequently sent me enamoured letters, and one of them was even more enchanting than the others... until I turned a page in *Clea* and realised where most of that letter came from! The relationship did not survive the test of time, but *The Quartet* still has a place on my bookshelves. After returning to Stockholm I read *Bitter Lemons*, but it left me with mixed feelings. Durrell's description of the purchase of his house was immensely funny, and the way he wrote about the ensuing rebuilding of it had a magic that made me feel very familiar with rooms I had never been to. However, when he started to lecture the British High Commission on how to rule Cyprus, I found him unbearably pompous and boring.

I had kept in touch with Panos, and when I decided on a second stay in Cyprus the following year, I asked him to help me find a house to rent, preferably in Bellapais. He did find one, Durrell's, although he no longer owned it. The 'Bitter Lemon House' had in the meantime been bought by a British couple who, I was later told, had only lived in it for two weeks. Very proud of its provenance, they had — soliciting an entrance fee — opened its enormous blue wooden doors to other tourists with an equal excitability for celebrities. When the new owners returned to England, they arranged for it to be leased, and it happened to be available for the period of my intended visit. It was too big, but my reading of *Bitter Lemons*, although only in part seductive, had left enough lingering charm to make the offer irresistible.

My idea to go and live in a remote village in the Cyprus mountains caused some uneasiness at home in Stockholm. That must surely be dangerous! My father raved and ranted, and Bergman, a man of habit who did not very much like travelling outside of Sweden, very sweetly told me that if I did not like it, I only had to send him a telegram. He would then insist on starting some editing right away, and I could come back without losing face. I was very touched by his concern but doubted that I was going to take him up on the offer, convinced as I was that I would have a great time.

I had some experience of Swedish village life, and as my first visit to the island had indicated that this would be a vastly different education, I was eager to try it. You can probably live well in many sorts of places, but if your ancestors have not been known there for at least a couple of generations, in some important ways, you will always remain a foreigner. I do not necessarily regard it as negative; it allows you to look at things from an outside perspective, often interesting. As my stay in Bellapais proved, being curious about the place, and showing at least a minimum of sensitivity to local mores, takes you quite a distance. To the villagers it seemed strange that my parents would leave me alone like this, something they would never do to their unmarried daughters, and so they took it upon themselves to look after me. The Cypriots, Greeks and Turks alike pride themselves on how they welcome visitors, and I do not think I have ever lived in any other place where I was as safe as I was in Bellapais. I was a guest — albeit a self-invited one — but had I been in any way harmed, it would have put a stain on the whole village, not just on the perpetrator of any aggression. Sadly, I doubt that it is still the same, but these were very different times.

The Mayor, who was addressed by the Turkish word 'Muchtar' even in Greek Cypriot villages, almost every day, early in the evening, held office at one of the coffee shops down in the square. He played backgammon, gave advice, and listened to and sorted out grievances between neighbours. The coffee shop, one of three in this small village, was also the post office, and every evening, returning from his work in Nicosia, a villager would bring the mail. The sack was emptied on the counter among glasses and coffee cups, and the names on each and every envelope read out loud. If the Muchtar or his cousin Nicos, the forester, were there when I came for my mail, it was unthinkable not to sit down with them and accept their offers of coffee. From time to time Nicos would take me along when he patrolled the forests, and he taught me about local flora and fauna. Since the end of the troubles the use of privately owned rifles was forbidden, and that had made the bird life bounce back, but only a few years later, when the ban on bird hunting had been lifted, these same forests became almost totally silent again.

All this was good fun but what counted even more was that I managed to get to know some of the village women. They would never come to the coffee shop, not even to collect the mail, and if there was not a boy or a man in the house, a neighbour would bring it. My evenings in the coffee shop, I am sure, provoked some discussion, but no disrepute ever reached my ears, nor did I ever, but for one exception, feel shunned. Slowly, slowly my neighbours started to involve me in their daily tasks. They would stop at my house on their way to the church-yard to light the oil lamps for their dead, invite me to come with them to collect greens and wild herbs for cooking or bread making. Few of them had but a sliver of English, and my beginner's Greek made for much laughter and, on my part, also for some slow learning.

In most households bread making was no longer a daily habit, but for Easter, weddings, or funerals, the old big baking-troughs would come out of storage and several women always came together. The big round oven in the yard would be fired up while we all took turns kneading the heavy dough of flour, olive oil, chopped mint and whole, ripe black olives. When the massive, round loaves finally were set to rise in their beautifully carved wooden forms, we all sat down for a well-earned rest. When the oven was hot enough, the embers were pushed to one side, the bottom swept clean, the big round breads put on fig leafs and shoved in. After a while a heavenly smell started to waft over the neighbourhood.

When I first lived in Bellapais you never locked your door during the day, and returning home, I would often find gifts in my kitchen. In the beginning I was at a loss to figure out who the kind giver could be, and after the mutual embarrassment of returning a plate and the linen it had been wrapped in to the wrong house, I realised that guessing would not do. My neighbour across the street, Maroulla, who as part of the leasing agreement also cleaned the house, turned out to not only be useful in that respect but she never erred in her knowledge of who the rightful owners were and always showed me the right direction. She was friendly and even-tempered and a gold mine of useful infor-mation. At the time the house did not have electricity, and the fridge was a kerosene-driven beast that with irritating regularity covered the kitchen walls in black soot. Maroulla would come in, survey the disas-ter, eye the guilty party and exclaim, '*i pagånie´ra, i pagånie´ra, lipo´me, lipo´me*' (the fridge! the fridge! I am sorry, I am sorry) then leave, but soon return with a bucket of whitewash and a lot of determination. My kitchen was the most well-painted room in the house! Her seemingly unflappable way of dealing with life's disorders was however only half of it. One evening when I was preparing supper, a big commotion outside made me fling open my wooden shutters. The narrow street between the house and a big triangular water basin was filled with a black-clad, wailing mass of women. I took my pan off the burner and went out in search of an explanation. Eventually I found Maroulla, but her usual rudimentary English had drowned in tears and loud cries. Her never easy, rapid Cypriot patois was now next to unintelligible. I understood something about a dead girl, but that was all, and after a while I returned home none the wiser, but the age-old drama of wailing and crying went on unabated for hours.

The next morning Maroulla was better disposed to explain the events. A child-rich but income-poor village family had sent one of their daughters to better-off relatives in Nicosia, but the girl was homesick and had time and again begged her parents to let her return home. The father insisted that she stay where she was, and late the day before, a telegram, saying she was dead by her own hand, had arrived. What I had witnessed was the village response to the tragic news, but the next two days would bring even more drama, although of a different kind. The girl was not deceased at all, but had herself concocted the story and sent the telegram, hoping, I guess, to soften her father's heart! Now Maroulla with much animation recounted how a very angry man, first thing in the morning, had left for Nicosia refusing to let his begging, crying wife come with him on the bus.

Before returning to my working life in Stockholm, I had a serious talk with the Muchtar and told him of my wish to buy a small house in Bellapais. He promised to keep it in mind and would let me know when something came up for sale. It did not happen very often; Bellapais was a well-functioning village with a stable population, but if anybody would be of any help it certainly was the Muchtar. If anybody sneezed he would be the first one to be told, but he also was a man who knew the virtue of discretion. Land speculation had not yet started on the island, and although tourism had improved, house prices were still very low. It took a good year before I would hear from my trusted delegate, and that was probably just as well, for I had not given any serious consideration to the financial side of my dream.

As so often happens, coincidence came to pass. Greece and Turkey, with the help of local elements, squabbled over Cyprus. The Turks threatened to bomb the island, tourism ceased and FAO[21] personnel were evacuated. They had been renting the Bitter Lemon House, and the British owners were not only now deprived of an income, but also faced the unpalatable possibility that their famous house in one strike could be changed to a heap of rubble. In their rush to sell the house, they had written to the Muchtar inquiring if he knew of a likely buyer. He sent them my address in Stockholm, and late one evening returning from work, I found that through the mail slot had dropped an offer to buy Durrell's former house!

I made an appointment with a solicitor, who came highly recommended, but after hearing me out, his enthusiasm for this new client was not great. This elderly, soft-spoken man pointed out with emphasis that he could not in good conscience advise me to buy a house in a country at war. That was not a way to handle an inheritance! The looks and the voice were different, but the words could have been my father's! He was right about the money being an inheritance: It had been willed to me by my grandparents, and by coincidence the sum had been transferred to my bank account only a very short time before I got the first letter from England. I took a deep breath and started on my list of objections: with all due respect, I had *not* asked for his advice, and I had no intention to buy the house — just yet! What I wished him to do was seek clarification about the asking price, which had not been mentioned, and also to fire off to England a string of letters with all sorts of lengthy questions. This way I saw a possibility to stall until it became clear how the war was going and if it would end in the foreseeable future. He actually did a splendid job, and several months later, having read a reassuring letter from the Muchtar, he started to cut through the considerable amount of red tape encountered when I, a Swedish citizen, endeavoured to buy a house in Cyprus from British owners! It took a lot of time and perseverance, and when I eventually bought 'The Bitter Lemon House,' the event had no comparable enter-taining elements as the ones Durrell had written about, but by then my solicitor and I were really on speaking terms. Although he neatly nego-tiated a price that fitted the sum of my inheritance, I do not think he ever changed his mind about my use of the money. I did not for a sec-ond think that it was a misuse, and I was convinced my grandparents would not have thought so either. They might have been surprised, but I have always felt that they would have understood and sanctioned the joy that came out of this windfall.

In the village I never detected any lingering, overwhelming sympa-thy for Durrell, but when the tourists eventually returned, his *Bitter Lemons* was a highly appreciated sales item by the souvenir shop own-ers. Only hinting at the idea of renaming it 'Ulla's House' was an almost too easy way to win any arguments with the plumber or the electrician, who both seemed to have financial interests in the shops. As the years passed, I melted into village life in a very pleasant way. When I was not in Bellapais, Nicos saw to it that the house was aired and in good repair, and each return unavoidably started with a prolonged stay at the cof-fee shop. Before I was even allowed to get up to my house, I had to say hello to all I knew, accept offerings of yet another cup of coffee, telling them all how happy I was to be back. The only person who never greeted me was the priest, and I think I know why. During the armed uprising against the British, the church had been a driving force of resistance. Anything British, like the small hospital in Kyrenia, was boycotted, and although it meant some hardship, people did respect the dictate. The war had eventually come to an end, but it had left a dead-ly legacy: Greek and Turkish Cypriots alike, although in small num-bers, but with painful regularity, still killed each other. Family feuds, personal animosity and/or revenge, rather than political reasons, seemed to dictate the slayings, and as long as the tally of dead bodies did not square on both sides, the slaughter continued. Most people had some degree of English and did not seem to dislike using it, on the con-trary. Because my Greek was poor, I mostly spoke English, and in the eyes of the priest, I suppose this equated me with the old enemy. The

Papa lived above me in the village, and in our comings and goings we crossed paths ever so often. I always politely greeted him — in English, then Greek, and finally even Swedish, but to no avail. Always leading his donkey, he went on his way, as if I did not exist. When one year my stay in Bellapais coincided with Easter, I wished to have the priest's approval before I, not a Greek Orthodox, went to his church, and I solicited Nicos's help as a go-between. He came back with the answer that I was welcome, and on the evening of that Good Friday, when just before the mass I came to buy my candle at the church, I was greeted with a loud 'Good evening!' Finally the ice was broken, and from then on the Papa would not only speak to me but if he happened to pass by, also join the welcoming group at the coffee shop.

That same Easter another favour was also bestowed upon me: The Muchtar's daughter invited me to join her and the other younger village women in charge of the flower decorations. On the Thursday morning in Holy Week, a lorry dumped a full load of laurel branches outside the church, the children brought flowers from their gardens, and we started to cover a big, arch-shaped wooden frame, first with the laurel and then with flowers until no more wood showed. Inside the church the Papa laid strand after strand of rose petals around the edges of an icon: a Christ figure painted on a considerable slab of blueish glass. When night started to fall, a procession emerged from the church, winding its way through all the dark, narrow streets of the small village. Big candles were carried in front, then came the priest, and behind him the icon resting under its heavy, flowered arch carried by six sturdy men. Then followed the villagers, old and young, everybody who could walk. When the procession reached the church, the icon was first carried inside, followed by the priest. The arch was then held high, and we all passed under it into the church. During the mass, one by one people went up to the icon, took a rose petal, received its blessing with holy water, and then returned to their place. When my turn came I hesitated; my neighbours poked me in the back, but when I did not move, the woman next to me went. I did not know her, but when she returned she handed me one of the two rose petals she had taken. That night and in the nights following, I stood with the rest of the village through the liturgies that went on and on until early into the mornings. The night of Good Friday offered an unforgettable moment when all the lights in the church were switched off and all the candles, save a big one in front of the congregation, blown out. The mass continued for a short while in the near dark until the first man in the first row on his side and the first woman on her side went up to the burning candle, lit their own candlesticks on it, returned to their places, and passed the flame to the person standing next to them. In this manner the lights slowly coiled their magic way through the whole church.

Everyday life in Bellapais did not denote any fervent religious priorities; the Papa regardlessly held his masses several times a day, but his congregation was only a couple of old men and a few elderly women with some grandchildren in tow. At Easter the church was filled, the whole village came. Very few people appeared to fast anymore, and if they did, it was only for a day or two, but the respect for the rules, or at least some of them, was still in place. From Thursday on, nothing stronger than coffee was either asked for or served at the coffee shop. Save for my married years, the Sweden I lived in and knew was quite secular and becoming more and more so over the years, but that did not prevent some services — like the one on Christmas Day at 7:00 AM — to fill the churches. If you lived where the Christmas was white, you might even go to church by horse-driven sledge and afterwards return home to coffee, the season's special goodies and the presents from the night before. It was a time-honoured, pleasant ritual but very seldom seemed to be an important religious one, and that was for me the big difference in Bellapais. These villagers seemed to still have a belonging, a living spirit of their religion, and their presence in the church had an internal meaning far beyond any routine following of a tradition. Besides the sheer beauty of certain parts, what made my Easter experiences so moving was the strong authenticity that prevailed.

The mass on Friday night only ended at two in the morning and then I had the soup, which traditionally breaks the fast, with Maroulla and her family. After the morning mass on Saturday, I also made my way with them and their friends to the next village, down the mountain side, where Maroulla's parents had invited us to share their big Easter meal. At the outskirts of the village, our party met a gaping hole. One of the big wooden poles, needed for the electricity that was brought in, had only days before Easter disappeared into a cavity and the work had stopped. The custodian at the castle in nearby Kyrenia had come up on his motorbike, inspected the big hole, and climbed down to its bottom, which was a gravesite. He had fenced off the area and alerted the archaeologists in Nicosia, and now he was only passing by to see that the fencing was intact. We knew each other, and once the customary Easter salutation 'Christ is risen!' was exchanged, he invited me to take a look at the grave. A ladder was fetched, and we climbed down. The pole had struck at the opening of the grave and left a small half circle of clay pots and figurines intact. The votive offerings were not very spectacular but at least undisturbed, indicating that grave robbers had not been here. The most intriguing part was an indication in the inner cave wall of yet another burial chamber.

It is customary to dress in new cloth for the Easter Saturday morning mass, and I had put on a white, knitted cotton dress and my last pair of stockings without runs, but when I finally reappeared my party gasped. No white was visible! I was covered from head to toe in the reddish dust from the copper-rich Cyprus soil. No amount of bleach would ever bring back the original whiteness of that dress. So what! The world is full of white dresses, but how often do you get a personal invitation to the Bronze Age!

The travel agency which arranged the charter flights to Cyprus also offered excursions to Lebanon and to Syria, and when they were not fully booked I sometimes got an offer to come along. My first visit fell on a New Year's Day when, yet unbeknownst to the rest of the world, Beirut had seen an unsuccessful coup during the night. One of the three insurgents was apprehended before daybreak, but the search for the other two was still continuing. As the city was calm, nothing prevented you from moving around, but at irritatingly frequent road blocks I had to explain my Swedish passport in full before being allowed to pass. A taxi driver, who was stopped two days later, most likely had even more questioning waiting for him. He took to his heels but did not get very far, and the 'passenger' in the trunk of his car was found to be one of the insurgents. After that the control eased, and the night curfew was lifted. In Lebanon's volatile political history, this was not even a tempest in a teacup. The few shots that had been fired during the first night were only very faint precursors of the ravages that were to be visited in the near future, not only on Beirut, but the whole Middle East.

The highlight of the Beirut season was the New Year's Eve opening extravaganza by The Monte Carlo Ballet, and this year had been no different. While the un-bloody coup took place in central Beirut some twenty kilometres down the bay, at the casino, the unaware bejewelled guests had dined, danced, and gambled away. It was only in the small hours of the night, when the immediately imposed curfew prevented them from leaving, that they learned about the event. The morning had seen the exhausted revellers sleeping in chairs, on stairs, and in other uncomfortable places before they were finally allowed to go home. I was often told that once you penetrated its international gloss, Beirut was both interesting and attractive, but my stays were not long enough for an affinity to develop, and I never seriously took to the city although I found it interesting enough for a couple of visits. One night the casino spewed enough money into my lap to allow me to return to the antique shop, where some days earlier, I had seen a gem beyond my reach. It was an antique bracelet in a technique called 'The Paradise Bird's Nest.' The Druse believe in reincarnation; the final state being a Paradise bird, and to carry some jewellery crafted in this technique supposedly helps you to get there somewhat quicker than you otherwise would.

In Beirut I stayed in a very charming hotel, co-owned by a Lebanese man and a British couple who had been song-and-dance artists in their younger days. A short distance from the noisy centre, it had a beautiful big garden that ended in a beach where you could swim. The former owner had been a sheikh who had exchanged this attractive property for a gleaming, sterile, glass-and-steel tower across the road. He was never home when I was in town, but the place was always ready to receive him. I could observe the daily morning routine when seven or eight big black limousines would line up in front of the entrance. A single person got into each vehicle but for the last one, reserved for two small boys struggling with a number of big baskets. Once they were in, the caravan set out for the market and the daily food shopping that attested to the readiness to receive the owner and his entourage.

Returning from the antique shop with my trophy, I proudly showed the Lebanese owner the bracelet and also told him how I had managed to buy it. He obviously knew what he was looking at, and when he finally handed me back the armlet, he also presented me with an invitation to stay on at his hotel with, he assured me, no obligation other than to accompany him every night to the casino! A gambler had met his Lucky Charm — or so he thought. My arguments that I could not afford the life of a mayfly fell on deaf ears. I was welcome to stay as long as I wished, I would have credit for room and board until I won at the Casino, and what had just befallen me was a sure sign of my winning powers. Flattered, but not seriously tempted and still listening to my annoying little voice of reason, I opted, when the time came, to return to the somewhat more manageable thrills of my editing room. I still have the bracelet, and if I do not end up as a Paradise bird, it must be because I have not been wearing it as regularly as I ought to.

If I was looking for something that immediately presented itself as authentic, I certainly found it in Damascus. Geographically, Beirut and Damascus are not that distant from each other. In the morning I would be swimming in the sea in Beirut, and only a couple of hours later I would be in the Syrian capital — at least if snow did not stop me at the border. There, the big highway turned into a modest road, and it usually took a single, smallish snowplough some hours to make it passable. Damascus had nothing of Beirut's international gloss; it was dusty, hot, and noisy, but still it somehow appealed to me. To the north there were some archaeological burial sites with the most amazing range of big sarcophagi that had recently come to light. The site had not been able to accommodate any heavy machinery for the digging, but the archaeologists had devised an ingenious way to lift the heavy stone coffins, one by one, by pouring sand under their bottoms and thereby slowly raising them up to the surface. In the city, in what was not much more than a hole in the wall, I found a whole stack of colourful, storied paintings done by a then eighty-year-old Syrian artist who always seemed to take his inspiration from the oral history of Anthar and Abla. In some versions, Abla is Anthar's beloved, in others she is his cousin, but, whatever her status, she always rides an orange-coloured horse, and at all times, Anthar, on his big black steed, fights the 'white dogs' while defending her honour. From one trip I brought back one of these paintings and still take pleasure in the sight of the fighting Anthar. His sword has penetrated the enemy's face and, slightly crooked, is sticking out of the back of his head, splattering pale blood.

Over the years I got to know people in Nicosia, among them the director for Cyprus Broadcasting Corporation, the poet Andrea Chrystofide. He eventually suggested that I should come and work at the station, and toward the end of 1969 I arrived there from Montreal. For the first time, I had come to Cyprus not for a long holiday but in order to make documentaries and train some younger employees at the TV station. Since Greek and English were used simultaneously all the time, my still vapid Greek was not regarded as a drawback, but I soon discovered that two of my 'students' did not speak any English at all. The time had come for me to be serious about some proper language training. The Minister of the Interior directed me to an excellent source, housed in a beautiful old building next to Archbishop Makarios's palace in the heart of the city. The head of the School For Retarded Children, also its only teacher, accepted an adult student and kindly offered to give me lessons at noon when the school closed for the day. This perfect arrangement allowed me to come during my lunch break, and the short drive even had an additional benefit: I would be passing the market before it closed.

In Bellapais every household grew their own fruit and vegetables; the village shop had no reason to carry any. If I asked my neighbours to sell me some, they insisted on making it a gift, and with hardly any way for me to reciprocate, it was not something I wished to do regularly. I now stopped at the market for some quick shopping, and when I arrived at the school I parked the car and honked my horn. There were always a few pupils still waiting to be fetched by parents or older siblings, and the teacher would let the kids come out to the street. They bustled around my big basket, and when they all had at least one hand on it, they carried it in to the cool of the high-vaulted entrance. Then they followed me into the classroom where they seated themselves behind me. Because their teacher was trained in a special way of tutoring, I was taught exactly as his other charges, and it was immensely effective. I don't think I have ever taken the first difficult steps into a foreign language, in particular one with a different alphabet, as quickly as I did with Greek, and moreover, I amused the kids to no end without even trying. To their master's horror, they laughed, clapped, and hurrahed every time I made a mistake of something simple, which they had already mastered. If they had to leave during my lesson they would come up to where I sat, and we would exercise our parting phrases in the most polite way. They were an adorable lot!

The shortest distance to Nicosia was the main road that went due south from Kyrenia, but it passed through a couple of Turkish enclaves where the Greek-Cypriots, after the partial Turkish occupation of the north part of Cyprus, were no longer allowed to travel. Every morning a convoy, led by UN peacekeepers, travelled from Kyrenia to Nicosia and in the early evening, in the opposite direction, thus allowing the Greek-Cypriots with work in Nicosia to use the road. Their alternative, outside convoy hours, was the narrow, heavily trafficked coastal road, but it was three times longer, full of sharp bends, and it made its way through several villages where dogs and kids commanded it. With my Swedish passport, I could travel the main road whenever I liked, and to avoid the slow speed of the convoy, I usually started out ahead of it. Once I began working at the TV station, the Turks very quickly learned to recognise the daily comings and goings of my little blue VW; most of the time, they just waved me through. If I was stopped from time to time, it seemed to be more a case of the sentry being bored than of national security, for their interest in my passport was always minimal. But the chance to exercise their few words of English — or Greek for that matter — and to try to chat up the single woman driver was not.

One Friday night after a very late dinner in Nicosia, I had turned down an invitation to sleep over in the capital because I *had* to be in Bellapais first thing Saturday morning. My Cypriot hostess and her husband begged me to take the coastal road back, but once in my car I baulked at the ordeal of an hour and a half on that miserable road in the middle of the night. I turned the car to the shorter road to Kyrenia and passed through the first of the three Turkish villages without being stopped, nor was I stopped in the second one. The sentry's cubicle was dark, but when passing it at low speed I heard a strange thudding sound. The car pulled toward the other side of the road. I managed to straighten it up and then sped away until I was well out of the village. At first I had no idea what had happened, but it slowly dawned on me that somebody, hiding in the dark, might have taken a pot shot at the car. I stopped, reached for my flashlight, and got out of the car and started to walk around it. Each door had a hole in it! I was obviously not hurt, the engine was running, and I could not smell gas, so presumably the tank was okay. I got back into my seat and sat there for a while wondering what to do next. The two options, driving through the last of the Turkish villages in the dark or sitting where I was, waiting for daylight, were equally unpalatable, but was there any alternative? Finally, I slowly drove on and into the village, stopping at the sentry's unlit cubicle. Nothing stirred, nobody came out, and then I made a very quiet exit. Once out of the village, I charged home to Bellapais and there, in the dim light of a street lamp, took a closer look at the holes. A bullet had entered from the left, passing so close to the back of my car seat that the upholstery was singed, and then had gone out through the other door. At the time, Volkswagen had not yet moved the gas tank to the rear of their cars, and you were virtually driving with the tank between your knees. Two days of contemplating the what-might-have-been scenario was not very relaxing, but by Monday morning my fright had given way to a rage.

On my way to Nicosia, I parked outside the cubicle in the middle village, stormed out of my car and dragged a very perplexed sentry around the vehicle showing him the bullet holes and, I am afraid, showering him with a plethora of invectives. He finally shook loose of my grip and ran into the building behind the cubicle only to reappear with an officer whose knowledge of English was not much better. He got what was left of my anger before I dashed off to Nicosia. Tuesday morning I was stopped at this check point and by sign language made to understand to stay where I was. The sentry left, and I started to have second thoughts about my Monday performance when the same officer I had seen the day before came out carrying an enormous bunch of roses. Excuses were lavished on me, and I got a promise of repair to my car. This was Cyprus in a nutshell. What could I do but love it?

Considering the island's relative remoteness, the TV station was not badly equipped, but sadly, a lot of useful gear bought abroad only collected dust on the shelves. The fear of losing face was stronger than curiosity and prevented any experimenting with new tools. It took some delicate manoeuvring to try to change the attitude, and my speedy, Western efficiency had to be slowed down. I needed to find ways that would not be construed as criticism; comparison became a very useful engine. I encouraged and led small series of tests that clearly showed that some of the new equipment gave a better result than the old. As in all places, some people resisted, some went along, but this being 1969, the idea of gender equality had not yet reached Cyprus in any noticeable way. That I was able to set in motion any change at all was in itself no mean feat. In the long run I think I was possibly the one who learned the most, as I eventually got a deeper understanding of the difference between 'to impose' and 'to inspire'.

While working at Svensk Filmindustri I twice had the opportunity to direct short films of my own design, and as that was a line of work I wished to develop, the offer to make documentaries in Cyprus had carried considerable weight in my discussions with Andrea Chrystofide. Every time I returned to Cyprus, more ideas were added, and I now handed him three short outlines: one suggested a film about the island's

most famous monastery — the one at Kykko — where an icon attributed to St. Luke can be found. In the Orthodox world there are only
three monasteries which have a claim on the Evangelist, but the one in
Kykko has an added attraction, at least for the islanders. On a too-often
drought-stricken island, for centuries the icon has also enjoyed the
greatest reputation as a bringer of rain. The Archaeological Museum in
Nicosia was bursting with treasures from all ages, and I wanted to take
a group of children from the school for the blind to the museum and let
them 'see' with their hands. The idea to make a film about Bellapais,
including some of the Easter celebrations, was probably no surprise,
but all three ideas were enthusiastically received by the director and
committed to production. Everybody in the upper echelons was, however, not as open to new ideas as the director himself, and I soon started to experience never-ending problems with planning and equipment
allocations. This way the only film that came to fruition was the one
about Bellapais, but because of all these machinations, there was no
filming during Easter, and the final film lacked the focus point it would
have provided. The finished film also in no small way suffered from the
fact that the editor — unfortunately myself, without any input from a
reliable second opinion — did not kill her darlings!

Galling as this cleverly disguised sabotage was, my anger *was* mixed
with some understanding: I was dealing with a very old culture in
which the hereditary values so far had only received a very thin, cos-
metic layer of revision. Being a foreigner and a woman to boot, I could
not see that it made any sense, or that I had any right to judge them
from my European, more equality-informed background that did not
go totally scot-free either. Throwing stones sitting in a glass house only
creates shards with sharp edges on which your opponents are going to
cut themselves, breeding more bad blood. My choice of setting an
example, combined with gentle resistance, is I believe in the long run a
much more effective way. Stupidity has no gender, and obtuse men tire
me as much as insensitive women. The fact that men and women *are*
different, to me is a source of richness and delight.

One of my trainees, the only female director at the station, was a heartbreaking example of what can happen when a new value system starts to infiltrate old cultures. She was a bright young lady in her early twenties, the daughter of a well-to-do lawyer who had sent her to finishing school in Switzerland. Back home for a year or two she was working at the station as a junior director. As a person she seemed unhappy and lonely but was good at her work, soaking up knowledge and quickly processing it. Her Swiss education had been a very strict and rather conservative one, but some of her international co-students had opened windows to freedoms she, as a Cypriot girl, had had no idea existed. Eventually back in her parents' house, where it was taken for granted that she should adhere to and obey to the old Cypriot rules, she felt the conflict. Even to be allowed to work had been a battle, but her father had finally given in, although there was on his part — as well as on her mother's — a tacit expectation that she would, in the not too distant future, marry the man of their choice. He was the son of one of her father's confrères, and there were old bonds between the families. Although the young people were good friends, neither seemed too keen about the idea of a marriage. She loved and respected her parents, and she knew that a refusal on her part would hurt and sadden them.

Although she doubted that they would force her against her will, the assumption was only of temporary relief: she felt trapped and saw no way out. As much as I sympathised with her plight, all I could do was lend an understanding ear, but I also pushed her into as much training as possible; if one day she would decide to fly the coop, proficiency would be her most useful luggage. I thought I had a pretty good idea who was behind the troubles I encountered, but as a junior director, my trainee was still too unimportant to be another victim of this untalented director's fears of competition. I had, however, no doubt that if she stayed long enough her day would also come — unless she had been able to navigate her way up the ladder without making enemies. Compared with me she also had the definite advantage of being Cypriot.

After about a year and a half on the island, life in general was still very pleasant, but work had lost at least some of its appeal. Resentment that I had been unable to appease quite clearly would continue to prevent me from making my own films, and as that was what I really wished to do, staying on did not carry any great attraction. With the sad news of John Grierson's passing, a return to Montreal was less pressing, and I felt the time was appropriate to learn French properly. To that end I started to investigate the possibilities of finding work in France, and while doing so, I got involved in a real local 'circus.'

A Cypriot, the young director George Pan Cosmatos had learned filmmaking in Rome, and he was at this time preparing for an Italian-Cypriot co-production. Cypriot locations had been used in a few foreign films, but this made waves; not only was George a son of the island, but it was also to be the first feature film made there. The essential film crew would be Italian, and George had made a surprising scoop: signing Racquel Welch as his leading lady. She was to play a Cypriot woman who, by not obeying the moral code of widowhood, is subjected to the wrath of her village.

George's wife was a Swedish painter, and I had met them a couple of times over the last year, but now I started to get invitations from George's parents with whom they stayed. Delectable dinners were combined with concerted efforts to tie me to the project, and when finally it became evident that work in France would not materialise very quickly, if ever, I accepted the offer to first do the continuity in Cyprus and then edit the film in Rome. The big carrot was the prospect of working in Rome.

I never saw the finished film, but as soon as the filming started, one could clearly see that if his leading lady was a scope for distribution, she also was his Achilles heel. Racquel Welch, her looks notwithstanding, was not a very good actress and not very convincing as your average village woman. From the day of her arrival, she tried her best to move Hollywood to Cyprus where it was not much needed. Still, she had one remarkable performance, although I think it was real horror more than good acting that finally did cut a tear in her usual lacquered Hollywood demeanour. In one scene a vengeful villager has suspended a dead chicken over her door, and when she steps out of her house, blood drips on her face. George insisted on a freshly slaughtered chicken and filmed the scene without rehearsing it. Just as well, for Miss Welch, in hysterics, would never have agreed to a second take!

Another of our bloody undertakings was the sacrifice of a bull, and for that sequence the set designer had chosen a windblown stretch of cliffs with the sea as a backdrop. It was indeed a very dramatic location on a vast, stony coast. The only negative aspect was its difficult access. No road went that far, and we had had to lug all the equipment a considerable distance. When finally ready to film the scene of the sacrificer thrusting his knife in the bull's throat, I was not very comfortably 'coiled up' on the tripod under the camera. Perfect continuity was a must, and in order to be sure of it when clicking my Polaroid, I had to be as close to the action as possible. The man raised his hand and lunged, but no blood spurted from the sack hidden on the bull, instead a gush of blood hit the actor in the face, and he was squeezing his thigh where the knife had imbedded. One of the gaffers rushed forward, grabbed a piece of cloth, and applied a tourniquet. A makeshift stretcher was quickly assembled, and our rather pale and, for once, unobtrusive actor was carried as quickly as possible all the way up to the road and then driven at breakneck speed to Kyrenia's hospital. Luckily the knife had missed an artery, if only by a hair, and he was soon on his feet again. This idiot, who thought a lot of himself, had secretly changed the theatre knife he had been supplied with for a real one. 'It has to be real to feel right' we were later told. He had never been much liked, and this stupidity did nothing for his reputation, but the thought of what might have happened haunted us all. After the accident, it was difficult to get the shoot back on track, but eventually we finished the filming and moved to Rome. One week later, a crying George told me that he had been duped by his Italian co-producers and could raise no more money. In order to finish his film, he had to sell it to the Americans, who for union reasons insisted on using an American editor. I was paid off and let go.

THE HOLES IN THE SWISS CHEESE

It is a strange irony that I should be so totally captivated by a profession that clearly is a city activity, when at heart I really am a country person. Despite these contradictory feelings, Rome is a city where I feel at home, and for the next few days I nurtured some dreams and made inquiries about work. With surprisingly short notice, I got an interview with the head of the United Nation's Film Unit. My CV had lingered in the UN archive in Geneva for quite some time — or so I thought — but I now discovered that it had been in a very 'personal filing system' for at least a year. After some considerable time with the organisation, this gentleman knew far too well how easily the mega-structure lost track of papers. If he came across a file of possible future interest, it went straight into the bottom drawer of his desk! He explained that my CV was going to stay there until the regional policies of the UN made it Sweden's turn to submit candidates. Presently it was Africa's tour, and as their mandate lasted for another year, he put it upon me to keep him posted of any change of address. At the time I had few contacts in Rome, and it did not take long before I had to admit to myself that my film future in Rome was just a pie in the sky. My procrastination-prone ambition to learn French properly finally nagged me into action. France, after much delay, had finally come clean: I was not going to get a work permit there, but Switzerland was nearby, and I had a contact in Geneva. Arne Boström was a filmmaker who had also left Sweden in 1968, establishing a small but successful animation company in Geneva. A telephone call solved my problems in no time. Arne was up to his ears in work, badly in need of help, and implored me to get on the next plane! Without a work permit, I had to enter Switzerland as 'a tourist,' and we arranged for my salary in such a way that neither he nor I would land in trouble should the authorities be inquisitive.

To call Arne's studio busy was an understatement; we worked from early to late, often seven days a week. I edited, directed commercials, kept laboratory contacts, and learned to paint animation cells. After three months, just before my tourist visa was due to expire, I went to Amsterdam for a couple of days to supervise the dubbing of a commercial into Dutch, then continued on to London. A prolonged general strike had cut telephone, telegraph, and mail service between Switzerland and the UK; the only way to reach the London factory in order to buy the animation table Arne badly needed was by turning up in person.

On the plane an article about Luxor in an in-flight magazine caught my eye and reminded me of my dreams of a never-realised trip. Reading *Justine,* the first book in *The Alexandria Quartet,* whet my appetite to go to Alexandria, with the book as a guide, and then sail up the Nile to see Nubia before the immense dam construction at Assouan would set it under water. It was a lingering fantasy that never worked its way into reality, but before my week in London was over, I had an enigmatic encounter. I was a house guest and one evening, without much enthusiasm, I had tagged along to one of my host's dinner invitations where I found myself sitting across the table from an elderly gentleman. He looked as British as they come and kept polite conversation. To this day I do not know what possessed me to suddenly answer one of his questions in Greek! He showed no surprise but started to talk about the Mediterranean world, and now things became interesting. He had lived in Alexandria for a long time, and during the Second World War had been in charge of its waterworks. He talked about the city and people he had known there with a love that had kept important details alive, but he also acknowledged, with noticeable sadness, that the life of the pre-war city was gone and the city itself was very changed.

After ten days absence, I returned to Geneva and the animation studio, starting a new three-month 'tourist' period. This arrangement was, however, of limited duration; after a third 'tourist' period, I would not be admitted to Switzerland again for some unspecified time. The work was interesting in its diversity, which added skills to my register, and my boss was easy to work with, but I made very little progress in French. Arne spoke it reasonably well, but between two compatriots their common language was closer at hand, and since he was constantly in a hurry, he mostly spoke Swedish. For obvious reasons my presence in Geneva was not trumpeted from the roof tops, but working in the studio I, of course, met people from the film and TV business. I discovered that, until recently, La Télévision Suisse Romande had filled its quota of editors by importing them from France, Belgium and Germany. That avenue was no longer available since the cry of the day, in some xenophobic haze, had become 'Switzerland to the Swiss.' I have no idea how they thought they were going to live without all the 'guest-workers' who did all the jobs the Swiss themselves had no taste for, but the TV station had eventually realised that they needed to establish their own in-house training. As there was nobody qualified already on staff, they were in dire need of somebody who was. I fit the bill, and shortly after my return from London, I was offered this new position. What I had seen of the station's output did not exactly make the offer irresistible, but it was undeniable that, employed by La Télévision Suisse Romande, I would get a proper work permit and no doubt a better chance of finally getting on with learning French.

The station wanted me to start working as soon as possible, but I was not going to leave Arne in a bigger jam than necessary and left it to him to set the date. The station promised they would, without delay, apply for a work permit, but as the rules stated that the person concerned must not yet live in the country, I provided them with a suitable address in France. That, however, did not prevent some scatterbrain from giving my Geneva address, and as could be expected, the application was turned down. Then the station repeated the exercise, this time using the French address and were, surprise, surprise, again refused any permit. The canton's bureaucrats might have been bureaucratic, but they were at least not stupid. In the end, management had to go to Bern and apply on a special federal quota list for qualified technicians, and then after roughly six months, they finally obtained this elusive piece of paper. By that time I had been working at the station for a couple of months already, and now, before anything else, they had to get me out of the country as a tourist and then back in as a legitimate worker.

My immediate boss — who at this point had had enough of disrupting incompetence and who did not wish to lose me — decided to see to it himself. We drove to the nearest border crossing where my passport was duly stamped *Departure*, continued, and entered France where we celebrated with a lunch worthy of the occasion. As it was imperative that we returned to Geneva via a different border crossing, we did some sightseeing before turning homewards. It had started to rain, and at the crossing into Switzerland, the guard from inside his dry cubicle just waved us on, but as the entry stamp on my work permit was the most important part of the whole exercise, we stopped and sat in the car until he eventually came out and fulfilled his duty. I was finally on a legal footing, but I was never able to find out into which pocket the tax money, which had been duly deducted each month from my paycheque, had disappeared. As I had not officially existed as a working person in Switzerland until this rainy afternoon, it was not very likely that the amounts had been delivered to the canton's income tax department!

La Télévision Suisse Romande was a small station, and when I started there, it did not have its own building but rented spaces in different parts of the city. The editors were housed in a former office building with windows that did not open and an air conditioning system that left a lot to be desired. As a result, everybody left their doors open, and it was a terribly noisy place. From time to time you did not know if it was the sound in your own editing table or one from a nearby room that you heard. When we later moved into a newly built TV tower, the noisy overcrowding was replaced by near to total isolation. The only places where you might see people were in the elevators or, possibly, on your own floor when taking a walk to or from the washroom. We had a good laugh the day the personnel were invited on the grand tour of the new facilities for, when the tour came to an end, someone asked, 'Where are the directors' offices?' Dead silence. It turned out they had been forgotten in the planning, and changes were hastily made, but as somebody quipped: 'It really does not make that much of a difference whether or not there is a director.' I am afraid that, over time, I detected that on the whole this was the sad truth. I do remember one or two directors who really did make a difference, but generally speaking, at the time, the production was very, very pedestrian. And there were some very bizarre rules that badly needed to be changed.

My job was to supervise and train the editors, but I had from the start talked my boss into also letting me edit. He was one of the rare exceptions among the bureaucrats who, with the help of some technocrats, were driving this station. Working as an editor was the only way to get a realistic understanding of whether or not the imposed time limits were reasonable and my work might also set an example for the other editors. Beyond that I hoped that the contact that I, as an editor, would have with the directors might lead to a better understanding on their part of what kind of images they had to bring to the tables if better programs were to see the light of day.

Especially coming from Cyprus, with their sometimes less sophisticated work methods, it was no small irony to find now, in Central Europe and in the country of advanced technical expertise, that time had been made to stop like any old clock! After complaints about unsteady film projections, caused by badly applied tape in the splices, the editors had been forced to revert to the old hot splicers. Instead of a ten-minute lesson about the correct way to use the tape-splicers, they were forced into a time-consuming, dirt-collecting system that virtually added insult to injury by preventing them from opening a splice and lengthening the image. To convince the powers that be that this antiquated habit had to be stopped did not seem possible. I talked to deaf ears until one day I discovered by chance that one of the editors used a tape-splicer and had done so for quite a while. She was French, had earlier worked as a freelancer, and owned her own equipment. As she was an intelligent and accomplished editor, there had been no need for supervision, and I had never observed how she worked. I was delighted! As there had been no complaints, I now had irrefutable proof that the tape-splicer was fine — if correctly used. Dumping a number of her tape-spliced programs on the right desk finally lead to a change, and eventually all editors got a tape-splicer.

My endeavour to change the totally detrimental rule that shooting time equated editing time took even longer, and although I won a couple more battles, the war was never really won. I was incapable of coming up with any arguments that made the bureaucrats understand that the quantity of interview material you were able to shoot, in say three days, by far extended what in equal time you could — without transcripts and hardly ever any worthwhile cutaways — successfully shape into a visually interesting program. Close-ups of twiddling thumbs were the standard cutaway fare but something with more significant aspects hardly ever showed up, with one almost comic exception. One young director always brought his editors this otherwise lacking variety of cutaways, but they were invariably shot from the wrong angles and thereby completely useless. Most of the station's cameramen did not seem to either know better or bother when he directed them to camera positions that did not cut with the rest of the footage. He was the unvanquished master in the kingdom of 'Crossing the Axis.' I explained his errors again and again, I drew diagrams, I spliced in his wrong images, and then he seemed to see why they did not fit. He promised never to do it again, but during the next shoot, he was still incapable of getting it right. From a teaching point of view, he was a complete failure, but because of all his good will and ambition to learn, it was impossible not to like him.

The generally poor footage made for acrobatics at the station's editing tables. We did not yet have the help of online magic, that would eventually solve much more than jump cuts, and from time to time, in the effort to establish a comprehensible narrative, we could not avoid making them. These disjointed cuts where heads jumped did not have any place in the bible of good editing, but they were the only way out. At La Télévision Suisse Romande, they appeared so regularly that they even acquired a name — 'a Godard.' I could see why the French filmmaker had been 'honoured' this way, and a meeting with the man himself only strengthened the perception. Jean-Luc Godard had accepted an invitation to come to Geneva, show us one of his films, and discuss it. He was expected by ten o'clock on a Sunday morning, and there we were waiting for him when the delegation at the airport reported that the plane from Paris had landed, but without Godard, who had simply missed it. It was then arranged for him to come on the next flight. When we reassembled, Godard had arrived, but forgotten his film. What followed was a dreadfully tedious 'discussion' between our guest and one of the station's senior directors; yet another demonstration of the truth in *The Emperor's New Clothes*.[22]

One day someone lugged a number of boxes into my editing room, and in them I found roll after roll of great music and interesting footage once shot at a Duke Ellington concert in Lausanne. It had been filmed with three cameras — two from the station and one rented from outside — and an editor had started to synchronise image and sound but soon realised that something was amiss. Nobody had been able to figure out exactly what, and the footage was packed up and banished to storage. Its resurrection was due to a report that Ellington was seriously ill and not expected to live much longer. Marking identical frames on the images as well as equivalent points at the sound tapes revealed the roots of the problem: the two station cameras had run at their normal speed of 25 frames/second while the rented one had not been changed from its 24 frames/second film speed. The hour-long program the station wanted had to be reduced to half its length. I raved and ranted and moaned over great shots of The Duke and some divine music I could not make use of.

When this bungling station ventured into its first-ever international co-production, it became *the* event of the year. A musical comedy with a number of bilingual French-German lyrics, as well as songs in French only, later to be dubbed to German, was bankrolled by a television station in Munich, Germany, but produced by La Télévision Suisse Romande. The station's most capable director was in charge, and as the editor, I for a change had eminently cuttable footage. We both had a really good time, and once the show was finished, I went to Munich to supervise the dubbing. It was not just the contrast between efficiency and inefficiency that made this trip so memorable, but to personally experience the much-touted German drive and precision was a good professional experience. Not only had they told me just to send them the footage and they would attend to all the preparation of it, but they also forecasted that the dubbing would take 'at the very most two days.' Based on earlier experiences I had estimated five, if all went well!

Neither subtitles nor dubbing are, from an artistic point of view, desirable tools when you have to present a film in a language other than the original one, but I had taken a monumental lesson from Marcel Ophuls's incredibly ambitious documentary about French resistance, or lack thereof, during the Second World War. Four-and-a-half hours long, *The Sorrow And The Pity*[23] is never dull; its American version, also closely supervised by Ophuls, is equally enjoyable. How many films, dubbed for American consumption, can you say that about? The secret of the success lies in the choice of the voices used in the dubbing. Each and every one has a timbre that is, if not identical, always very, very close to that of the original voice. This also minimizes the irritation over lip movements lacking exactitude. In conversations with Munich, I had stressed this point, and they seemed to understand what I was talking about.

They had indeed! I met with perfection. The chosen actors specialised in dubbing; you would never encounter them on a stage or see them on the screen — their whole talent was in their voices. When I arrived they had already been rehearsed to flawlessness, and the few times I asked for a second take, it had to do with intonation, never with a false start or messing with the text. Once a loop was finished, the next was ready to roll. By five o'clock we had only one more loop to go, and I was asked if I would mind working until six o'clock! We had started at nine, had one hour's lunch break, and by six o'clock, without any noticeable stress, it was all in the can. After dinner I was given a taste of the nightlife in Munich. The following day, before returning to Geneva, I was shown around the city and given the grand tour of the station, where the very high efficiency level seemed to stretch beyond the dubbing studio; nevertheless the atmosphere was pleasantly friction free.

The greater part of the year Cyprus was a warm and sunny place and people were easygoing. When moving to Geneva, I had been aware that some adjustments awaited me, but the gap between reality and what I had imagined was considerable. The fact that The League Of

Nations — the precursor to The United Nations — was born there in 1920 and that direct democracy, in the form of the referendum, had age-old roots in the country, even before its modern introduction in 1848, had made me naively presume that I was moving to the cradle of international life and democratic policy. I was quickly proved wrong on both points: the international influx had not opened up the Swiss — it seemed to have had the opposite effect. At least in Geneva they kept to themselves in small 'coteries' and, scratching the political surface, a fascistic leaning seemed to emerge. 'Guest workers,' mainly Spanish and Italians, who toiled in the building and agricultural industries, where the Swiss did not want to put their hands, were not treated in a very pleasant way. Housed in dreary dormitories, they had nothing to do after work and had hardly any outside contact; they were not allowed to bring their families with them until they had worked for several years. When eventually they were given permission, the wives had to sign a three-year contract to work as housemaids. That clause was eventually abolished, but Switzerland had an air of feudalism that I found heinous.

Geneva of the early 70s had no permanent local theatre or opera company, no art cinema, and only a few movie theatres with mostly mainstream American films on their repertoire. No restaurant admitted you after nine o'clock. One of the few things to recommend in this clean, orderly, and utterly boring city was the museum housing old musical instruments. Some were even kept in working order, and on Sundays the museum gave concerts. To suddenly hear the music of Mozart and his contemporaries, played on instruments of their time, was not only very different from what I knew, but to listen to what sounded simultaneously both familiar and intriguingly new was hugely stimulating.

Life in Geneva and at La Télévision Suisse Romande was, on the other hand, not very exciting, but at least it did fit the bill: I earned my bread-and-butter and was finally learning French. The majority of the editors were friendly, but save for one exception, we did not have much contact outside of work. When I arrived, Najet Ben Slimane was in

Tunisia due to her father's death, but once she returned things changed. With an amazing capacity to move between two very different cultures with both sincerity and grace, she was unparalleled to anybody I have ever met. I was very lucky to be honoured with her friendship. She had not only worked at the station for several years, but also created a large circle of friends and I was very soon included. Najet also quickly took my language training in hand and she was — and has always been — the only one with a way of doing it that never embarrassed me. I had a tendency to speak before thinking about the French grammar, and Najet put an effective curb to it. I was allowed the same mistake twice, then there were penalties. The first recurrence would cost one franc, the second was double the amount, and so on. In the beginning the kitty grew quickly, but the sheer cost soon made me think — at least some times — before opening my mouth. We used the money to indulge in our mutual liking for good food, so my shortcomings also helped to give me some insight into the restaurants in Geneva. Whenever I hear the French exclamation 'Génial!' it brings Najet to mind.

That most of my salary did not go into our 'grammatical-punishment' kitty was, to a very large degree, due to the efforts of Marianne Jeannet-Resasco, an excellent language teacher who taught phonetics at the University. I had been lucky enough to find her when I started to work at the TV station, and understanding that my kind of job was not a nine-to-five one, she always did her best to accommodate me when last minute emergencies forced a change of lesson time. She constantly grumbled over my accent, and I am afraid she still would, but for the rest she engineered considerable progress. We also discovered similar tastes and matching interests and in time developed a real friendship. As a foreigner, I was not allowed to rent a flat before having lived in Geneva for a certain time, and when I finally got into one it happened to be situated across the street from where Marianne lived. After my lessons, we often cooked together and shared our dinners, and over and above the pleasure of it, this certainly added to my language training.

One Easter Marianne had been given the use of a house in a small village on the east coast of Spain, and she invited me to come with her. For Good Friday we went into the nearest little town where we attend-ed an elaborately staged passion play that slowly made its way through the streets. Flats covered with flowering white heather and red flowers carried statues of saints; a Christ figure toiled under his cross followed by other characters out of the Bible. At each station toward the cruci-fixion, the procession came to a stop and performed a short play. All the people involved were ordinary citizens, but many performed the same role year after year. In Cyprus I had met religion in a very pure form; here I encountered high drama made religious.

Another ineffaceable holiday ensued when Najet invited me to spend the summer's vacation with her and her family in Tunis. I again took in a new country and a different culture, but living with Najet's family meant insights that ordinary tourist life would never have pro-vided. While Najet visited friends who were not bilingual, her sisters and brothers took me around Tunis, and I went to the market with her mother, a remarkable woman who, in her early forties, had lost an arm in a car accident. Najet had told me that, from being very elegant and outgoing, she had then for years withdrawn into a depression nothing could shake. But she had eventually emerged and with great determi-nation adapted to a work-filled life. Widowed two years earlier, she had taken the place as head of her household and now guided her children with a firm hand but also with much love. When I met her, she was in her sixties. Her grey hair fell in a long braid down her back, and she was always dressed in the simplest of dresses but looked beautiful. She cooked one-armed, did her sewing and anything else with an ease that made me with my two arms feel clumsy. While all her children spoke impeccable French, she only had a few words, and as I had no Arabic, ordinary conversation was not possible, but it did not seem to matter. She possessed an understanding that went beyond words. I am con-vinced that if I had been left alone long enough with Najet's mother, I would have learned to speak some of her language. Among all the charm and beauty I met, the place that finally stole a little bit of my heart was Sidi Bou Said. Although a well-known meeting place for

Tunisian artists and musicians, it was still a small, genuine village with a great view of the Bay of Tunis. It will forever be linked to long happy days and nights of sweet dreams with a small bouquet of jasmine flowers on our pillows.

For the last holiday week, Najet went to Paris, and I made a tour to the south of Tunisia. On the tour bus, I found myself sitting beside a Frenchman from Marseilles who turned out to be both interesting and pleasant, although mysterious company. He was not very talkative, but eventually I picked up that he had spent the war in North Africa, and this trip seemed to be born out of a desire to return under different circumstances. Whatever his reasons, he certainly did not seem an ordinary tourist, and I soon discovered that he spoke Arabic fluently. His way of looking at things and remarking on people and events went deeper than usual small talk.

Arranged tours are normally not my cup of tea, but I had chosen this one because it left a certain flexibility and more options than ordinarily expected. It would also, at least on the surface, show me much more of Tunisia than if I had tried to do it on my own in the short time of a week. On the third evening, we were in Tozeur in the west, near the big sandy desert, and the following day's program included a camel ride and a visit to an oasis where dates were grown. My mysterious companion, however, offered to share a much more interesting agenda. He had rented a jeep, and we drove past Nefta and into the desert. I did not ask, and Pierre did not tell, but I was convinced that we were on some sort of a pilgrimage. What he got out of it I will never know but this endless expanse of golden sand, patterned as if a last, never to be repeated outgoing tide had once passed over it, inspired fear in me. Although I have always had a great respect for vast expanses of water, they at the same time evoke feelings of freedom and choice; this 'sea of sand' only gouged out terror.

Eventually Pierre turned the jeep around, and just before leaving the desert, we stopped at a coffee shop in a small village. When we had finished our coffee, a new set of cups were brought to our table, and the boy indicated that a tall Bedouin, standing near the entrance, had sent them. Pierre asked the boy to invite him to our table but the man did not move, although he accepted a coffee. When we finally got up and left, the Bedouin followed us to the jeep and struck up a conversation. I was never let in on what they had been talking about, but after a while Pierre turned to me and asked if I wanted to see the hidden city. I nodded in astonishment, for Pierre had earlier mentioned its existence but also that a great secrecy surrounded it and all questions about it were always met by silence. What was known, was that long ago this land had regularly been invaded by foreign tribes who burned, looted, and took prisoners. The diminished local tribe finally found the solution to its survival: they built an underground city and disappeared into it when the invaders came. Nothing but empty houses was left above ground, nothing to kill, nothing to carry away.

I am equipped with a reasonably good sense of direction, but even to save my life, I would not have been able to retrace our route. Our guide led us up and down several lanes, across yards, through a couple of what seemed inhabited but empty houses, and finally down a long, curbing, slowly descending, corridor that got darker and darker. At its bottom he lifted a big slab, which to the unsuspecting eye looked just like the rest of the floor, and invited us to climb down a sturdy, long rope ladder. He went last and only stopped long enough to put the slab back in place and roll up the ladder. We stood in a small space where, in contrast to the heat above, the air had a pleasant freshness. Our guide started to lead us through a vast complex of rooms: kitchens, store rooms, washing areas, sleeping quarters, and more. There were water wells with fresh-tasting water, shafts that let fresh air in and others that kept the whole area lit in twilight. Time seemed to have come to a standstill while we wandered through this underground city from one house to the next, our footsteps and echoing voices the only sounds. Eventually our guide left us waiting while he continued into a new corridor, but he was back quickly enough and then took us with him into an upward slope where a rope ladder was hanging. Pierre climbed up, I followed, and when the Bedouin ascended he rolled up the ladder behind him and placed it in a space you would never find, unless you knew where to look. We walked through a door and out into the open, and I guessed that we were now on the opposite side of the village. Before us lay a shimmering green oasis where we sat down. Our host plucked some oranges that he peeled and offered us. He then seated himself between the two of us and explained, now in fluent French, that the secret on how to access the hidden city was carried in one single family from father to eldest son and had been so for generations. He, in due time, would pass the secret on to his eldest son.

This was not a day like any other, so I was not even astonished when the Bedouin took my hand and for a long while looked at its lines before saying: 'You have travelled a lot, now is the time to stop.' I had kept it to myself, but shortly before leaving for Tunisia, I had been contacted by the supervising director at the United Nations Film Unit. Her term was near its end, and since she was determined to see the job go to another woman, she had started to pull strings. Evidently my earlier interview in Rome had something to do with it, and she strongly, at length, urged me to apply for the upcoming job. Her calls had left me undecided. The work would, I was sure, bring me to some interesting places, but was I really tempted? My temperment is not suited for the delicate diplomacy that I suspect is a requisite to successfully work inside the UN. The whole idea of having to make documentaries that please all sides, or at least did not offend any, was surely a recipe for a blandness that had no appeal. Besides, there was a large administrative side to the job, and that did not have much allure either. The woman had been very insistent, and she wished to come to Geneva when I returned from Tunisia. I had finally promised to think about it, but mulling it over did not in any big way change my first perception. Finally I decided to put it out of my mind until after my holiday. I, who would never seek advice from card readers or glass-bowl gazers, now listened attentively to an unknown Bedouin's words and then and there decided to go back to Geneva and stick it out until my French was good enough, and then return to Montreal!

Each time I went to a cheese shop in Geneva, I was reminded of something from my childhood. Before we were old enough for school, my mother would take my brother and me for a morning walk, while at the same time doing her food shopping. My favourite place was the cheese counter where we were always offered a small slice from a couple of different cheeses. Although it meant another admonition from my mother — 'You just take what you are offered!' — and the ridicule of my brother, if it was Swiss cheese that was presented, I would, without fail, ask for a piece with many holes in it. My mother would later measure out some minor punishment, and my brother never tired of pointing out how stupid I was, not understanding that this way I got less cheese. He was undoubtedly right, but the holes, for some inexplicable reason, held an ineffable magic, and although I loved cheese, satisfying my fascination was even more important than filling my mouth. My readiness to follow the scent of fascination and my love for cheese are still unabridged, but my childish fixation on holes is no longer the same. The questionable honesty, the callousness, and thinly veiled Fascism I sometimes detected in the fabric of Swiss society not only emitted a lasting malodour, but also forever took something away from my fascination with the holes in the Swiss cheese.

MONTREAL REVISITED

Eventually my proficiency in French reached a stage where I was able to return the snootiness that seemed to be a common trait among the sales ladies in the elegant Geneva boutiques. It was 1973, and I felt ready to follow the advice I had been given in an oasis in the Sahara. I returned to Montreal, where it was easy and pleasurable to settle in. On the surface, it first appeared to be the same charming city that I had left four years earlier, but day-to-day living soon revealed that *something* essential had changed. With the October crisis of 1970 and Prime Minister Trudeau's use of The War Measures Act, the city had lost some of its innocence; the optimism and confidence Expo had created in 1967 was no longer present. The boom economy never established itself firmly, it only made short-lived appearances and then again faded into difficult times. Not just Montreal, but the whole of Quebec, would have to live with this pattern for the rest of the century and beyond. The National Film Board, as well as the CBC, suffered yearly budget cuts, and it was difficult for the private industry to find financing. The French Canadian feature film industry all the same clawed its way up. In 1971 with *Mon Oncle Antoine,* Claude Jutra gave it a noticeable niche that, two years later, was further strengthened by Jean Beaudin's *J. A. Martin, Photographe*. Both Jutra and Beaudin had taken their inspiration from a province of the past, but in 1975 Denys Arcand emerged as Quebec's first truly contemporary storyteller. *Gina* was not only contemporary, but also an intelligent, mocking revenge on the Board for having, in 1970, censored his documentary, *On Est Au Coton*. The powerful owners of the cotton mills in the Laurentians were not amused by Arcand's critical documentary, and the Board's commissioner at the time, Sidney Newman, gave in to their pressure and censored the film. The negative, or a copy of it, must somehow have fallen off the back of a truck, for it was easy enough to get hold of a print, and the film I am sure, got a much wider viewing than it otherwise was likely to have had.

The documentary side, on the contrary, had to constantly manoeuvre in economic uncertainty; the majority of the small companies barely survived on producing series farmed out by TV and/or government-requested educational films. My interest in documentary film had only grown so it was natural to continue in this field. The difference was that now I had settled on the francophone side. At the time, it was a very unusual move; the fence between the Two Solitudes had hardly any gates at all and certainly no swinging doors. People were puzzled and, in a few instances, rather hostile. When I could so easily have continued to earn my bread and butter on the anglophone side, why on earth had I gone to all this trouble to learn French? All I could say was that it had to do with affinity. I had an understanding of and a liking for the francophone filmmaking, and there was no hidden agenda. Most of the time, the anxieties abated, work was offered, and in general there was an interested and often warm acceptance. When work brought us together, a couple of individuals treated me with ice-cold correctness, while two anglophones at the Board called me a traitor to my face. The hurt from that insult was, in sharp contrast to the depth of my contempt for their stupidity, only minimal.

Not that discrimination is ever amusing, but an incident at the French language TV station Radio-Quebec all the same became dangerously close to laughable. A director there had asked to have me employed to edit a series he was going to direct, but the head of the editing department disapprovingly told him that if he wished to go outside the station, he at least ought not to choose 'a foreigner.' The director refuted that skill, and nothing else, was the only legitimate yardstick and, in a very balanced tone with just a hint of mockery, continued by pointing out that, when it came to being or not being Québecois, he himself was 'a foreigner.' He was Belgian! That ended any further obstruction, and the job was mine. At the time, Quebec still did not have educational opportunities in all fields and importing French-speaking specialists was a common occurrence. It was a necessity, and as such had to be tolerated, but it was never very welcome.

Fernand Dansereau, who I had met at the Board in 1968, by now had his own company, Inmedia, on St. Paul Street in Old Montreal. He soon employed me for some editing, and that was the start of a long-lasting collaboration. I became Inmedia's 'permanent freelancer.' I edited, directed, produced, and helped to teach the young talent who Fernand, with great generosity and a sometimes economically danger-ous optimism, gave a chance. The company's financial situation was most of the time precarious, but the atmosphere was pleasant and the challenge constant. One of the great attractions working at Inmedia was that both Fernand and Iolande Rossignol, his then-wife, were very committed to a community-oriented cinema, which I so far had not come across. One of their interesting series was *L'amour Quotidien*, made with ordinary people instead of actors. Through a workshopping method, they participated from the start of the project, developing their 'characters' and thereby also the plot line which, from the start, was always left open. This kind of improvisation was not common at the time, and with amateurs, lacking the accuracy of trained actors, the work method, interesting as it was, made the editing an even greater challenge than usual.

The contracts with Radio-Canada[24] were mere slave contracts. The station exercised its control over the script, the footage, the editing, and the final mix, and still, in the end, had the right to refuse the program, in which case the company had to return the money already paid out! To my knowledge, it never went that far, but Damocles' sword always seemed to hang over your head. The TV station had two 'controllers.' One was a friendly, level-headed person who listened to what you had to say and thankfully had no need to always be the one in control, but his colleague was quite the opposite. You never knew which one would oversee the next production, but you very quickly learned that if it was the Blockhead, there would be suffering.

My worst run-in with this zany troublemaker occurred during one of the early episodes of *Les Jeunes Scientifiques*, which was a multifaceted and, in parts, very dynamic series. *Pascal et le Vidéo* was a film of a film made by a group of thirteen- to fourteen-year-olds, based on their own script. The boy who directed was the son of a filmmaker, and he had surely been hanging around Dad's sets more than once, for he knew every bit of the job! In spite of his age, he also knew something about Hollywood B-movies! The script he and his friends had concocted was a boy-meets-girl story, with action provided by a successful robbery of a jewellery store. Rich, the boy then married the girl, and they escaped to a sunny coast, living happily ever after. The whole gang constantly cursed, pestered, and smoked like chimneys. The young director would put a cigarette in his mouth and then waited for the assistant director to come running and light it for him! Their image of adulthood left nothing to be desired.

The youngsters used an uncomplicated video camera, a so-called Port-O-Pack, and their work was documented on film by a director at Inmedia. Some of the video sequences were later incorporated into the final film, and the newness of Fernand's idea lay in the mixed use of video and film. For the video to be transferred to film stock, we had to send it to the USA, and even there the process was still in its infancy. Not only was it expensive, but it produced images that were very grey and grainy and not very attractive. In this case, as they represented the film in the film, it passed reasonably well. What passed less well was the content, for to my horror the Blockhead came to the screening of the rushes. No laughs were heard in the cinema, and when the lights came on, the man got to his feet, and declared that he would not tolerate any smoking or swearing in the film! I interjected that in that case we had better put all footage directly into the garbage bin. Blockhead glared at me and barked: 'No swearing and as little smoking as possible!' where-upon he left.

On principle I do not agree with censorship, and although this man's rigid value systems always irked me, in this case I could understand some of his concerns. The program was aimed at a young audience, but notwithstanding, I felt that a certain flexibility could and should be applied. If all that was typical of these boys was taken out of the film, what was the use of showing it at all? Instead of 'dry cleaning' them, would it not be more constructive to use their not-so-wholesome and rude habits as a base for discussion between kids and concerned adults?

I cut and cleaned as best I could until one day I came to a sequence where common sense told me that if it had to be cut we would lose the essence of the entire film. Fernand usually only looked at my final cut, but now I asked him to come to the editing room. I knew that my only hope of saving these images was dependent on Fernand being present at the screening and arguing for it. The ruse worked. I mixed the film and sent it off to Radio-Canada with a sigh of relief, but my joy was premature. The next day saw the can back at Inmedia with a terse note saying that one could hear a swear word. I went to the mixing theatre, and together with the mixer, played the reel at extra-high volume. We could not hear anything untoward. During a second run, the mixer detected the very, very faint sound of a forbidden word among a lot of traffic noise. It was barely audible, but Blockhead had of course heard it! We drowned the offender by mixing in a noisy car toot, and the can was on its merry way back to Radio-Canada. The self-appointed 'courier' was Inmedia's accountant who was in dire need of the Radio-Canada paycheque.

Fernand one day suggested that I show him some film I had direct-ed, and I had to ask Cyprus Broadcasting Corporation to send copies of two of my films to Montreal. Today you would, for a minimal cost, secure a video copy of what you had done, but my work in Cyprus hap-pened before the occurrence of video, and a film copy meant a consid-erable expense. In the fullness of time, the parcel from Cyprus arrived, and I passed it on to Fernand. He placed it on the windowsill in his office where it rested undisturbed for the next four months. When Fernand finally looked at them, I had already directed the last three films for the series. Of the thirteen half-hour programs stipulated in the contract for *Les Jeunes Scientifiques*, ten had been made by different directors and duly delivered, but during the summer all Fernand's energy had been engaged in a feature film, directed by one of his broth-ers. By the beginning of August, the film project was abandoned, and instead of giving Inmedia the economic boost Fernand had hoped for, the unfinished film left the company in a very serious economic situa-tion. To add to his worries, he had a December 23 deadline for the

Radio Canada series, and nothing at all had yet been done about the three remaining films.

Although my track record as an editor and/or producer showed that I delivered quality work on time and could be inventive in tricky situations, Fernand knew nothing about me as a director. All the same, he offered me the job as writer-director of these three remaining films. It was a baptism by fire, for not only did they all need to be made on the thinnest of shoestring budgets, but if the contract deadline was to be met, each film could only be allotted thirty days from conception to final product. On my to-do list was finding three groups of students with ideas that lent themselves to visual stories which were not too complicated or expensive, write the scripts, get the okay from Radio-Canada, shoot the films, and supervise the editing and the mixing — all times three. Negative-cutting and the making of final prints also had to be taken into account. Already, on paper the schedule looked impossible, and thinking back on it, I doubt that either Fernand or I deep down believed that it could really be done, but what we had in common was that it *had* to be tried.

For a day or two, I racked my brain in order to find the themes for the films, but then I realised that, with the restraints I faced, it was not a question of what I would like to do, but rather an exploration of work the students already were toying with and even may have started on. Les Jeunes Scientifiques was actually the group name for an activity started by some science teachers in a couple of Montreal schools. On their part it was a voluntary effort to keep their students off the street after school, and the variety and the number of activities were impressive. I turned to one of the teachers and asked about the possibility of having a meeting with these young inventors, the more of them the better, and a few days later I met with an impressive number of ambitious young talent. With differing degrees of eloquence, they described what they were working on, and that served me in several important ways. Ideas too close to those already filmed were recognisable and quickly eliminated, and the same happened to the ones of little visual interest. Their presentations gave at least some idea about how well they expressed themselves, but if the ease would still be there when the camera started to roll was of course only a guess. The process was effective and left me with a shortened, and much more manageable, list of subjects, but the culling had to be draconian.

My spaghetti budgets allowed for an unusually low ratio of raw stock, three days filming maximum, hardly any props, only nearby sites that did not eat up travelling time, and as few exteriors as possible. My trust in co-operation from the Montreal weather was very limited. After these acrobatics, I could allow for one week's editing, and that did not seem too much of a problem as the job was to be done by Frances Pilon. She was a freelance editor at the early stage of her career, and I had already seen some of her work at Inmedia. Editing suited her extremely well, and she worked with an intelligence and a feeling for the material that was very reassuring. If my three programs came in on time, it was in no small measure thanks to Frances. They also came in on budget and, if I remember correctly, one of the three even a proud, very proud $50 under budget! To later be told that these three films were among the best-selling in the series, was very nice.

As if the economic restrictions imposed on the assignment did not create enough difficulties, the laboratory had an accident, the weather played a dirty trick on us, and I made a stupid mistake that would gall me every time I was forced to look at it. The first film was about two boys who had developed a surprisingly simple but effective way to determine the composition of the minerals in rocks. The opening sequence in *Le Goût d'une Pierre* was situated in the vast Mirron quarry in the north of Montreal. The boys arrived on their bicycles and started to collect rocks for their experiments that were then shown in interiors. But the morning of the filming, there was no rock face to be seen because the quarry, like the rest of the city, was blanketed by a thick layer of fresh snow! It was too early in the year to even suspect an odd snowfall, but here it was, and it had gone on all night. I had become aware of it the evening before and passed a sleepless night rewriting the beginning of the film. By five o'clock in the morning, I called Fernand who was sound asleep and had no idea of what it looked like outside. He approved my revised opening scenes as well as my firm intention to bypass an okay from Radio-Canada. At the quarry the boys feigned great surprise at this 'local' snowfall, pretending to have seen nothing of it on their way out from the central city. They then amused themselves throwing snow balls and clowning around until they were completely white. Hopping on their bicycles, they started out for the city, and we picked them up in our interior location and continued to film as planned. This new beginning had gained me half a day in shooting time, but it also felt as if the anxiety had shortened my lifespan by much more than that.

The next film, *Balune*, featured a group of young, very enthusiastic amateur meteorologists who were sending up helium-filled balloons for temperature readings in the atmosphere. By its nature this had to be a complete exterior shot, and I had been in two minds about the implicit risk, but the boys were animated and the visual possibilities very attractive so I had taken a deep breath and settled on them. During the filming, the balloons of course showed a will of their own, greatly helped by a bit more wind than we would have preferred, but the shoot on the whole went well, as did the post-production.

If *Le Goût d'une Pierre* had tested my mettle, *Vivre à la Quatrième Dimension* excavated it right down to its core. Among the students, I had met a young man who was into mathematics in a serious way. By presenting infinite mathematical series, he had been that year's winner in both the local and the national contests among *Les Jeunes Scientifiques*. He had obtained the results by starting with a line, moving to an angle, then a triangle, a square, a pentagon, a hexagon, etc. He had observed, measured, and compared sides and angles between bodies of different shapes, and based on these observations, he had then constructed his series. Neatly folded paper models of his own construction helped him to explain in a very visual way how his observations had led to the series. There was no doubting that you were dealing with an intelligence well above the average, and later during the filming, his mother told me that he had not been an outwardly active child. One day, when she again saw him sitting outside on the kitchen doorsteps, she got impatient and asked him why he was not doing something instead of just sitting there? 'Ma, I *am* doing something, I am thinking,' said her son. 'That was the last time I asked such a silly question,' she laughingly added. Her son had a pale, delicate face and black shoulder-length frizzy hair, which during filming, even with liberal doses of hair spray, had an obstinate habit of obscuring his face — purgatory for a director who firmly believes in the magic of the camera lens looking into the eyes.

The idea for the film had come to me during the evening when the whole group had made their presentations. With much conviction, this young man told us that mathematics was *not* a difficult subject in itself; according to him it was only the way school taught it that made it difficult! It was then that I had the idea for the film. Three slightly younger, average students would join him, and he was going to explain to them how he had obtained his results. Their grasp of the idea and the interest they showed would be the proof of the accuracy of his statement. The funny thing was that nobody, not Fernand nor the TV people, ever asked me what was going to happen if the boy was wrong. I never posed that question myself, but that might have been because I had once chosen mathematics and shared his feelings about schools' habit of complicating things. Regardless, he was right!

Because I was so short on time, I had no possibility of scouting around for the three younger students myself, and again I relied on my helpful teacher contact. He sent me two lively girls and a very quiet boy who at first sight I was already very unsure about. I wished to exchange him for someone else, but foolishly fell for the time pressure — and paid for it later. He turned out to be just as dull as I had feared, and I cursed myself until a real catastrophe pushed anything else into the background. The laboratory lost one of my magazines in the developing bath, and that reel contained *all* my close-ups of the paper models. Normally, in a situation like that, you would go back and re-shoot the lost material, but 'normality' was not by any yardstick within my reach. My cameraman had gone to Europe the day after the filming finished, and the laboratory's only obligation is to give you a roll of negative for free. To add insult to injury, the cost to have it developed is on you! To reconstruct the shoot with someone else behind the camera would have been both costly and very time-consuming and the possibility to exactly match the light and the original camera angles was at best uncertain. My budget had no contingency — not because it had been forgotten, but the money had not stretched that far.

Frances started the editing, and when we came to the places where the missing close-ups should have been, she edited for sound information only, putting black leader on the film side. I went out of my mind trying to find a solution but did not even hatch any unsuitable ideas, and time was running out. Then suddenly I remembered what I had discovered years earlier during the editing of *Persona* — the possibility to mix different styles of storytelling. Promptly the ideas tumbled in and to find the solution seemed almost easy. Frances made a very detailed list of each of our black film bits, noting which model was used and measuring to the frame the exact length of each take. The student lent me his models and allowed me to pierce a hole in each so I could hang them on a thin thread. The differently coloured paper sheets he had used when originally folding the models had been visible on his worktable during the filming, and I now arranged them in a geometric pattern on a wall in the editing room. Against this background I hung model after model, and a new cameraman put a corresponding light on the new set. Before each take, Frances ran the nearly finished film in the editing table, showing our actor the wider shot leading into the black leader. This way he could see at each cutting point the angle of his hand, how it had moved, and thus repeat the movement in the new close-up. Guided by his own voice on the sound track, he turned the model as he had originally done, and we had instant control over the take: it would have the exact length as well as correct continuity. Our use of negative film must have been the most economic ever heard of! Ninety minutes later we had a new set of close-ups in the can, and this time the laboratory sent them back in good order. Not only did the new takes have a perfect fit, but they looked much more interesting than an ordinary close-up would and they lifted the film to a new height.

Years later, I would come across *de Bono's Thinking Course* published in 1982 by the BBC as an accompaniment to its TV series with the same name. For the first time I met the term 'lateral thinking,' and although Edward de Bono theorised about thinking and not about film, his ideas were highly applicable and very useful. Back in Montreal, what first had held me back was what de Bono called the 'intelligence trap,' and it was lateral thinking that had released me. Although pleased to have learned something new, or at least having found a name for what I had done, it in no way diminished the seriousness of the lesson from *Vivre à la Quatrième Dimension*: under 'normal' conditions I would *not* have done what my predicament had forced me to do, and that was a momentous realisation about the deadwood of habits.

By 1974 Inmedia's economic situation had become untenable, and it closed its doors. For some time I continued to work as a freelance editor but finally put down my scissors and grabbed a pen. I had obtained a grant from Le Ministère des Affaires Culturelles and started to write a feature film script based on André Major's novel *L'épouvantail*. Major's writing appealed to me, and it revealed a side of life that I perceived as typical for a part of the Québecois' rural society. My own knowledge of small villages in northern Sweden made for an understanding that went beyond simple appreciation of the characters and the events, and that doubtlessly was part of the affinity I had with Major's book. The person at the Ministry who negotiated my grant had a somewhat unrealistic idea of what writing was and held forth that, since I already had the story in Major's novel, it would not take me very long to write my script. He showed no understanding of the dissimilarity between writing for the page and writing for the screen, nor did he understand the vastly different conceptions of 'based upon' and 'inspired by.' My argument that a given text is often more of a hindrance than a help, a film not being a translation of a text but the rendering of an idea in a different dimension, fell on deaf ears. I ended up with a grant that was supposed to cover my living expenses for six months, but it would take me almost twice that time before I had finished the script.

It was my first feature film script, and I gave no thought to the need for a different mindset when writing 'shopping lists' for documentaries and on the other hand creating a dynamic narrative with a functioning plot and characters the audience would recognise and be interested in. My admiration for Major's book also made me all too respectful and finally — to give the death knell to my efforts — pure ignorance got me bogged down in a morass of technicalities about camera movements and the like. At the end of a difficult exercise, I was left with a clay-footed elephant that had very little resemblance to the lofty ideas I had had at the start. Years later, when I met Mike Leigh, the British director, whose films I greatly admire, I received an instructive lesson in how to sell your ideas. Delivered with his tongue-in-cheek approach, especially when expounding on his filmmaking, Mike talked about his early films at the BBC where he quickly discovered how an 'acceptable' script was supposed to look. Once he had been given the okay, he would then go and make the film he had had in mind all the time. It was very amusing and most instructive, although I do not think that at the time even this knowledge would have saved my bacon. My education and experience as a journalist had probably stood me in good stead on the documentary side, and I had forgotten to ask myself the crucial question: am I really of the temperament that makes a feature film writer / director? I eventually came to the conclusion that the answer is No, but at this early stage I was too green to realise it.

Nor had I made a conscious distinction between the hunger that is love and the passion that denotes desire. The love I brought to editing was platonic and did not prevent me from placing myself at a certain useful distance from the film, while the desire that pushed me towards fiction was a body of untamed lust, fantasy, fascination, and impulse.

A VERY MIXED BAG

Not that the shape, form, or content of my script really mattered, for when I finally surfaced among the work needy, there was hardly a single job to be found, and financing of a feature film script — even an excellent one — was not very likely. The economy had reached bedrock, and if the job seekers ahead of me were not always more experienced, they were all Quebec-born. With the economy showing no sign of improvement, after several months of total unemployment, I made the decision to leave the world of film as an active participant and recycle myself as a cabinetmaker. I applied for admittance to a course established to take people off unemployment and came face to face with a form of prejudice that tottered between the unbelievable and the truly ridiculous. Looking at my application form where under *present occupation* it listed *film editor*, the lady shook her head and declared that this course was not for me. Asked why, she declared that cabinetmaking was for the PRACTICAL and I was an INTELLECTUAL. I countered that editing was, if anything, a practical task in which you use your hands all the time. I wisely left the brain out of it but stressed that I was a very practical person and vaunted my liking for gardening and cooking. I had always liked to work with wood, and I finally made a big spiel about the artistic side, the design aspect of cabinetmaking.

Nothing I said seemed to have the slightest effect on this lady who once and for all had divided her universe into two incompatible worlds; it was all too clear that I was looking at someone who had found security in an intractable pigheadedness. It was time for another tack. I got on my high horse and told her that it was her job to get me off unemployment, and how would she like to have a complaint launched against her? That did the trick, for even if she was 'reason-proof,' 'threat-proof' she was not. Soon enough I found myself, together with eight unemployed men, in the care of an elderly Spaniard with an in-depth knowledge of the use of interesting and beautiful wood. Old, richly sculptured European furniture was his personal preference, but he was wise enough not to try to impose this taste on his much younger North American students. We started at the bottom of the learning curve, and the rigour and discipline he asked for reminded me of my laboratory teacher at Europa Film. I felt good at what I was doing, and it was an immense relief to finally be out of the doldrums.

I only knew one or two people in Toronto, so the day I received three consecutive telephone calls from the city, it came as a real surprise. I was spending a leisurely morning at home while our woodworking equipment was being transferred to a new locale and we were given a couple of days off. The first caller — whom I had never spoken to before — was offering a feature film editing job. I thanked them for thinking of me, but, sorry, I did not edit any longer. The second voice I did know. It belonged to the writer and TV personality Patrick Watson. In 1968, newly arrived in Montreal, I had edited a trailer for his writer and filmmaker friend, Gordon Sheppard, who had scored some interest in Hollywood with *Eliza's Horoscope*. He and the studio however, differed in their opinions of who should play the leading female part. Hollywood wanted a well-known actress of their own; Gordon lobbied for his girlfriend. In order to convince the studio how much more attractive his choice was, he shot a few scenes as a trailer, and when we worked on it, Patrick had often come to the editing room. The snippet did the trick — the girlfriend got the part! Over the years Patrick and I had run into each other a few times, and now he called as a friend of the McLuhan family. One of Marshall's daughters, T.C. — or Teri as she was usually called — had made a feature film in which a lot of things seemed to have gone wrong. Teri needed some expert advice, and would I be so kind to take a look and tell her what I thought?

It was not the first time this sort of request had come my way, and my reply was, as always, in the negative. Not having seen the uncut footage, how could I judge its full potential? What worked for the present cut did not need to be discussed, and to pontificate about the unsuccessful parts would amount to little more than adding insult to injury. I can, of course, give my reasons for thinking that something is not working, but seldom does that explain to the director and/or editor where and why the derailment started. You have to assume that they have done the best they could, or it might be that what came to the editing room did not lend itself to much more than what you see on the screen. Or it could simply be lack of imagination! Or there may have been a large discrepancy between the script and the footage, and instead of forgetting the script and letting the images guide the editing, they had clung to the script as if to the Holy Grail, ending up with a homemade disaster. A mitigating factor in this case might have been the all-around lack of experience. Teri was a first-time feature film director, and it was her editor's first feature as well. Whatever the reasons, I had never felt that the time and the costs of my involvement this late in the process would be worthwhile. Precise suggestions are what matters, and they can only be given by someone familiar with the uncut footage. So, just as in previous instances, I declined. It was nice of you to think so highly of my skills, but no thank you. What I had not remembered was Patrick's outstanding persuasive powers: A little later I heard myself agree to come to Toronto and 'take a look.'

The third call was not long in coming. A very grateful Teri communicated practical travel arrangements and then, at length, did her best to convince me that I ought to look at her existing cut. I declined, explaining that a viewing, unencumbered by any lingering memory of what I might have seen, would leave me in a much better position to come up with suggestions. I asked her to have her editor splice back together, in its original uncut shape, fifteen minutes of what she considered her best footage and an equal amount of her worst material. Teri finally accepted, and a couple of days later I flew into Toronto to a red carpet welcome, but the screening left me puzzled. If part of what I had seen was the worst of the material, why had they not been able to make something acceptable out of it? With a naivety that from time to time has landed me in hot water, I did not even suspect that Teri had cheated on me. But she had, and I would all too soon become aware that what I had been shown was all the good material there was.

Patrick might well have been honest, not being intent on implicating me further than a screening — followed hopefully by some useful advice. However, looking back on this first encounter with Teri, once I got to know her, I finally understood that, from the outset she had intended to make me her editor — by hook or by crook. At the end of the day, I flew back to Montreal having promised to think about the offer she had given me. I had no intention of changing my mind about taking a new direction, but Teri's offer was a challenge — something I have always found difficult to leave alone, often to my own detriment. My plan was to ask to be allowed to take a break from the cabinetmaking course, then be readmitted to a new course as soon as I had finished the editing in Toronto. Had I been denied that possibility, I would have turned down Teri's offer, of that much I was sure. What I obviously had not known, or at least never on a conscious level fully realised, was how 'film-intoxicated' I was — and still am for that matter. The reality is that I get high on film like other people get high on coke, alcohol, or other substances.

Taking time out from my course did not cause any problem, and by the New Year I was back in Toronto. One of my conditions for signing a contract had been to be provided with a new work print and a new sound transfer. Teri went to her backers and came away with more money, but they had set a condition: wishing to assure themselves of the progress, they had demanded screenings once a week! This was the time when the Ontario tax system allowed unprofitable investments to lower the tax burden for big earners, and as a result, at the end of each fiscal year, accountants, lawyers, and doctors among others, shopped around for film investment. The insanity of it was that, although they invested in a market that needed all the money it could attract, they only promoted the wrong end of the industry. The greater the possibility that the film might become a flop, the bigger was the willingness to put money into it. I am sure the backers were great specialists in their own field, but they came to these screenings with their wives, daughters, and mistresses, all brimming with an instant savvy about filmmaking. It was a very trying exercise to politely answer one stupid question after another without giving away the fact that I, in reality, was working in what more resembled a hospital's emergency than an editing room. Figuratively speaking, I was day after day performing open-heart surgery and putting limbs in casts — at least that was what it felt like. It was during these screenings that I was most deeply angered by Teri's cheat. In the editing room, there was only time and space for great doses of inventiveness — although I would not call it creative editing — in an effort to shape the footage into a story that hung together without too many incredulous turns.

When discussing my contract, I had had to make a decision on a thorny point. Would I keep the former editor's assistant or get a new one? As I did not know the Toronto scene, finding what I deemed to be a good assistant was equivalent to playing the lottery. The present assistant might come with lingering loyalties and hurt feelings, but regardless, she had one tremendous advantage: she knew the footage. When Teri told me she aimed for the Cannes Festival, the time factor went to the top of the priority list, and I decided to keep Sharon Lackie, who turned out to be a great assistant and a really nice person. Orderly and fast, she had a reliable memory and good judgement and loved film. Her commitment to the work was great, and she had a tenacity to match my own. Our first meeting had taken me by pleasant surprise. The night before work was to start, I was invited to dinner at Teri's parents' place, and before going there I had taken a detour to give the editing room an inspection. As it was New Year's Day, I had not expected to meet anybody, but the lights were on, and there were Sharon and her boyfriend as well as three of their friends, all working like beavers. The laboratory had been late in delivering the new work print, and rallied by Sharon, her friends had all been hard at work since early morning, synchronising the sound tape to the new print. My new and unknown assistant immediately earned my respect and it would only grow as I got to know her. Both Sharon and her boyfriend were unusual people, very likeable, and that they honoured me with their friendship made me proud and happy.

Teri was also a pleasant surprise. She was a thoughtful employer who showed her appreciation of our hard work in many different ways.

Every so often a delivery boy appeared with coffee-break treats, and there were more gifts on St. Valentine's Day. She had detected my love for flowers, and there were always fresh ones in the editing room. At the weekly screenings, she showed a knack for diplomacy with the backers, and as the director, she was unexpectedly docile, listening to arguments and hardly ever forcing any changes. For somebody who put her name on the credits for five different functions, this must have been a great exercise in self-control. Like most other people, film directors come in all shapes and forms, but from the outset, I nevertheless wondered what had made Teri choose this path. Neither her material nor her reasoning showed any irresistible passion for the medium, and I doubted that Teri would ever make a good film director. I eventually suspected that she most likely had gone into film in order to do something no other member of the McLuhan clan had done. I found it all the more sad because she had one exceptional feature: she had obviously never learned to spell the word 'impossible.' I doubt it even had a meaning for her and felt that all her tremendous energy might be put to better use in another field. Slowly gaining insight into all the different sides of filmmaking, I had seen enough things go wrong in spite of knowledge, intelligence, goodwill, and care, but I was at a loss to understand what had guided Teri in this film. Even if your story is based on the premise of a mix-up at birth of twins, why do you hire two British Shakespeare-trained actors, one with a very limited experience in front of a camera and the other with none? Because they happen to be twins in real life? Would not anybody in their right mind go for two good actors with film experience and for the rest rely on makeup? Especially as the two young men who stared at me day after day from the screen were not exactly like two same-sized apples. The questions burned my lips, but finally the instinct of self-preservation, which had let me down so badly when I allowed myself to be hoodwinked into this rescue operation, now at least cautioned me to let sleeping dogs lie.

Teri had prolonged her contract for the editing room with its the screening facilities, and that meant that the same projectionists who had watched the first cut now also looked at the new one. The change for the better surprised them, and word began to get around in one of the world's most gossipy professions. I started to get inquiries about the time frame for Teri's film, followed by offers for editing work. Eventually the nightmare ended, the laboratory delivered a glossy print, and Teri left for Cannes and its film festival. I did not see her again, but as far as I heard, her trip did not result in any sales. Later in the year, the film played in a Toronto cinema but disappeared from the screen before the week had come to an end. It was in no way an injustice to the film, but Sharon and I pondered the irony of it all: a good film or a bad film — the work required to. bring it out is, most of the time, much the same!

I was still convinced that I was a future cabinetmaker but my professional pride dictated — or so I thought — that my film career should end on a worthier note than a rescue job. Another interesting offer seemed always to lie in wait, and that way I kept up my delusions for a while. Between jobs I drove back to Montreal for a couple of days, saw friends, and looked after my house in St. Mathias. The economic situation in Quebec showed no signs of recovery, while Toronto was bursting with activity, and because I had started to work regularly with a small, interesting company, it took a while before I heard the knocks. Truth stood at my door loudly telling me that I was a film junkie and had better stay one. I wrote an apologetic letter to my Spanish teacher, sold the house, and moved to Toronto.

My working life once again was very satisfactory although I really missed Montreal's charm, its graceful ways, and lack of pretension. Toronto had none of this, and although it already had a considerable influx of immigrants, that had not given it any international flair. To make friends outside of work was not easy, but I was reassuringly told, 'Don't worry! Just give it a couple of years, and you will see the difference.' Nobody, however, told you how to survive in the meantime! The question soon took care of itself; time outside work virtually disappeared when I became the director of *The Sensational 70s*.

The production company Hobel-Leiterman had already made a very successful series about the 60s and had decided to continue with another one about the 70s. Both series were compilations of existing footage of politics, sports, art, entertainment, and other noteworthy events — with an hour committed to each year of the decade. Douglas Leiterman in Toronto was the Canadian producer, and in New York Philip Hobel was the American one. *The Sensational 70s* was primarily aimed at an American audience, and consequently, except for international occurrences, the content was, to a great extent, based on American events, but the company also had a pre-sale to Canada. The two versions would have the same final length, but the Canadian one would have a fifteen minute local segment. Economic reasons dictated that every version had to be formatted in such a way that an entire fifteen minute block in the American version could be lifted out in the Canadian one, and then substituted with the block of local content. In theory it did not sound too complicated, but in practice it turned out to be a very fiddly affair. Before you could even start to work on the American version, you had to understand what content you were later going to drop. Once that decision was made, an even knottier one emerged: how to edit these images together so they formed a rhythmic, informative, and entertaining entity with some logic to what surrounded it? It wasn't made easier by the fact that the Canadian content was seldom dramatically as strong as the American was, and consequently the switch had a tendency to unbalance the Canadian version. It took a lot of cutting and re-cutting before both versions felt as good as you could ever hope to get them.

My first job had been to compile a content list for every year, and this was where my old training as a journalist came in handy. My employers vetted the lists, rejected some of my choices, and added some of their own. The American and international footage would be bought in the States; where to find it was a question for much deliberation. The problem with enterprises selling archival footage, especially concerning big events in the past, is that their stock has been used so frequently, that it has the sad look of déjà vu. I went to New York, and having pinpointed a couple of events from different years, I compared the footage available from the leading seller of archival footage with that from one of the big networks, that normally did not sell such footage. The difference was so encouraging that Philip, with great tenacity, spent considerable time negotiating with the network and cutting red tape until we were given access to an archive that had so far only been used by the owners themselves. The films were stored in Fort Knox — also home to the American gold reserve, of which I never even got a glimpse — but what I had my hands on was also a treasure trove. The footage of all the big events of the decade, as well as some smaller, but amusing ones, paralleled my nearly ten years abroad in a nutshell!

When I first lived in Montreal, I occasionally went down to New York for a few days and gorged myself on ballet, theatre, and art exhibitions. My first encounter with Merce Cunningham's work had happened that way, and I had become an instant fan of the aged but still performing dancer himself, his ballets, and of John Cage's music. New York was intoxicating like nothing before, and now being able to work there was even more so. With an energy level in a class of its own, it made each return to Canada feel like a time warp where everything was set to another, much slower, and alas, less exciting clock. The Torontonians seemed comfortable with it, but the timekeeper in my editing room was of another temperament.

Knowing that Douglas had done a lot of editing himself and also liked that part of the process, I had wondered how close an eye he would keep on the editing room. As it turned out, I was left to work on my own, and Douglas only looked at the reels when they were finished; I can not remember that he ever even asked for any changes. Once he had given his okay, I went to New York for a screening with Philip, returned to Toronto, and continued the routine. The planning and design of the production had taken more time than anticipated — what's new? — and when the practical work started in earnest, the time pressure became enormous. In Toronto, I constantly worked fourteen- to sixteen-hour days, seven days a week, but as the trips to New York could hardly ever be completed in one day, that thankfully left me the odd evening free to go to a film or stage play — often with Philip and his wife. Although sometimes tired and irritated by the fact that everything took so much longer to get done in Toronto than in New York, I found this production by far the most interesting one I had been involved in for a long time. Douglas and Philip were both pleasant and easy to work with, but I think the greatest pleasure came from the footage itself. I had not tackled this kind of 'documentary' before, and already the research work had given me a much deeper understanding of the links between the big occurrences during the 70s and how they were born out of the 60s. My own experiences of North America fell in this time frame and became part of a pattern, that the work in the editing room made even more obvious. The French, when contemplating history, make a distinction between the big events and *la petite histoire*, the more anecdotal, often personal stories that give history its human face, but seldom finds its way into history books.

Toward the end of winter came a telephone call from Stockholm and on the line was Jörn Donner, who the previous year had become the head of the Swedish Film Institute (SFI). While still working at Svensk Filmindustri, I had edited some of Jörn's films, so we sort of knew each other. He had shown fresh ideas, looked at his own material with some degree of detachment, had a very wide range of activities and interests, and had a brain that worked on overdrive most of the time. His supply of patience was limited, but I had found him stimulating to work with. The reason for his call was that he wanted to fly me down to New York for a meeting to discuss some possible employment. He did not wish to elaborate on the nature of it over the phone, but I forewarned him that I was not interested in returning to Stockholm. That did not change his resolve, and some time later I was told the whole story over breakfast at the Algonquin Hotel. SFI had, for some time, been involved in international co-productions but had not exercised a very active control over how their investment was used, with the result that they more than once had been taken to the cleaners. Jörn's outlook had always been international, and he wished to continue on this path and, if possible, even establish more co-productions, but he also had to put a stop to the misuse of Swedish money. To this end he planned to employ somebody who combined language skills with a working insight into all aspects of filmmaking — somebody who could effectively act as facilitator but also as a controller. Sweden and France had also recently signed their first co-production agreement, and Jörn intended to actively work on and develop that opportunity. My skills fitted the profile of this new employee, who should on one hand 'police' co-productions from the script stage to the final print and on the other be actively looking for foreign scripts worth considering. It sounded as if there could be interesting possibilities, but I still was not prepared to return and live in Sweden. Jörn did not see that as a problem and suggested that I could be placed in Paris. It seemed sensible as it would let me work more intimately with the French film industry, and from a travel perspective, Paris would also be a more practical 'railway station' than faraway Stockholm.

I returned to Toronto with a lot to think about. Did I really wish to continue living in Toronto once my present work was finished? My chances of getting directing work there were not great, and although I still liked to edit, I had increasingly started to feel that I had seen enough of often mediocre footage. It would still be several months before the series was finished, and I did not wish to leave before it was done. Jörn had been flexible on many points, but he insisted on two: that I join the Swedish delegation at the Cannes Festival in spring and start to work in Paris in August. On these two points he would not budge, and although I could see the importance of being there during the Cannes Festival, I doubted that a month or two would make a big difference in Paris. Jörn's patience had obviously not increased over the years, and I did finally realise that if I really wished to accept his offer there was a price to pay: leaving the series before it was finished.

During my next screening in New York, I took it up with Philip who, without hesitation, encouraged me to take this opportunity. He did not like to lose me but the importance of the offer merited some generosity on his part. Douglas, who would be the one to find somebody to replace me, was less enthusiastic but all the same also showed great understanding, and we agreed that my employment with Hobel-Leiterman should cease by the end of July. I was also promised ten days leave for the Cannes Film festival. The narrator for the production had not yet been chosen, but because all the visual material was collected, I continued to get more years through the editing room. When I left for Cannes, the search for a narrator was still on, and I at least had the satisfaction of knowing that my absence did not delay anything. Ten days later I returned from European spring to Canadian winter and continued with the editing until summer came and it was time to say bye-bye for good. I have never liked unfinished business, and this time was no different. Common sense told me that Jörn's offer opened up possibilities that were unusual and that *The Sensational 70s* would well survive my departure, but still I wished that there had been a way to untangle the Gordian knot instead of taking the proverbial sword to it.

NOT ALL IT IS CRACKED UP TO BE

'Imagine! To be able to *live* in Paris and to be paid for it too!' Followed by good wishes and some envy, I left Toronto and on August 1, 1979 came to Paris, as my new employer had dictated. However, what I met was only the façade of a metropolis. I had never been to Paris at that time of the year, and I can not imagine that Jörn Donner had either, but what had been driving him was probably, as always, to get his new idea up and running, the sooner the better. The timing was a grandiose mistake. The French treat their summer holiday with the same serious-ness as they do the rest of their habits, and everybody who possibly can is away on holiday. Offices and a great number of shops are closed for the entire month, and good luck to you if you need an electrician or a plumber! In spring, after a week in Cannes, I had gone back to Toronto via Paris looking at a number of apartments, some with a lot of charm, until I saw the kitchens and the bathrooms! Finally, I had been shown a pleasant and very suitable place on rue Falguière. Before my new role — as the sole employee of SFI International — called upon me to start making contact with the industry, I had a whole month to settle in and I occupied myself by walking around in Paris.

I was, however, not Jörn Donner's only Swedish gift to Paris that year. In his efforts to widen the confines of Swedish filmmaking and at the same time give the industry a greater international exposure, he planned to have an independent cinema where Swedish films could be shown unhindered by the cultural narrow-mindedness of French dis-tribution. His choice fell on Studio des Ursulines, an ailing picture the-atre in Quartier Latin which had for the first fifteen years of its exis-tence, and under several different names, been a nondescript neigh-bourhood cinema, each with a short lifespan. But then in 1926, its days of glory were set off by Armand Tallier, a young actor of an attested renown and looks that made women swoon. He named it Studio des Ursulines after the nunnery that had once stood on the grounds and for the next thirty years managed it as an enormously successful avant-garde cinema.

Surprisingly, Studio des Ursulines already had some old Swedish 'connections.' On the opening night, preceded by two shorter films, *La rue sans joie* had been the main feature, directed by the then still unknown G.W. Pabst and featuring a very young and equally unknown Swedish actress, Greta Garbo. The film brought down the house and stayed on the repertoire for two months — a duration previously unheard of. It was followed by years of interesting — but sometimes controversial — films leading to tumultuous scenes among the audience. Surprisingly enough, the police never intervened. Tallier showed a total disdain for the censor's edicts and invariably scored successes with his public. He also kept abreast of his time, and by 1930, the cinema was equipped for the new talkies, inaugurated by Josef von Sternberg's *L'Ange Bleu* with Marlène Dietrich, an even greater runaway success that lasted for fourteen months with daily afternoon and evening screenings! When Tallier died at the beginning of 1958, Studio des Ursulines could look back on an impressive list of films that, under his leadership, had been premiered with exclusive rights. Directors included René Clair, Marcel Carné, Howard Hawks, Man Ray, Fritz Lang, Roberto Rosellini, and the Swedish Alf Sjöberg, to mention just a few. At the beginning of the 50s, Tallier had been joined by Angéline Peillon who, after 1958, continued to run the cinema with the same astute eye and neverending love of the new that had guided Tallier. Luis Bunuel, Michaël Cacoyannis, Michelangelo Antonioni, Satyajit Ray, and Andrej Wajda had their films shown at the theatre and from Sweden had come *La Prison* and *Une leçon d'Amour* by the young Ingmar Bergman. But all that was now in the past, and the 70s' hardening economic climate, the advances of TV, and the changing tastes made it more and more difficult to keep Studio des Ursulines in play. Madame Peillon was deeply attached to her cinema; her love for, and understanding of, film was still surprisingly fresh, and notwithstanding her age, her economic know-how left nothing to be desired. She had been calamitously widowed at a young age, and the cinema had always been such an important part of her life that she, understandably, had some difficulties fully admitting that the golden years were behind her. Angéline Peillon and Jörn Donner belonged not only to different generations but also to specific cultures, and the negotiations between the two did not always go smoothly. Jörn proposed to lease the cinema, not buy it, which meant that Madame Peillon, with a look to the future, wished to have her say too. When he argued for a facelift with new, more comfortable chairs, thereby lowering the total number of seats, things came close to blows. At the same time, projections for a singularly Swedish cinema were not very promising, and after much hither and thither, Studio des Ursulines, in its new incarnation, was finally designed as a showplace for Scandinavian films.

The cinema was, thank goodness, none of my business, so I witnessed all this from a valued distance, but I was of course present on opening night, and that was how I first met Madame Peillon. By then there was not much love lost between her and Jörn, or the rest of the Swedish management, so why she took a liking to me I do not know. But she did, and I could only be deeply grateful because, as it turned out, she was not only a walking dictionary of French cinema, but also a very charming and generous person, as long as you did not get on the wrong side of her. She introduced me into the industry, which of course was most helpful, and through Madame Peillon I also met Véra Volmane, a film critic and at the time one of the presidents at the Cannes Festival. The two ladies, each of them a genuine personality, were old friends and by what appeared mutual agreement, took me under their wings. I certainly gained both a professional advantage and a deeper understanding of French culture and its quirks, than I would have done under less genuine and generous circumstances. Invitations to accompany Madame Volmane to the screenings she attended as a film critic were ongoing, and she always without hesitation shared her vast knowledge of the industry. Her interest in history was profound, and she adored her city, where she had lived all her adult life. With a depth of knowledge, humour, and great enthusiasm she, for my benefit, often expounded on *la petite histoire* which otherwise I would not have heard. Driving through the city as a passenger in Madame Peillon's small car was an entirely different story and not half as pleasant. She tore through the streets at breakneck speed, hurling invectives at all other drivers who, in her opinion, drove like idiots! Most of the time I was scared out of my wits, but at the same time, it was terribly funny to see this bourgeois, elegant, doll-like elderly lady behave like a fury when she got behind a steering wheel. At home, at frequent lunches and dinners, she was always a very graceful hostess.

The French film industry lamented the bad times at full volume, but the Paris I encountered was still a place where the cinemas showed more French than American films! The trade papers listed very few co-productions, a clear sign that there was money to be found, and even small companies, if they had a good track record, still could get new productions up and running. Two years later, the economic situation had worsened considerably, and there was hardly one single film made without the producer being forced to go hat-in-hand to French TV, different German sources, and even to the Italian RAI where quality and financing was in steady decline. The immovable French sense of national cultural identity, for decades protected by draconian laws, made its cinema withstand globalisation for longer than most other countries. Sclerosis, however, eventually showed, and France ceased to be the big player, not only at home, but also on the international market. After a number of lean years, the French government stepped in with a strong commitment to the industry, and even if the quality of the creativity was not always what it once had been, in 2001 a whopping 204 full-length feature films were produced by the French!

If Jörn Donner's perception of France and the French had had some lacunae, the same seemed to have been the trouble with the people who had cobbled together the Swedish-French co-production agreement. The money I could offer promised riches and marble halls — but only until the rules had been understood. Employing actresses like Bibi or Harriet Andersson, Ingrid Thulin or Gunnel Lindblom appealed to the French, and the thoughts of Max von Sydow and Erland Josephson were equally attractive, but when they discovered that the agreement also asked for the inclusion of some Swedish technicians, the enthusiasm very quickly faded, admittedly for a good reason. Producers and/or directors understandably balked at the mere thought of working with technicians who did not speak French, and I would have been hard pressed to find a single Swedish film technician at that time who spoke French. However laudable the idea to give Swedish film people exposure to other cultures, in this case it was a flagrant example of Indian-file thinking. How this clause had ever got into the agreement was beyond my understanding, but there it was, effectively blocking my ability to establish any co-productions.

As a central 'railway station' Paris was not a bad choice, and I certainly did a good deal of travelling. My first trip was to Madrid, where I had to oversee the editing of a co-production already on its way to completion. A more showy film would have been nice, but the rendering of the story was pedestrian, the camera work did not add any glamour, and the editor was in want of footage, especially close-ups. The director seemed to have given up. His editor dejectedly assured me that there was nothing more to be found among trims or discarded takes, and they looked to me to shake a rabbit out of my hat. I sat down with the editor and screened the film, primarily suggesting some changes but also stopping at all the places where a close-up would do us some good. He was asked to take note of these spots and assemble a reel of all trims and outtakes of the scenes in question. Perplexed but dutiful, he followed my instructions. With the suggested changes, we already had a slightly more acceptable film, and the atmosphere in the editing room lightened somewhat. The next step rendered the man speechless. We started to cut frames from the reel he had assembled and insert them in the footage. He now saw that by using any frames that conformed, even if they did not belong to the same scene or even the same sequence, he was able to disguise at least some of the paucity in the worst problem spots. He might have been an editor of average skills, but it was not beyond him to see what 'stealing and borrowing' from his own material added to his caché. The opportunity simply had never occurred to him, and if the operation had not made a silk purse out of the proverbial sow's ear, at least we finally had a film that was more presentable.

My next project was a script in progress, but the locomotion seemed to have stopped. Jörn Donner sent me down to Italy to try to coax a script out of Ingrid Thulin. We did not know each other and had hardly ever exchanged two words, although we had all been staying at Siljansborg during the making of *Winter Light*. I had only been able to observe Ingrid from a distance; she was an extremely private person and rarely mixed with the other actors and the crew. Usually she had her dinner brought to her room. As an actress she had always had my admiration, and the courage this still-beautiful woman showed by allowing herself to embrace, without restrictions, the rather unattractive exterior of the unhappy, red-nosed, snuffling school teacher in *Winter Light* had, if anything, only deepened my admiration for her as an actress.

Ingrid's tendency to isolate herself showed, I think, in the fact that she had not settled in Rome but in a rather nondescript countryside, away from the city. Her house was very comfortable and also had some self-sufficient quarters arranged to accommodate visits by her mother. I stayed in that part of the house, so we did not need to live in each other's pockets, but all the same we were not very comfortable together. Ingrid saw me, I think, more as a hindrance than a help, and although always very polite, she plainly did not want me there. My presence *did* advance her script, but I do not think it made it any better. Eventually she got it off to SFI, and a film ensued but did nothing to promote her as a director. The critics unanimously called the film 'a failure with some commendable details,' and at the box office it was a catastrophe. Her opinion of my work clearly showed: my name was not on the credits.

Viveca Lindfors was another Swedish actress who, for many years, had lived abroad in New York. *Viveka, Viveka,* her autobiography, had been published in 1978 in Swedish, and Jörn thought the book might lend itself to a film, so I started to make trips to New York. If Ingrid had been an introvert, Viveca was an extrovert, to say the least. At sixty she

191

still had enormous energy, took theatre lessons, found small parts on Broadway and outside, and was enthusiastically writing and doing workshops. The list was most impressive, and every time we met, she was on to something new. Our respective ideas of what constituted a viable film script differed considerably. Viveca felt her book *was* the script, but I could not agree. It was probably the actress in her that made her unable to understand the difference since her inner eye objectified the individual scenes, but she was oblivious to the need for these scenes to form on the screen a narrative with some logic, emotional or visual, that — however floating — hinted at elements of a beginning, a middle, and an end. We had long, wide-ranging, and passionate discussions when we worked, cooked our meals, and ate. Viveca was challenging and very good to work with, not the least for always being sincere, but in the long run she had too many distractions. Jörn tired of waiting, and the whole project came to nothing.

Another of Jörn's interesting ideas met with the same fate but, while in the making, gave me the thrill to work, at least for a while, with Lindsay Anderson in London. Admiring his films, Jörn thought that a film directed by Lindsay would bring international prestige to the Swedish Film Institute and at the same time be an important experience for the people eventually attached to the project. Considering the personalities of these two men, it was not at all surprising that their initial discussions had touched on a plethora of ideas. It was now left to me to coax Lindsay into making a choice and start on a treatment. He, however, only continued to put more and more ideas on the table, and whether this was Lindsay Anderson in a nutshell, or a clever delaying tactic to avoid any serious commitment while still leaving as many balls as possible up in the air, I was never able to figure out. I did, however, discover in Lindsay a pragmatism that all his quick imagination had so far kept hidden. But one day, Lindsay himself revealed it, talking about his 1969 film *If*, this magnificent, surrealistic portrayal of students at a boarding school. It was designed as a colour film, but on a fairly restricted budget, and when they came to a scene where the lighting for colour would have taken more time than the

NOT ALL IT IS CRACKED UP TO BE

daily schedule allowed, Lindsay without hesitation went for the less time-consuming black and white. 'Not done' was a concept that did not cut any ice with Lindsay Anderson, but I had not known this and ever since I first saw the film I had tried to find an answer to the 'significance' of this mixture!

Jörn, understandably, asked for something that could be timed and priced out, but it was like carrying water in a sieve. Lindsay, with no embarrassment but an impressive facility, only ran on. Although most of his ideas seemed to be worth a closer look, we got nowhere. After repeated visits to London and long telephone conversations, I started to have a growing suspicion that his interest in our project lacked serious commitment and passed on my impression. Jörn in turn told me that Lindsay's demands now exceeded the Swedish capacities, and it was time to call it a day. If you get depressed by such repeated setbacks, you better change professions because there is hardly anything in film that offers instant gratification. To get an idea up and running can take years, and very often, just as it all looks promising, one piece in the complicated puzzle falls to the ground and it is all for naught!

One project that came to fruition was the French part of Jan Troell's *The Flight of the Eagle*,[25] but, in the shrinking Swedish economy, the Paris sequence that from the beginning had been considerable, unfortunately had to be shortened. In the original script, as in reality, the balloons that would eventually carry Andrée and his team to the North Pole were made in France, and in the early script stage there was a visit to the factory just outside Paris, followed by a test flight over a country landscape. A whole evening at Moulin Rouge was preceded by a shopping tour to buy Andrée some Parisian elegance. My job was to find the right locations and line up possible French actors for a couple of small roles. It was a fun job, although not an easy one, because the period film required streets without electric lights, modern buildings or TV antennas. The original Moulin Rouge had virtually gone up in smoke, and the new one not only looked different, but also charged a fortune for the rental.

The extensive and intimate knowledge of Paris that was a requisite for this research was not something I possessed so I checked out the experts. Hélène Tierchant had gone through IDEC and as a freelancer worked in both the film and TV industries. She came highly recommended and was an energetic, very pleasant lady who, only a couple of days after her briefing, took me on the grand tour. A short drive out of Paris, she showed me a former brickyard, where a beautiful old building would be perfect as the balloon factory. Behind it stretched a bucolic countryside — an equally fitting location for the test flight sequence. Back in Paris, Hélène directed me to a restaurant where one long wall was clad in mirrors and all the rest of the interior was sculptured dark wood. It was an inspired replacement for the old Moulin Rouge. Once you entered you immediately felt transported back in time, and the cinematographic possibilities, thanks to the mirrored wall, were immensely rich. Troell's original script also included a visit to a shop where Andrée would buy a pair of white gloves that, in those days, were part of a gentleman's evening dress. Hélène guided me to the most amazing place: an authentic glove shop that had stayed the same since it was built, probably early 1800. A minuscule room, its four walls were covered from the floor to the low ceiling with drawers containing gloves in all shapes, colours, and sizes. As in the restaurant, the wood was beautifully carved, but here it had a lighter, elegant nut-brown tone. Every place was documented with photographs and measurements, and I was very pleased with what I could send to Stockholm. The sequences also asked for some local talent in small roles, and I screened several period films before contacting and interviewing a number of actors. Some were interesting old foxes who had their photographs sent to Stockholm. I was quite amused by a couple who, counting on me not being too familiar with the French landscape I assume, declared with force that they *never* acted as extras! 'Tant pis!' When this job was finished, Hélène and I continued to meet socially, and I was soon introduced to her producer-director husband, Serge, who was equally good company. Hélène and I had more in common than our interest in film; we were both enthusiastic gardeners.

A very attractive project was next on my agenda. Jörn wished to produce a documentary film about Sweden and had solicited scripts, but nothing he read evoked his enthusiasm. I was then told about the project and asked to find a suitable director outside Sweden. The idea was a real challenge, and working on it I became deeply aware of how much my own view of Sweden had changed. Time, distance, and the abundance of new experiences had very effectively cured my initial 'home-blindness.' Jörn, coming from Finland, had an outside perspective and had found the Swedish scripts uninspiring. The trick, I thought, would be to find an external observer with enough affinity to facilitate a degree of understanding of a typical Swedishness, coupled with an eye for what made the country unique. What place, I asked myself, would be likely to foster such traits? A country with an equivalent degree of industrialisation would be no good, so Germany was out. East European filmmaking I often found very skillful and highly attractive, but this was to be a documentary, and I thought the chances slim in avoiding a one-sided left-wing slant. Poland was reluctantly eliminated. As I certainly did not want a philosophical, intellectual discourse, France fell by the wayside. Italy would not have been a likely contender had I not then recently seen a film by a young Italian director, Mario Brenta. It was his first feature film, a tale of human misery among some destitute people in Rome selling their thin blood to a paying but not very discriminating blood bank. There was no blown-up pathos but a low-key visual narrative that had great impact, and you cared for the people up on that screen. I located Brenta in Rome and flew down to meet with him.

He was a mild-mannered, somewhat shy person who came to life when showing me some of the documentaries he had made. We talked about the film I had already seen, what had been his motivations, and how he had gone about the practicalities. Already guessing that it was made on a rather limited budget, although the film did not look cheap, now I got to know *how* scant that budget in reality had been, and that certainly was in the director's favour. I arranged for some video transfers and went back to Paris convinced that I had come up with a winner. Jörn got my report, looked at the videos, became interested, and I got the green light to fly Brenta to the upcoming Cannes Festival for a meeting between him and Jörn. The outcome was positive, and I was given a development budget for the project.

Brenta had never been to Sweden and knew nothing about it but soon found himself with an abundance of information. Anything I could lay my hands on in English or French — there was next to nothing to be found in Italian — went to Rome. Government departments and The Swedish Institute published statistics on almost anything you could dream of, but I also sent Brenta children's books, cook books, and novels I chose because the authors had written so descriptively about what they felt was characteristic of their small part of this elongated land. He got Swedish politics and history in condensed form, music cassettes, books about art and handicraft, and maps, anything I could think of, save Swedish films. Then I left him in peace for a while.

A month later we had a week-long working session in Rome, sorting out which parts of this information avalanche had made Brenta tick and what was the relationship between them? From day one we got into a working routine: I came to Brenta's apartment by nine o'clock, and we worked until lunch time. He disappeared into his kitchen where I was never allowed to give a helping hand, and after our lunch break we worked on until the evening when Erica, his wife, came back from her fashion boutique. The three of us went for dinner to places in working-class neighbourhoods where an ordinary tourist would never set foot, dinners unforgettable for both the food and the atmosphere. Long wooden trestle tables and benches under high tarpaulins allowed you to eat outside even if it rained. These unpretentious restaurants were jam-packed most of the time, but some good-humoured moving up or down the benches always found us some seats. The food was delectable, and Mario must have had years of these culinary experiences for he knew exactly what to eat where.

Brenta then had a fortnight on his own before I came back, and we worked on a preliminary script and drew up a list of places in Sweden that Brenta needed to research. The work met with Jörn's approbation,

Brenta was given a contract, and we were allocated a research budget. I had been pleasantly surprised to find that Brenta had chosen locations and subject matter that, had it been my film, I myself would have gone for. The research trip went without a hitch. I had the added pleasure of returning to a couple of places in northern Sweden that I had known long ago and always been very fond of. The severe isolation of these parts that I had once seen was now evidently mitigated, and when at one of our small, plain village hotels, I voiced my surprise over the bowl of lettuces that appeared daily at our dining table, I was told that they could now afford them because the freight costs of fruit and vegetables from southern Sweden was subsidised by the government. Equality had reached unexpected heights, and by now all Swedes shared not only the astronomic taxes but also a balanced diet! The construction of a new Parliament building in Stockholm had made the street where I had lived for ten years disappear, while other parts of the city seemed entirely unchanged. Talking to people, I did not find that attitudes had changed very much, but at the same time, I felt that the American influence on eating habits and dress styles had taken an even firmer grip on Sweden than what I remembered. This was my first extended return to Sweden in a decade, and I could not help feeling a bit smug when looking at my return ticket to the wider world, where most of the time I felt freer and more contented. Not that I had ever felt a need for it, but now I had a verifiable confirmation that my decision of 1967 had been the right one.

. While in Stockholm, we met with Jörn, who stressed that, in order to accommodate SFI's other plans, our script delivery deadline was absolute and could *not* be changed. This did not seem to faze Brenta; I was not worried either. So far he had delivered although I suspected that without my presence in Rome he would in all likelihood have taken more time. He told me he now wished to work on his own and promised to send a draft to Paris in two weeks time. Nothing came. After a couple of days, I called him. Where was the promised draft? It was not finished yet, and most alarmingly, he admitted that he did not know when he would be ready. Would it help if I came to Rome? No. Would it be easier for him to write in Italian and not in English? I would be happy to arrange for a translation. No. I had noticed from the very first time I met Brenta that he had an almost excessive need to get things right, down to the last dot, before he could leave them, but I had never seen it as an obstacle. I assumed that this was what was blocking him and tried to reassure him about the possibilities to later change details. All that mattered *now* was to respect the deadline, or we would lose the project! This inflexibility might have been incomprehensible to an Italian mind, and I was never to know if Brenta expected a last-minute reprieve or not. The crucial date came and went, but no script. Among all the aborted projects, this was *my* Waterloo. Jörn's was still to come.

When SFI started to take an active interest in international co-productions, the Swedish economy had been booming, but when I came to Paris, there were already signs of a slowdown that would in time be more and more noticeable. Being familiar with the milieu in which Jörn was working, I doubted that his internationalism had met with any great enthusiasm, but as long as the economy was good, it had at least, from what I understood, been endured. With less money to spend, he started to encounter some opposition that during my second year in Paris took a nasty turn. Part of my job was to be on the look-out for film scripts that would lend themselves to co-productions, but so far I had not found anything suitable. Now I had, however, come across an unusual French script that I felt could also enthuse a Swedish audience. It had an active plot, vibrant and developed characters, and interesting, well-written dialogue, but it was important that these elements would, to their full extent, survive the necessary translation, before the script could be presented to the Swedish commission. I had seen some of these translations, and not feeling that they ever did the original script justice, with Jörn's approbation I now wrote the Swedish version myself. He liked the script and had agreed on its potential, but when presenting it to the board of commissioners, they threatened to step down if Jörn used his chairman's vote to promote it. What was most upsetting was that quality had no place on their agenda; there was no evaluation of the script, only insistence that the money available should go to Swedish films and nothing else. This prejudiced

Swedishness was not new to me, and by all logic it should not have surprised me because Sweden can be, and often is, just as xenophobic as the rest of the world. But logic was not on call that day, and to see my native country behave in this dismal way *did* hurt.

Jörn had initially offered me a four-year contract with SFI, but I had preferred and negotiated a two-year one, with an option for renewal — if things turned out to our mutual satisfaction. Jörn's enthusiasm for the French project was both urgent and sincere, but he had a habit of being fervent about a great number of things, when they were new. It was not that he lost interest, but eventually his plate overflowed, and some projects did not get the follow-up they needed. I both understood and admired his quest to make Sweden, or at least Swedish films, more known to the world, but I wondered if there had ever been any tangible proof that the French, with their cultural and intellectual self-sufficiency, felt that they needed *us*? When I met Jörn in New York, I did not think of it, but later in Paris, it came to my mind that, as early as 1649, the Swedish queen Kristina had summoned the French philosopher and mathematician René Descartes to her court with the hope that his presence might help to refine it. Descartes died in Stockholm a year later, and it was, from his point of view, a miserable year. Swedish climate, way of life, and philosophy were too far removed from their French equivalents, and I doubted that time had done much to shrink the gap. I am sure that I was not even half as miserable in Paris as Descartes had been in Stockholm, but one aborted effort after another certainly did not make for the dream job it was cracked up to be.

As a student I had spent a couple of happy months in Paris and in the Loire Valley, and although I had no expectations of the same easy life, the changes were very different from what I had envisaged. And they definitely were not for the better. The country was ossified in its ways of thinking and for the most part unwilling, or unable, to cope with what time had brought about. The important social changes that had taken place on the other side of the Atlantic had not had much inspirational impact in France. The embryo of social change that the country experienced in 1968 fizzled out quickly enough. The students left the barricades for their summer holidays and afterwards went back to their universities as if nothing had happened. The workers remained in the same unsatisfactory void that for years to come would incite disrupting strikes. Never a very friendly lot, the Parisians were now stressed and tired, and the political upheaval did nothing to make things easier as the unpredictable intruded on organised life. The Metro and buses went on sudden strikes, scheduled meetings were called off with hardly any notice, and getting hold of people was even more difficult than it used to be. Suddenly there would be no water, or gas, or electricity. It was annoying and time-consuming, but there was one aspect that I, the foreigner, found quite amusing. If you woke up to a day without gas and/or electricity, these services would, without fail, come back between noon and two o'clock! Obviously, no true Frenchman, not even a striking blue-collar worker, would forego his or her hot midday meal. Military trucks occasionally replaced Metro and bus service, but standing on the backs of these trucks with nothing to hold on to — save the next fellow creature — were only a last resort in extreme circumstances. Taxi drivers often could not find enough gas and simply stayed home when you needed them the most. France seemed an unhappy, unruly, and ungovernable country, and this certainly also left its mark on its cultural life. I, on the whole, found little vibrancy in writing, painting, dance, theatre, music, or film, and if any theatre put on a play of interest, tickets had to be booked months ahead. With my frequent absences from Paris, such long-term planning was always difficult.

But, of course, all was not gloom and doom. As part of the tax imposed on Picasso's estate, a considerable number of paintings and drawings from different periods had been consigned to the state and now formed an extensive exhibition in Paris. Ever since my visit to St. Petersburg in the 60s Picasso's art has inhabited a very prominent space in my awareness. During a visit to the Hermitage I had — by the simple act of lifting a foot and then placing it on the other side of a threshold — entered Picasso's blue period. In a square room, not very big, the walls were covered with smallish paintings so close to each other that one hardly saw any wall at all. The misery of his Parisian life in the first years of the 1900s was the subject matter, and the palette took my breath away. In the next room, identical to the first one, I was engulfed in rose; Picasso had left Paris behind and spent time in Holland. These two rooms made me, for all time, a willing prisoner in his artistic world. However, the first time I went to the exhibition in Paris, I stood confused in front of a fairly big painting in different brown hues. What was a Braque painting doing in this show? My amateurish eye had not at first distinguished it, but it was of course a Picasso. Looking at the date, 1909, it was painted shortly after he had met Braque and seriously embarked on the cubist's path. But most irresistible among all this abundance were two minuscule mixed-media collages from the same period, impregnated with Picasso's own pictorial inventiveness.

Another pleasure was to discover Gérard Depardieu as a stage actor. Until I came to Paris, I had only seen him on the screen, and although he had been very compelling in some roles, too often I had asked myself what it was that had made him yet again agree to play another lacklustre part in a film of very limited interest? On stage it was much more than his hulking frame that filled the space, and whatever you thought of the plays as such, his characters were mesmerising and stayed with you long after the final curtain call.

I also took with me one unsurpassed memento from the afternoon of Thursday, January 22, 1981, when I listened to Marguerite Yourcenar's inaugural speech to L'Académie Française. Established in 1635 by Cardinal Richelieu, L'Académie had by sheer good luck until now been spared the agony of having to contemplate the almost insurmountable step of admitting a woman. The three women worthy of L'Académie's observance were — besides the abominable fact that they were female — for very different reasons, out of the question. Mme de Staël, although born in Paris, was of Swiss lineage and into the bargain married to the Swedish ambassador in Paris, thus she was not looked upon as eligible. George Sand — Aurore Dupin, by marriage Baronne Dudevant — lived what was regarded as a scandalous life. Colette, possibly the most worthy of them all, maintained that a woman does not visit a man in order to solicit her candidature. Steadfast in her beliefs, she therefore cut herself out of the race before it could even start. Although thirty years younger, Marguerite Yourcenar shared Colette's attitude, and she had not solicited her nomination either — a fact she made altogether clear in her address. What now obviously made the difference was that, in conjunction with an undeniably strong literary production of a rare quality behind her, she had enough gender-unbiased friends inside L'Académie. Jean d'Ormesson, in his ensuing response — after first allowing himself a discrete mea culpa on behalf of L'Académie — even evoked the probability that had Mme Yourcenar been of the opposite sex, the seat would have been offered much earlier.

This being France, the importance of the literary event had had to share its place with another question, purported to be of at least equal significance. The French fashion world stood on its head debating for months how the ceremonial uniform for this male bastion now had to be recreated to suit its first woman. The occasion might have been dramatic, but there was nothing theatrical about its central figure. This elderly, straight-backed, somewhat rotund, and not very tall lady had poise, sincerity, and an impressive simplicity about her. Her hair brushed back in its usual bun, her face devoid of makeup, wearing an ankle-length, dark, very simple but utterly elegant coat-like dress and supported by her cane, she made her way to the chair where, contrary to habit, she addressed L'Académie sitting down. Except for the cane, nothing visibly indicated that her health might have been delicate, and her voice carried a strong, calm confidence — pride without the slightest trace of affectation.

After having thanked L'Académie for the unprecedented honour it had bestowed upon her, Mme Yourcenar paid homage to all the women who, through the ages, had influenced the arts: the noble women with the means to be patrons, the women who had motivated and inspired through sociability and friendship, the women who were talented writers, precursors of taste and ideas. Without being particularly misogynous, but in accordance with the time, L'Académie had placed these women on a pedestal but not accorded them a seat in its midst. As Mme Yourcenar herself had done nothing to advance her candidacy, she obviously felt free to give the august institution a lashing, gracefully and elegantly formulated, but all the same a reprimand for not leading, for not being inventive but, under the cloak of tradition, only continuing to follow old habits.

In her eulogy over her predecessor, Roger Caillois, Mme Yourcenar noted that the two had only met a couple of times, only shared a few meals, but, she continued, 'I have done what is even better: I have read his books.' The disciplined, tireless researcher had done her homework, and not just for this occasion. It was clear that her reading had started way back and continued over the years, and her reward had been the recognition of shared tastes, the grasp of a multifaceted man and the comprehension of his steady progress on to new roads. Her voice had a previously absent warmth that revealed a bond and a deep admiration for the man. I, who had never heard of Roger Caillois, let alone read any of his work, sat up and took an interest. As always, Yourcenar's deep sense for the essential showed: she was not the message, only the messenger. In order to publicly express her gratitude for the first time, she took us back to 1943. Caillois, in exile from German-occupied France, lived in Buenos Aires and published the revue *Les Lettres Françaises*. He had printed a long essay by Yourcenar who then felt a deep gratitude for his efforts to give free French literature a voice, albeit a small one. We were taken through Roger Caillois's entire oeuvre and in an effortless way made to understand what, at each turn, had informed his writing and its philosophy. Like Marguerite Yourcenar herself, Roger Caillois had toward the end of his life been profoundly shaken by the contempt for logic and the barbarism the world demonstrated. The only things that did not change were the rocks Caillois for a long time had studied and passionately loved. Yourcenar shared this love and ended her eulogy: 'Dear Caillois, when I strive to listen to the stones I still think of you.'[26] This tour de force covered twelve full-page columns when *Le Monde* printed it the following day.

Jean d'Ormesson's welcome speech was slightly shorter, very graceful, and in parts interesting as it, among other things, traced the ten-year-long, drawn-out birth of *Mémoires d'Hadrien*. He also mentioned, apropos Roger Caillois, whom he had known for twenty-five years and deeply admired, that he had wished that Caillois, as had been done for Goethe, would have had his name given to a stone. It had not happened, but instead a butterfly had been named after him. At the end of this remarkable Thursday afternoon, I could not help feeling that d'Ormesson was a butterfly, albeit not the most ordinary one, while Marguerite Yourcenar was the real gemstone.

THE YEN FOR EXPERIMENT

One day Véra Volmane brought me a script written by Laure Mergault, a long-time friend of hers. Laure was a painter and had come to writing in an unusual way. A heart ailment had sent her to bed for nearly a year and she had not been allowed to paint. She was bored stiff until one of her friends — who always had found her a very entertaining storyteller — suggested she try writing. Back on her feet, Laure had a good number of pages to show for her efforts and she was convinced that it was a film script. What Véra passed on to me, however, was a novel, and a thick one at that. It had very well-defined locations and a lively plot, but the characters, although interesting to some extent, were too thin. After several readings, I shared my impressions with Véra, and it did not take long before she brought me an invitation to meet with Madame Mergault.

I made my way to rue Grange in the 5th Arrondissement in central Paris and entered a typical Parisian old, well-maintained building where nothing hinted at anything other than the bourgeois solidity, mostly sombre, that I had met in other Parisian homes. However, I was ushered into a surprisingly bright and sunny room with elegant white Italian leather furniture and, as I later discovered, a few of Madame Mergault's own paintings on the walls. She was a pleasant but ordinary-looking woman in, I guessed, her late forties or early fifties. We sat down and I offered my thoughts. Madame Mergault listened very attentively but without taking notes or uttering any counter-argument. My monologue finished, she got up and brought us tea, and now we had a lively conversation extending to all sorts of subjects — save writing. As script editor I had had all manner of meetings, but this was a new variety.

After a week or two, I got an invitation, again with Véra Volmane as go-between, to dine in her company at the Mergaults. I was introduced to Jean, Laure's husband and a professor in English at the Sorbonne.

They were an interesting couple with greatly contrasting temperaments but also an apparent rapport. Although otherwise not overly formal, as French formality goes, they still adhered to the old local habit of addressing each other with the formal 'vous' instead of the common, informal 'tu.' I had perceived the invitation to be Laure's way of thanking me for the interest I had taken in her writing, but the dinner conversation did not at all touch the subject. When, after an unhurried, good dinner, we moved to the living room, Véra and Jean discreetly left the two of us alone, and then Laure brought up the subject. Would I like to co-write a new version with her? I had never before co-written anything and was not really sure how such an arrangement would work out or even if I would like it at all. My experiences from the NFB in Montreal had left me with a rather deep distrust of filmmaking by committee. Only very rarely had I seen anything whole come out of it, while an inordinate amount of time and effort had usually been wasted. Explaining my reason for not being hot on her offer, I volunteered to become her script editor. The difference between the two concepts was no secret to Laure, but she insisted: she wanted me to co-write. I asked for a couple of days to think it over.

My contract with SFI was still worth another six months, but it did not take any great imagination to figure out that I would be getting fewer and fewer work orders — if any at all — from Stockholm. As things had turned out both there and in Paris, I thought it a foregone conclusion that, once my contract expired, my position would cease to exist. Nobody had brought it up, but I had decided that the coming months would be best spent making concrete plans for my future, and it was not one in Paris! Accepting Laure's offer would not exclude other work if, unexpectedly, something would manifest itself, and the challenge to try something new was not lost on me. To discover how much self-discipline (or lack thereof) I would possess in the give and take of co-writing was tempting, and working with somebody as interesting and multifaceted as Laure had considerable appeal. Last but not least it would, without question, also be beneficial for my proficiency in French. Being absolutely honest about it, my ultimate reason for taking it on was to be found in Laure's own script; its main character slowly slipped into a deepening depression and eventually went mad. Every time I saw another sorry Ophelia, or strange Kafkaesque renderings of 'madness' on screen or stage, I was once again reminded that to 'play mad' did not work, but what would? How does one convincingly show the breaking-down process that finally leaves a broken mind; which are the believable images of 'madness?' Finding the answers to these questions was still on my to-do list, and co-writing with Laure opened a tempting possibility.

I do not know what a psychiatrist might say, but I see 'madness' as being on the other side of a two-way mirror where one side of the glass has become defective — and it is not my side! Unaware of my changed mental status, I perceive my actions as 'normal' and catching sight of them in *my* mirror helps to strengthen my perception. But in the other mirror they are seen distorted — as something that is not 'normal.' What figuration can make this believable? The Swedish actor and director, Hans Alfredson — also a producer of hilariously funny cabarets — once had the genius to juxtapose, without any trickery, a realistic presentation on a mythic content. In *The Simple-minded Murderer*[27] Alfredson created a prodigious sequence where The Avenging Angels from the Christian Bible have taken visual shape: three tall and handsome angels, clad in white, with big, feathered wings, shod in high boots with pistols stuck in the legs, purposefully stride over the stubble-fields of autumn. With faces resembling those of a Botticelli painting and their unlikely mixture of religious and cowboy elements, the images were not only breathtaking, but they also effortlessly push you towards the acceptance of the mental breakdown that makes a simple-minded boy, under physical and mental pressure, lose his grip on reality. He sees the angels as real, as messengers who have come to tell him to take an axe to his and his sister's tormentor. And he does! Not until later, when I met Dennis Potter's *The Singing Detective*, would I again see similar spellbinding magic. I was yearning to find out if I was able to create something different, but equally magical, and that finally pushed me to accept Laure's proposal.

We started almost immediately and worked with purpose and regularity. Having read the script and seen her paintings, I was aware of
Laure's love for the symbolist poet Guillaume Apollinaire. His admiration for the early cubist painters in France also seemed to have been one
of *her* early painterly inspirations, but these notions had not prepared
me for the depth of her attachment to the classics. Her script comprised
clashes between generations, a child's despair when feeling abandoned,
but surprisingly, also free sex, a rejected pregnancy, and two young men
who, although not sure of paternity, are together taking on fatherly
duties in a serious way while the mother is conflicted between her acting career and her child. I never learned anything about Laure's background or where she had grown up, but Le Midi — as the south of
France is often called — as well as Paris with its university milieu felt
authentic. Knowing that Laure and Jean had a son, their only child,
who at the time was in his early twenties, might also have played to my
imagination. Regardless, I felt that her classic attachments played too
strong a part and needed to be somewhat diminished. What really
counted was that Laure was a vivacious storyteller but had difficulty
giving her characters necessary depth. *Songs for the Sirens*[28] in its initial
form, spanning from 1960 up to the present day, could just as well have
been a novel, but her wish to write a film script seemed to be born in her
painterly self — in search of images.

Laure was indeed very pleasant to work with, and although physically not very robust, she had perseverance and a profound patience.
Our work progressed, but as always, the writing took longer than
expected, and in late spring, when Laure and Jean were to leave Paris
for their country house in the south of France, we still had work to do.
The Mergaults suggested that I should spend my holiday month with
them so we could finish the work. Not normally eager to be a house
guest, this time I was all the same delighted. The three of us, over the
past months, had developed a very pleasant friction-free relationship.
Their invitation would also take me to Languedoc, where I had not
been. Photographs from their 'mas' showed a charming old farmhouse
in a garden where not much had been done. It was not lack of interest,

but both Laure and Jean had delicate health, and could not do heavy garden work. This did not preclude their vivid interest and an enduring appreciation of the embellishment of the garden — my 'thank-you-gift' for their generous invitation. Hélène Tierchant introduced me to an excellent nursery, and as they are the only places where I find shopping really exciting, I had a ball! When later I pointed my car south on the Paris-Lyon autostrada, it was filled to the roof.

Their 'mas,' situated not far from the small town of Eyragues, had been modernised to allow for a comfortable life, but its old beautiful exterior was still intact. I went to the neighbours and borrowed the tools I needed, and after a week of early rising, digging, and watering, everything I had brought was in the ground. The garden had a new look. The Mergaults were very pleased, and, because nothing seemed edible, their farming neighbours looked at it with amusement. It had been several years since I had had any opportunity for this kind of 'real' gardening, and I had sorely missed it. The planting of a *hydrangea petiolaris* against one of their whitewashed walls had been a truly inspired choice; its summer-lush greenery with clusters of white flowers seemed as highly appreciated as the winter's ornamental 'Japanese' patterns — projected by its cinnamon-coloured, denuded branches. For years I got progress reports from the garden and the hydrangea was always mentioned.

We did a good deal of rewriting and in the process the main character's descent into madness was cut out. It was not a great loss and it did not really matter, for this month was one of the most pleasurable during my two years in France — its calm, unhurried existence for a change felt purposeful. Every day in the cool of the morning, Laure and I worked on the script, took our daily siestas, cooked enjoyable meals, went for walks in the countryside and shopped in Eyragues. With my hosts as informed and animated guides, I was taken to Avignon, detecting in all its magnitude and beauty one of France's most significant cities from the Middle Ages.

A few days before my return to Paris, we finished the script and celebrated with a trip to Camargue — a scenic mix of pools and salt marshes. I had always longed to see this landscape where wild horses still roamed, and the magic that photographs of the area had imparted now revealed itself as the reality. A diminutive whitewashed chapel on a small parcel of land had always been an important meeting place for the Roma. Entire families regularly came here to offer their prayers and whisper their requests to its Blessed Virgin. In the windless afternoon of this day the place seemed empty, and I stood in the doorway looking at the life-sized sculpture of the Madonna with a kneeling worshipper. Suddenly the devotee disengaged herself and stood up! In surprise I took a step back. I had looked at a human being, but the stillness of her body was so deep that even her breathing had escaped me. Passing, I do not think she even noticed me; she still lived in the moment when she was bringing her thanks — or had it been a supplication — to the Blessed Virgin.

The return to Paris was not very exiting until one day, out of the blue, came a telephone call from Sydney, Australia. On the line was Storry Walton, the director of The Australian Film and Television School, as it was then called, offering me the position as head of its editing workshop. He promised to send me a long letter in the next few days, explaining everything. He also mentioned that he was going to come to Paris in a month's time, and suggested we meet. This was a total surprise, and I did not even know how or where he had got my name. When I lived in Toronto, the Film Festival had one year championed Australia, so the little I knew about this faraway continent was related to my own field. Fred Schepisi's *The Chant of Jimmy Blacksmith*, Peter Weir's *Picnic at Hanging Rock*, and Gillian Armstrong's *My Brilliant Career*, plus one or two more films were shown outside the competition, and this way Australia had belatedly found a place on my world map of film. It surprised me that I could have missed it all since *Picnic at Hanging Rock* had been made as early as 1975, but there probably were not any French language versions, and consequently Australian films were not screened in Montreal where I then lived. The promised letter from Storry Walton never came, but with little to do over and above renewing my old contacts in Montreal, I felt it could not hurt to find out a few things about his country. As the Information Superhighway was not built yet — I would have to wait for some twenty years before it would become available — I had to make my way to the Australian Embassy where I got an abundance of folders, publicity, statistics, and propaganda, as well as a map. Once most of it was digested, I went to a couple of newspaper archives to read up on politics and daily life, while with some curiosity waiting for Mr. Walton himself to arrive in Paris. I read a couple of Patrick White's books and fell in love with *Voss*, with its unusual, complicated, spellbinding story, and dramatic characters. When I eventually went to Australia, I discovered that the landscape itself was an immense drama, its light most unusual and extremely filmic. I also learned that I had not been alone in thinking that *Voss* was film material: over the years, several people had been holding options, but they had all lapsed sooner or later — none with a film in sight.

Eventually, Storry Walton did arrive, and we had a couple of so-so meetings. I was offered the school's usual five-year contract but stuck to my old habit of wanting a two-year one with a renewal clause and also demanded some changes to paragraphs regarding both parties' rights and obligations to severance. They all of course followed local rules but nobody seemed to have been entertaining the fact that if you 'imported' somebody from overseas some adjustments were necessary. Storry assured me that the school would have no difficulty obtaining a temporary work permit, and he was highly surprised when I observed that if I did not get a general work permit I would not come. But why? Without a general work permit, I would not be allowed to work in the industry, and it made no sense to me that I should educate people for an industry I could not be fully part of. If I was not willing and able to participate on all levels, I did not see that I had anything to do in Australia. I was far from convinced that Storry really understood my motivations, but he promised that the school would undertake the necessary negotiations. They eventually did, but with an unbearable tardiness that, until the very last minute, jeopardised my departure from France.

That Storry was extremely proud of his institution had been evident, but our meetings had not given me any clear understanding of his judgement and/or artistic values or how he saw the school's future. That had left me not only with a very blurred image but also with a feeling of unease, and when shortly after Storry's departure, the school wished to fly me to London for a meeting with Richard Thomas, its newly appointed rector, I welcomed the idea. I might have come with recommendations — from the Film School in Stockholm, as I later discovered — adequate for Storry, but Richard was insistent: he was not going to okay any new employment before he had met the person and formed his own opinions. He had worked at the BBC for a considerable time but had recently been at the Australian school on an extended leave and had personal experience of the situation. Ten years into its existence, most methods and habits had outlived their worth, and Richard had extensive plans for a necessary renewal. Listening and talking to him clarified certain things, but I would also later realise that I had only been given — or heard — half the truth. Never very good at discerning the subtleties of the English language and, as usual, taking things at their face value, I did not suspect the degree of malfunction that was awaiting me. True, I had already been involved in one messy film school, but that experience now lay some good ten soothing years back in time, and then I had seen the problems as a teething fever. In Sydney I was to meet something very different and probably worse — the ravages of time. Richard and I talked for hours, compared our value systems and approaches to teaching, and finally, after many cups of tea, agreed that it was worth giving it a try. Richard took me to the airport for my return to Paris; when I saw him next it would be at the airport in Sydney, Australia.

Although my curiosity about Down Under was great, my love for Montreal had not died, and I still hoped to return there one day. As an immigrant I could only be away from Canada for a limited number of years before losing my status. At this point I only had one year of grace left, and what would happen if, after two years in Australia, I wished to return? I took my question to the Canadian High Commission where an immigration officer gave me a thorough interview, opened a file on me, and then pleasantly told me not to worry; all I had to do was to come and see him when I wished to return, and everything would be okay. With this reassurance, I felt free to accept a two-year contract with the school in Sydney and set about being fingerprinted by the French, interviewed by the Australians, and generally collecting proof of my non-criminal existence from all the places where I had lived for the last ten years! It was quite an exercise, and a far cry from how uncomplicated it had been to become 'a landed immigrant' in 1968. When I moved to Paris, the French police had not asked for any fingerprints, but now when they took them on behalf of the Australians, they smartly secured one set for themselves and did it without even asking permission! Had I not asked what the second set was for, I would not even had known that I was going to leave such a personal imprint in Paris.

Before departing Europe, I planned to spend two weeks in Spain, and then a couple of days in Paris in order to pack up and evacuate my apartment. All the dates were fixed, the tickets were bought, but the school still had not sent me any papers at all. A telephone call to Storry Walton was elucidating: Ulla Ryghe?? I reminded him that we had met in Paris and that he had offered me employment at the school. He had forgotten that I existed, and the administration had not done a thing to secure the papers needed! I curtly told him that if my contract, in every detail conforming to my demands as discussed, together with my work permit were not delivered to Paris in the next seven days, they could not count on my services. My flight to Sydney was routed over Montreal, with a ten day stopover, so I figured that if Australia was not going to be my destination, all I had to do was give the transport company a new address and change my flight to Montreal as my final destination. Six days later, the Australian papers arrived, but it took two more versions before my contract was finally correctly written.

DOWN UNDER

The move from Stockholm to Montreal in 1968 had felt like taking a big breath of fresh air, but returning to Europe ten years later did not feel anything like it. France of the late 70s appeared imprisoned by its history; the overwhelming importance it was accorded acted like a noose. The political determination that sets change in motion did not exist, and I deplored its absence. If I craved change, going to Australia was an effective cure: I not only met something totally unexpected, but for the first time I was also to live in a society grappling with its growing sense of identity. Although Australia was no longer a colony, a surprisingly great number of people still to me appeared to feel colonised. It clearly influenced their thinking and when after some years, I finally read Robert Hughes' *The Fatal Shore*, I better understood where the roots lay. Still, considering that more than two hundred years had passed since the first convict transports, this part of present day thinking startled me.

One of the first, if not *the* first question I invariably had to answer was: 'How long are you going to stay?' When I replied that I was not intending one of the usual 'six-months-of-a-warmer-winter interludes,' confusion and suspicion followed. That I would have *chosen* Australia seemed incomprehensible. Could I not make it any longer in Europe or North America? Had some undisclosed reason left me no other choice? What saddened and maddened me was that this happened in a place where there was creativity in abundance. Australia had writers, painters, dancers, musicians, and a small but growing number of definitely interesting filmmakers! Compared to what I knew from Europe and North America, all this without question held its own. Six years later, when I decided to leave Australia, on these points very little had changed. A very mixed bag of insecurities and xenophobia still too often seemed to inform creative decisions and/or actions. My artistic productivity had hardly any freedom.

The school was pleased enough to have acquired my expertise, and Storry did his best to parade me as his trophy around the bigger cities. For me, the most valuable part was that these trips gave me in a short time at least a fleeting impression of different parts of the country. Although everybody was impeccably polite, it also left little doubt that the Australian film and TV industry on the whole was not very enthusiastic about my presence, should it be permanent. My colleagues at the school, some of the administrative staff, and most of the students more than made up for it. Knowing that I had no family or connections in Australia, my students figured out the date of my birthday and every year threw me a big party. Their friendliness and generosity also manifested itself on a regular basis, including me in their out-of-school activities. As the weather most of the time allowed for a great deal of outdoor activities, social life was easygoing and unpretentious. The students were fun-loving and gregarious, but inside school they were also serious, very ambitious, and tremendously hardworking. To my delight no one ever tried to take undue advantage of my often double role as friend and teacher. This life also made for some surprising discoveries of the human psyche. Shortly after my arrival, not yet aware that one particular third-year student from the production workshop was very close to the top in our collection of problem students, I unfortunately became her executive producer. She would hurl abuse at her own workshop head and at me too, if and when we had any objections or simply insisted that she keep her schedules. As a former law student, she thought she had it all figured out and would even threaten to take us to court! But come Sunday I was often invited to go sailing with her and her boyfriend, and then she was a very pleasant, intelligent, and reasonable human being. Go figure!

Looked at from the northern hemisphere, Australia was not only down under, but it was also a massive mileage from anything but New Zealand and some Pacific islands. Flying time between Montreal in Canada and Sydney in Australia was more than double the distance from Montreal to Paris. Unlike some places and institutions in Europe and North America, there was no glamour or advantages earned by a prolonged stay. Naturally it limited access to foreign influences, specialists, recent films, you name it. In my experience distance had rarely been an impediment, but in Australia it suddenly was. An immense land mass with a relatively small population and a proportionally small film and TV industry, both concentrated to only a handful of bigger cities, also made the recruitment possibilities of staff quite limited. As well it impacted on the composition of the student body, who invariably came from the larger cities, and I wondered whether possible talent from middle-sized and smaller settlements did not risk being overlooked? The film school itself, after ten years existence, was not only ossified but also carried a very heavy academic superstructure. An ideal location, close to the theatre school and pulsating with life, would have been the old, big, and beautiful wool stores that stood empty in the centre of the city, but the school was tucked away in the middle of nowhere in a commuter suburb on the north shore. If I had regarded the troubles at the Film School in Stockholm as teething troubles, here I was faced with full-blown caries, and Richard Thomas had taken on a Herculean job, as had the rest of us. Collaboration between workshops had not really existed, but as the school started to slowly take a different shape, they were introduced on a regular basis. It not only greatly benefited the students, but as I would later find out, also myself. Good craftsmen from the film and TV industries, all with a generosity and will to share their knowledge and ideas, were, by a new and more flexible employment policy, being enticed to the school. That slowly pushed it from its crippling academic staleness to a more industry-related reality.

The school's three-year full-time program implied that I 'inherited' a second and a third year. Before my arrival, an initial selection for the new first-year students had already taken place, but I had my say in the final choice. The second- and third-years suffered similar problems, but what I could do for the third-year students was very limited. Their lack of knowledge, together with bad habits, were so ingrained, and they were so heavily occupied with all their final year chores, that there was hardly any time to effectively re-educate them. Some were quick to pick up on what I could pass on while overseeing their editing; others seemed to feel I was more trouble than they needed. After a disappointing first year, the second-year students were rebellious, and to make them take an interest in learning and to master better editing habits was an uphill struggle at first. However, we had a full year ahead of us, and when they graduated, I was confident that they were skilled enough to do reasonably well in the industry.

To 'teach' equates with to 'show,' if one looks at the roots of the two words, but in 1981 when I went to Australia, I lacked material to show my students. Because of the language dissimilarity, nothing of my Swedish material was of any use and as the need for new material was immediate, I did not have time to recreate it. The exercises that had been put in place when the school was established had never been upgraded or renewed and now lacked any relevance and/or attraction. The students grumbled more loudly as time passed, and in the year I arrived, they finally made their palace revolution and refused to work on this footage. I had taken a look at it and then threw the trash out. As an editor I know how much surplus footage every film leaves behind and as I had no reason to believe that Australia was different in this respect, it seemed natural to turn to the film and TV industries and offer to relieve them of some of this surplus footage that now only took up space in their vaults. I made inquiries all over Sydney and Melbourne — only to encounter a depressing number of more or less polite rebuffs. These people, as it was later explained to me, had no wish to risk seeing the students under my guidance perform better than their editors had done! I did not know whether to laugh or cry at this utterly stupid idea, but whatever I thought, I was stuck with their refusals.

Breaker Morant, directed by Bruce Beresford in 1979, had so far been the most successful Australian film, and looking at it, it was obvious that the courtroom sequences had been filmed from an extensive number of angles. Thus it was also a reasonable guess that there had to be a good deal of footage never used in the final edit. Adelaide had, for some reason, not been on the initial tour Storry gave me, and I had therefore not met John Morris, the Director of the South Australian

Film Commission. Now I called him and explained what I wanted and why. He gave no direct answer but suggested that I come down to Adelaide and meet him. Richard Thomas, who, from my very first day at the school, had done everything in his power to help me turn my workshop's disastrous conditions around, gave his permission, and I went to Adelaide. I was in for a real treat! Not only did I get to know a surprisingly open, intelligent, and charming human being, but I also, because of the timing of my visit, was regaled with one of nature's great displays. An amazing number of streets in Adelaide had once been generously planted with *jacaranda mimosaefolia*, and in early spring the long clusters of mauve-blue trumpet flowers hang from bare grey branches. Under a magical canopy filtering light I walked on a soft, blue carpet of fallen flowers. Then and there I decided that it would be an utterly blissful way to die falling asleep sitting under a mature jacaranda tree in bloom.

John, although extremely busy, still took time to arrange a perfect two-day visit. I spent my days viewing films with an eye to what might be useful for my students, had interesting and informing lunch meetings with members of his staff, and before leaving the office, had serious discussions with him about my intentions and needs for the school. Both evenings I was also invited to dinner with John and his companion and enjoyed the most entertaining conversation, great jazz music, and good food in the best company I had had for quite some time. I did not get any material from *Breaker Morant*, but came back to Sydney with more than enough other footage to keep my students busy. Over and above the great generosity already shown to me, John promised to send me films he thought would have teaching potential and also encouraged me to ask for more footage if need be.

As the name indicated, it was a film *and* TV school, but the teaching on the TV side had so far been kept to a minimum. The training consisted of a short technical course on how to use digital editing equipment and how to construct a simple edit. This was well taught but in my opinion far from sufficient. It was not their dream, but you could foretell that the majority of the editing students would end up working in

TV, and I saw it as imperative that they developed as editors to become equally proficient in both film and TV. There were already enough sorry button-pushers with scant creativity out there in the real world — not only in Australia — and I wished my students to leave the school as astute technicians with a creative mind and a will to exercise that mind on whatever material they might be handed.

The American Motion Picture Academy had material that was perfectly suited for what I needed. They were selling duplicate negatives of the abundant footage of the old TV series *Gunsmoke* that was produced before the industry had found its specific, multi-camera TV shooting style. Stylistically it was a hybrid that in this instance was advantageous because the footage allowed for both a TV cut and a big-screen cut. The Academy also offered three different edits: the final one that had gone to air, another that had a big-screen look, and a third version that showed little talent and for style and format was neither here nor there. I ordered all the *Gunsmoke* material and each student received two copies of the uncut footage: one on film, the other transferred to videotape. In a given time they had to edit a big screen version of 80-90 minutes duration and then, also in a specified time, a TV version of a fixed length. It was an excellent teaching tool. The edits of the different versions could be compared among themselves, and thanks to the uncut footage, the choices could be discussed in a meaningful way. The students first looked at all their own versions and then at the American ones, and as usual, we collated them, pinpointing strengths and weaknesses. All this viewing, looking at each other's work, and admiring and criticising without malice had two objectives. Besides the basic learning, I also wished my students, if they were to make steady progress, to become aware of the necessity to be able to both receive and deliver critique. Out in the 'real' world, in both the film and TV industries, there is a general absence of these discussions — one does not dare to criticise, fearing that it might be detrimental to one's future. Some of the mediocrity of the daily offerings on both the big and small screen I reckon has its roots in this unwillingness to realistically and honestly look at what one has done.

If very few students were intent on making a career in TV, documentary film did not have many takers either. The great majority aimed at, and dreamed of, a future as directors in the feature film industry. I came to see the school, at the time housed in a former toothpaste factory, as a big machine with six openings at one end, one for every workshop: writing, directing, camera, sound, editing, and production. After three years in this magic contraption, you arrived, more or less happy, at the other end where there was one single outlet — miraculously labelled DIRECTOR. I certainly had no wish to facilitate this tendency, so when I gave my editing students a filmmaking exercise once a month, it was for a very different reason. My aim was to develop their imaginations and strengthen their understanding of how a narrative can be realised in *images* without gratuitously leaning on dialogue. They were given a key word on which to construct a simple story. The first one was 'post' — anything with a connection to mail could be chosen — but with each month, the complexity increased, as did their skills. Until they got key words with emotional content, I do not think they all cottoned on to the fact that the first requisite was to start thinking differently. Instead of racking your brains to find the best lines, do it to find the most telling images! They were not obliged to write conventional scripts if they did not want to, but they could not start shooting before they had presented an extensive 'shopping list' of images. The rules for the exercise were simple: each student received a small, uncomplicated camera with three film cassettes. To mitigate the absence of sound — that otherwise would have helped them to feel a certain rhythm — they were encouraged, both when filming and when editing, to listen to music cassettes of their own choosing. Shooting, as well as editing time, was fixed, and they were given a minimum and maximum length for the finished product.

The students loved these exercises. They got out of their small and windowless editing rooms and, most importantly, felt that their creative efforts for once were not hampered by their co-students' 'crummy' footage. For some it also came as a not so welcome but necessary revelation that even they could come up with crummy material. The

monthly screenings of the latest 'masterpieces' became social gatherings, and together with a glass of wine, the necessary criticism was usually swallowed without too much pain. All this had a built-in consequence: they became more critical of what they looked at. They
watched in a much more detailed manner, they started to question, and
slowly they learned to observe and to reflect on what they were seeing
and thus started to evaluate the material in their editing rooms, on their
TV screens, and in the cinema with a new awareness. Seeing does not
necessarily lead to ideas, but observation, if processed, will!

The real beneficiaries of the new regime and its improvements were,
of course, the first-year students, but the second-year ones, whenever
possible, were also involved. They all had, as could be expected, grown
up on a diet of mostly American films and/or American-inspired TV, but
on the whole they knew very little about Central and East European or
Japanese film. In the beginning they also had great difficulty analysing
what they saw and verbalising *why* they liked or disliked something.
Inviting all the students, not only my own, I started film screenings followed by open discussions. This slowly opened up new horizons, and
beyond the cinematic aspects, it had the added value of showing how
differently various cultures deal with similar problems. Because of the
Australian remoteness, this was an eye-opener for most students, and
when the other workshop heads realised the changes, they suggested
that the screenings should be part of the school's general program. I
was happy to oblige, but when in my second year I tried to book the
films again, I found that a couple were not available. But why? Talking
to the distributors, I discovered to my horror that when their distribution rights expired they thought it too costly to send the copies back
overseas and instead of that, they burned them. BURNED! Gone up
in smoke! And this in a place thousands and thousands of miles away
from any film library. This had to be stopped! Some way had to be
found in order to save such films for teaching purposes. I started to
holler and bang on doors. Storry Walton concurred that it was horrible
and sent me on my way. Richard Thomas was sympathetic to my des-
peration and agreed that something ought to be done. But nothing ever

was! There were days when the Australian Film and TV School could drive you to drink. Even after all these years, I still fume when I recall the inaction in front of the ongoing destruction of irreplaceable, invaluable teaching material.

With a new intake every year I always had fifteen to eighteen students in my own workshop, and from the day I arrived I had been in demand as executive producer for students from other workshops. It added considerably to an already heavy workload, but I had an important reason for accepting. At first I saw it as a way to get to know students other than my own, but I quickly discovered that it also gave me insights into how other workshops functioned. With the editing workshop moving along entirely new lines, my own students made noticeable progress, some in a surprisingly short time, but what did not greatly improve was the footage coming from the other workshops. The school worked on the principle of self-sufficiency: the writing students wrote the scripts that the directing students realised with the help of the production, camera, and sound students. Looking, as executive producer, at the original scripts from the writing workshop, I could easily see that the problems with the final product were less a result of it being made by people in training than with the scripts themselves. Some of them had literary merit, but they were not visual. This came as no surprise because none of the students had ever done script work before coming to the school. They had had to show their skills as writers in order to get in, but their experiences lay with newspapers, magazines, and the like. The new workshop boss, who was an interesting writer and a very witty man, once told me, late at night at a big wine-soaked party, that he did not know the first thing about screen writing and had accepted the school's offer of employment with the hope of learning something about it! It might sound like *Alice in Wonderland*, and to some extent it is, but it is also the reality when working in faraway places with small industries and limited economic resources.

It was a tricky situation: unless you could get at the root of the problem, the scripts, nothing was really going to get better, and the scripts were clearly not my domain. I had a long talk with Michael Stedman, a

New Zealander who had come to the new team as curriculum adviser to Richard Thomas. He and his wife, Peggy, made me feel welcome as soon as I arrived and I often found that Michael had interesting ideas. Another thing I appreciated was that he was 'a doer' and there were not too many around! I was of course hoping for a solution to my problem, although not exactly the one Michael came up with: I was mandated to devise a course for the writing students. Now I had to ask myself: how do you effectively teach script writing? Can it be taught at all? If it could, why was America, where 'creative writing' courses can be found in every nook and cranny, not overflowing with excellent scripts?

With my mistrust of these kind of courses, I felt like the fox in charge of the henhouse, but I also know the eternal truth of Goethe's aphorism 'When ideas fail, words come in very handy.' Lecturing or writing yet another manual about Beginning, Middle and End, Development of Characters and Plot, Tempo — and whatever else goes into the soup — would hardly inspire the writing students to produce more fulfilling scripts. The writers, in contrast to the majority of their fellow students, did not show any desires to become directors — they were, and intended to stay, writers. As verbal expression was their main tool I could hardly take the words away from them — as I had done with the editors. The trick had to be to make them use their words in a different way; that is to say change their method of thinking. Instead of struggling to primarily find 'the right word' they had to learn to visualise, to 'see the image,' the one that would pass on their message. It is a mind game. When, on the book's page I read 'Joan hesitates,' she does it the way *I* see fit, but if Joan hesitates in John's script, it is a different story. 'To hesitate' has a multitude of degrees, and as a result, images imbued with this action are also multiple. Before putting the letters h-e-s-i-t-a-t-e down, John better figure out the precise image that in this instance fits *his* script. Proceeding this way, their scenarios would be pictorially richer and deprived of all — or at least most — of the seductive adjectives that makes reading so pleasurable. Being descriptive in a more precise way, they would probably also have a greater chance to, in the final film, see their intentions genuinely realised.

I knew I was onto something essential, but I had to find a way of teaching it. When in the end I remembered what a useful tool comparison can be, the idea emerged. Using a book and the film that is based on it, I could use 'role-playing' in a novel way. Having the students first deconstruct the book into action parts, descriptive ones and — if present — philosophy or 'inner voice' and then, looking at the film, take note of what had, or had not, made it onto the screen would give us a rich possibility for discussions about how differently 'information' works on the page and on the screen. Michael found the idea useful, and the writing students started a new chapter in their lives. As did I.

Looking back I realise that it was this work that would eventually lead me away from the editing table and firmly place me at the script editor's desk. Having had the good fortune to learn my trade on mostly high-quality footage, that over the years had became scarcer, I was no longer certain that I was at the right place. As a film editor, I had early on discovered that when things did not add up it was not often the result of unlucky circumstances during the filming, but because of a fragile script. I have also always been convinced that writing for the printed page and for the screen are *not* the same. The page is 100% words, whereas film, not counting dialogue, has no words, but telling images — if all is well.

There are a number of book-film combinations to choose from, but I opted for Ken Kesey's *One Flew Over the Cuckoo's Nest* (1962) and Milos Forman's film (1975) with the same name. Later I gave the course using other works, but, as long as the language is English, I still find *One Flew Over the Cuckoo's Nest* the unbeaten combination. Between its publication to enthusiastic reviews and the making of the film, the book had already made the transition to a stage play. Kirk Douglas, who retained both the stage and the screen rights, played Randle Patrick McMurphy and, after a long absence from Broadway, met with big success. But that feather in Douglas's hat was still tiny compared with the triumph of the film that won five Oscars in 1976. It has also aged extremely well, and to my taste Jack Nicholson's performance as McMurphy is still his all-time best. The fact that the book, from beginning to end, consists of an inner monologue also suited my purposes because it instantly raised the intricate question of how thoughts, observations, and thinking best transpose to action. The book is rich in detail, has well-defined, interesting characters, action, and human drama, and is, like the film, very entertaining, which does not hurt either.

The students were asked to read the book before we started, and on day one we opened with a film screening. Then each participant told the group how he or she felt about the two works, and we videotaped this discussion with the intent to replay it at the end of the course. The aim was to verify if the exercise had changed their perceptions and if so, in what way. We debated the use of inner monologue and asked a million different questions until we got answers. Living by the dictum that the more one knows the better, I was unprepared for the negative response I got one day from my (until then) very enthusiastic students. It was defining the differences between subjective and objective camera that met with loud opposition; they were writers, not technicians, and did not know anything about cameras and had no wish to learn anything either! However, little by little, it dawned on them all that this had nothing to do with the technical intricacies of the camera but with the all-important question of where you place it. The choice strongly affects the storytelling and how we, the audience, understand what we are seeing. Objective camera shows the action from the viewer's point of view, while subjective camera reveals what a character sees, as if the camera has moved into the frame and taken the place of the character's eyes, and we are more or less forced into empathy. The objective camera will show the fugitive running for his life, and we fear for him, but our fright might double if realising, at the same instant as the runner does, the dangers ahead. Some might say that the choice between objective and subjective camera is the director's choice, and there is no doubt some truth in that, but if it does influence the writing, I believe it can be the writer's choice.

The confusion created if the rules are not respected is evidenced in the highly acclaimed BBC TV series *Edge of Darkness*, long ago penned by the Scottish writer Troy Kennedy-Martin. The journalist Craven, who smells a rat when his daughter Emma dies while looking into a nuclear scam, has started an investigation of his own, and he in turn is exposed to radiation. In the actual scene, he is sick in bed, hallucinating, and in his confused state of mind believes he sees Emma at the foot of his bed. He also, in his feverish confusion, thinks he hears her saying: 'Don't mix the white wash with the colours!' Emma, being a hallucination, obviously is only perceived by Craven — i.e., should be subjective camera from Craven's point of view. Troy was on the set daily keeping an eye on where the director placed his camera, and all went well until the day Troy had to stay home and rewrite some pages. The director, left to his own devices while shooting the last scenes in this sequence, used objective camera, and suddenly in a wide shot I saw Craven in his bed and Emma standing at the foot of it. I jumped in my chair! Was Emma after all not dead? Had she miraculously come back to life? I was totally confused and in trying to sort things out lost most of the rest of the segment. The whole series was of such a delightfully high quality that it never entered my mind that it could be a technical mistake, but when I later met Troy I got to know that it was. He had been very unhappy and begged for a re-shoot, but budget limitations excluded it. Mistakes generally come in two categories: the sloppy ones which are just annoying and the dangerous ones, dangerous, because they confuse you, which in turn breaks your attention and your emotional attachment to the screen.

Once questioning and collations were behind us, we looked at the videotape from the beginning of the course. If this was the pudding, it was indeed very tasty. Detailed observations and in-depth analysis now replaced what earlier had been rather shallow judgements. When the students completed their last assignment, this became even more evident. Tongue in cheek they were asked to forget, as much as possible, that they had seen a film called *One Flew Over the Cuckoo's Nest* and to make their own choices for a short synopsis based upon or inspired by Kesey's book. At the beginning of the course, some students had mistakenly thought that they were going to learn only to transpose a book into a film script, but as time went by, they all realised that there is only one difference between that and writing an original film script. If you are doing the latter, *you* will have to come up with *all* the ideas, but whether they originated in your brain or were first put on paper by someone else, they have to be scrutinised and treated in exactly the same manner.

The writing students were an intelligent and very enthusiastic group, and their ability to analyse both what they read and what they looked at on the screen improved virtually by the day. The 'I like' or 'I don't like' without further qualifications progressively abated, and as this new awareness started to penetrate their thinking, it also coloured their writing. Like the editing students, they started to look at TV programs and films with different eyes and much more critical minds, and their input in the discussions after film screenings began to interest other students who became more questioning. For me this was a great relief because the year David Lynch's *Blue Velvet* was released in Australia the prospective new students, when questioned about what films they had seen lately and what they thought of them, drenched me in an avalanche of 'I love it.' No future camera student had anything to say about how Lynch used light and colour, no future director remarked on his particular, disjointed narrative. They were all seduced by the gloss of the film, and with their lack of analytical faculties, they were not inspired, but only on their merry way to become copycats.

Probably the most encouraging part of all this effort was to see that the writers, even after the course was finished, continued with their efforts and got progressively better at finding images that were representative of thought. With their growing awareness, the qualities of their scripts accrued, and my initial problem had found a solution. Eventually, what reached the editing students from other workshops was footage that lent itself to proper editing instead of rescue work.

If the film or TV editor has an advantage over the script editor, it lies in the fact that the former *knows* what they have got. Their footage might be splendid or a total misery, but it is there to be seen, evaluated, and handled. The script editor has none of this, and although I have never had to deal with a turkey of a script that was transformed to a peacock of a film, I have spent more than one evening in the cinema in awe of what was up on the screen but then later, with some trepidation, also wondered if I, as the script editor, would have recognised its potential.

A FIRST TASTE OF NEW ZEALAND

The Film School's repeated, but so far never fulfilled, promises of some form of assistance to Auckland University's film course had, over time, turned into a lingering embarrassment. Early in my second year, Richard Thomas found a possibility to solve the delicate situation and at the same time prevent me from, as he saw it, working myself to death: I was seconded to New Zealand for two weeks. My host had to carry the air fare and accommodation, but I would come free of charge. In order to reduce its costs, Auckland University invited the New Zealand Film Commission, the Film Unit in Lower Hutt just outside Wellington, as well as two or three private film companies to share in both the costs and my services. The University also left the organisation of the two weeks to the Film Commission where it was handled with aplomb by Helene Wong.

How much rest Richard had counted on I do not know, and I suspect he only knew Helene by name, but she had organised a murderous schedule that certainly gave all the participants their money's worth. It was, however, also extremely well arranged which — together with the warmth I encountered — mitigated most of the fatigue. Helene and I had met in Sydney when my visit was still in its early planning stage. She had impressed me with intelligence, humour, and a Chinese gracefulness that effectively camouflaged an unusually high energy level. I do not think she was at all familiar with my method: looking at footage with full participation of those present, but none of the usual expositions from behind a lectern! Helene had listened carefully and not raised any objections. She had also promised that scripts in different stages of completeness would be sent to Sydney, giving me enough reading and thinking time before I arrived in New Zealand. Once back home she succeeded in talking a number of filmmakers into showing their work in an editing room where we could spool the films back and forth depending on where the discussion took us. It was a real achievement on Helene's part, for nobody seemed to have 'lectured' in this way before and few directors feel totally comfortable meeting their audience at such a close range. When all the participants come from the film community, it does not become any easier, but there were not even any close calls. Most of the time the participants were good at asking pertinent questions about both content and technique. From time to time directors, to their own great surprise, found that their visual eloquence was much less clear than they had imagined. My introduction to New Zealand went very smoothly, and there seemed to be a happy feeling of achievement all around.

While there I did script editing with writers. I sat in editing rooms with editors and directors discussing their work and tipping them off on possible changes where I saw variations that to me appeared preferable. Analysing content and form, as well as discussing the relationship between these concepts, I went through a couple of feature films and a great number of documentaries. The participants showed interest and a willingness to listen, but while the feature film directors seemed to conscientiously have included form in their deliberations, most of the documentary makers admitted that 'it mostly happened during the editing.' Reading them my synonym list for 'form', or at least part of it — structure, plan, build, substance, construction, fabric, skeleton, etc. — they did realise that considerations about this element had its place at the beginning of the process and not in some haphazard way at the end. Later, when acting as script editor for a couple of the people I worked with during these two weeks, to my delight I discovered that our discussions had not been left unheeded.

That the National Film Board of Canada had a small replica in the Film Unit in Lower Hutt was news to me, and there I met, among others, Joan Isaac, its then newly appointed head. Comparing notes from my Montreal experiences, it quickly became evident that the same problems that plagued the bigger model in Canada also festered here. Joan had her work cut out for her, and, with her clear head, was in no doubt about how much things had to change before *her* institution would do its work as it was meant to. We had long discussions about the pros and cons of 'institutionalised' filmmaking and secure, lifelong employment, pondering the possibility of maintaining social security, without it in the long run leading to complacency.

As in all small countries with limited economies, financing in the film industry was a constant problem limiting the production possibilities. All the same, between 1975 and mid-1986, an impressive thirty-nine feature films, five feature-length documentary films, as well as many shorter ones were produced. New Zealand also participated, to varying degrees, in more than ten internationally financed features shot on the islands. The two which still linger in my memory are *Vigil* written and directed by Vincent Ward and Geoff Murphy's *UTU*. Ward, in both his writing and direction, showed a rare understanding of a child's world and also a profound insight into the feelings of a young girl who sees the man who accidentally shot her father eventually replace him in her mother's life. This was a deeply touching human drama where, miraculously, humour had also found a place. Alun Bollinger's admirable camerawork made a remote valley with a brutally dangerous landscape an integrated part of the story and not just the splendid backdrop it so easily could have become. *Vigil* was selected for competition in Cannes, but that was probably not the best thing for Ward; not only was it characterized as an art house film, a red flag for wide distribution, but — being Ward's first feature film — it also burdened him with unreasonable expectations that *The Navigator* and *A Medieval Odyssey* — despite a few very inspired sequences — did not live up to. To me he appeared to be an unusually gifted filmmaker, but he was evidently also known for a stubbornness that made backers stay away.

UTU is an historical drama in which a Maori warrior seeks retribution for the massacre of his village while a Pakeha[29] farmer does the same for the death of his wife. One of New Zealand's most expensive productions at the time, it was also the country's first film to be selected for the main program at a Cannes Festival, but its critical acclaim was not great. The bringing together of these two distinctive New Zealand societies — the Maori and the Pakeha — was my first glimpse of Maori culture beyond the inescapable tourist clichés of Maori warriors in their battle bodypaint. Although I found the film both moving and interesting, it gave the editor in me a shock. Nobody had asked me so I kept my mouth shut, but every fibre in me screamed: can't you see that what is now the beginning has its proper place at the end! The opening of the film showed the outcome of the battles and thus eliminated the suspense that otherwise would have carried the film. Would I have recognised it at the script stage? I am not so sure, but I would *never* have missed it in the editing room, nor would I, without putting up a real battle, have let an idea from the script override what the footage on the screen so irrefutably revealed.

I had been in Australia long enough to have picked up on what seemed a general attitude inferring that the New Zealanders were the poor cousins. Economically there might have been a certain truth to it, but as far as I could discover on this whirlwind trip, other aspects did not in any way attest to the veracity. I had assumed that the two countries would be fairly similar, but save for the outdoors that showed a resemblance in its splendour, I felt I met a very different atmosphere. Unlike in Australia, nobody in New Zealand seemed interested in the thorny questions about staying in the Commonwealth or becoming a republic. The New Zealand forefathers had purposefully taken with them all things British, down to their cats and dogs — and thereby unwittingly destroyed some of the uniqueness of their adopted country. Some flightless birds, formerly lacking predators, slowly disappeared, as did some native flora, but the relationship to the 'mother country' had always been taken for granted, and still was. Ideas about 'freedom' caused no soul searching, but not surprisingly, I would find that in comparison the New Zealanders on the whole were infinitely more conservative.

I met with producers, writers, directors, and editors, and whether it was in editing rooms or at working lunches or dinners, the best thing about these gatherings — the good food aside — was that almost all of them lacked the appearance of only social niceties, and instead were thought-provoking exchanges over problems that we all shared. Of course I also met some old stodginess, but surprisingly little, and felt very encouraged by the willingness to learn going hand in hand with an acceptance of critique that I found somewhat unusual. Or was it the result of geographical isolation, a pent up hunger for knowledge and contact that I mistook for openness?

OUT OF THE FRYING PAN
AND INTO THE FIRE

When the day to renew my contract approached, I had made up my mind to leave the school, at least on a full-time basis and as Workshop Head. I deeply missed my active participation in the industry and still doubted, as once I had back in Sweden, that one could stay a good teacher without — at least from time to time — working in the trade with its constantly changing trends. In order not to cause unnecessary disruption to my students, I promised to stay on until the end of the school year, but once I had seen them go I began to establish myself as a freelance director, editing consultant, and script editor. In a place where I had precious few contacts outside the school, this may have been foolhardy, but word about my course for writers had spread, and the Australian Film Commission was quick to give me work as script assessor and script editor. Eventually, they offered the writing course to a small group of new writers, and the Australian Broadcasting Corporation (ABC) also signed up the directors in their drama department for such a course. On what should be the creative side of TV, people unfortunately often concentrated more on the technical perfection of their images than on content, and as a result, much of their work had the sad look of illustrated radio. It intrigued and excited these directors to find out that by changing their thinking processes they could produce richer work without higher costs.

Soon after leaving the school, I also received an invitation to join a group of freelancers who had come together around their need to have a workspace separate from their homes. They all knew each other well and had figured out that the most economical way of solving their common problem would be to rent a house where everybody could have their own office but share the rest of the space. They had found a suitable, big, old house not far from central Sydney. Because one room still had no occupant, Geoff Burton, the cinematographer whom I had got to know when he was at the school, had suggested that I be asked to join them. My introduction to the group — as well as their inspection of me — turned out to our mutual satisfaction, and I was more than happy to accept their offer. They had this extensive list of contacts that I, as a freelancer, badly needed but still lacked, and they became an easily accessible and very generous source of information. I am sure that being part of the group also sometimes landed me contracts that otherwise might not have come my way.

Australia had for a considerable time neglected its sagging economy, and as a consequence it had gone from bad to worse. In the mid-80s it came to a head, and budget cuts started to fall — not the least on ABC, and as usual the freelancers were the first to be hit. One of our members had to let his office go. Not long thereafter, number two had to give up the luxury of his workspace, and for the rest of us, at the same time as our own work opportunities diminished, our financial burden increased. It was evident that we were not to see better economic times for quite a while, so when our lease expired, we reluctantly closed down our co-op and went our separate ways. A couple of us kept in contact and from time to time also managed to work together, but the daily, pleasant camaraderie and the Friday lunch barbecues in the garden were a thing of the past. But the worst was yet to come, and when a new round of budget cuts hit the ABC my future as a freelance director·in its drama department came to a sudden end. Having just finished directing a documentary for the department, I had finally got a foot in the door, but with their diminished budget, the department could not afford to pay freelancers, and my two forthcoming contracts were cancelled.

An obituary on October 19, 2000, over 'Australia's Martin Luther King,' the activist Charles Nelson Perkins, took me back in time. Of my two aborted scripts, one was a satire mocking the droll discrepancy between lust and morality; the other was a series of five documentaries looking at the engines for change. Five Australians — two women and three men — were at stations in life where their beginnings had not indicated that they would ever be, and I wanted to find out both what had triggered the change and what coping with the consequences of it had meant. One of my proposed subjects was Perkins. When I met him he was the head of the Department for Aboriginal Affairs, the single person of colour in the whole Australian bureaucracy, which he had entered as a research officer in the late 60s. His father was white and his mother aboriginal, and he was born in a shack near the central Australian town of Alice Springs in 1936. Perkins had been a first at a number of things: at Sydney University he had been Australia's first indigenous university graduate, and later, inspired by Rev. King's protest marches, in the mid-60s he started to lead freedom rides to Outback towns in New South Wales to confront discrimination and segregation. At a time when the majority of white Australians had little interest in social injustice and preferred to look the other way, it was big news when the town of Bourke was forced to end the ban on aboriginal children at its public bath.

It had taken both patience and a fair bit of insistence before I finally got an appointment with Perkins. The Australia where I had arrived was still very slow in its willingness to offer aboriginal equality, and I guess I was the first filmmaker who had ever sought his participation. He was puzzled and somewhat amused, but not very willing. Perkins was known to sometimes show a gruff exterior, and I was prepared for that, but to discover some shyness in this man with so much confrontation behind him surprised me. He obviously did not know how to politely tell me no to my face, but as he at the same time showed scant intention to say yes, I did not think I had much to lose by finally informing him, 'You do not have the right to say no.' Perkins was clearly surprised, and looked at me for a while before asking what I meant; I explained that the way I saw it, he was a role model for indigenous people in Australia and beyond. You would probably have been hard pressed to find an aboriginal who did not know who 'Uncle Charlie' was, but white Australia on the whole had little or no idea. I have always thought of acceptance of others as a two-way street, and felt a documentary film would be an effective way to show that there was another side to his community than the always trumpeted brawls, drunkenness, and the disproportionately high percentage of aboriginals in prison. I was patiently heard out, and left with what sounded like an honest promise that he would think it over.

I kept myself from calling Perkins' secretary, and three weeks later patience got its reward. She called and told me that Perkins had decided to participate. Hurrah! It was the very next day that my producer at ABC phoned and informed me that my contracts were among those eliminated by the budget cuts. Richard Thomas, who by then had become head of the ABC, kindly called and commiserated, but I fully understood, for among Richard's shortcomings, nepotism was not one.

In my capacity as educator, I eventually got another contract with the network. Richard had taken over a station where regeneration had not happened for a long time, and his problems were now akin to the ones he earlier had met at the Film School, the pool of young talent inside Australia was still very limited. He cleverly decided on a new tack, and instead of looking for experience, he went in search of brains. Eight promising individuals would be given the in-house training they needed in order to become good directors. Of the final selection, one had done some camera work, but the rest were, or had been, university students with no TV or film experience, and I was asked to design a course and also teach part of it. The idea was interesting, and it felt good to be able to start from scratch without first having to eliminate what I often saw as old, bad habits. They were a motivated group and quick learners, but they also made me make an appointment with a nose, throat, and ear specialist. Much of the time I could not clearly hear what they were saying and thought I was losing my hearing. The doctor was a scrupulous man, who after having satisfied himself that I had no cancer in my middle ear, sent me to another specialist who performed a number of tests that were both amusing and fascinating. I came away with some more insights into the complexities of sound, together with the welcome reassurance that there was nothing wrong with my hearing. In the final analysis, it was my students who, insecure in their new roles, were too shy to speak up! I never told them about my visits to the doctors but started to feign great deafness that miraculously disappeared the day they made themselves clearly heard on the set.

Toward the end of 1986, I got an unusual proposal from Melbourne. The National Screenwriters' second conference, to be held early in the new year in Queenscliff, Victoria, invited me to give a lecture. I suspected that the driving force behind this had been Anne Deveson, by then the Director of the Australian Film, Television and Radio School. She was to be one of the two moderators during the conference, and although I did not teach at the school any longer, I had regularly been called upon to help select the new recruits. The invitation was a pleasant surprise, for normally the contact between the film communities in Sydney and in Melbourne were almost non-existent. Incidentally, the same was true for all the different Australian film communities, although Perth, the single city on the distant west coast, was the only one I ever heard voice concern about the predicament. Each time I was there for some script editing, I got an earful of complaints over how isolated they felt.

Initially the Melbourne people had asked me to talk about how to edit a film, and it took some arguing to make the organisers understand that this would only be theoretical, useless, and boring. Script editing, on the other hand, dealing with concepts that can be understood even if you have not seen or read the script, was in my opinion more appropriate given that it was a writers' conference! After some hesitation, it was accepted that my lecture would cover the script editor's work: the necessities and the pitfalls, the need to wear two hats, that of the audience and that of the technician, but never the one of the writer. This would also lead to my favourite topic, 'visual writing,' how you achieve it and how it can make a good script even better.

One would be forgiven for thinking that after so many years of working as a script editor and with so much teaching behind me, I would be able to talk coherently about these things in my sleep, but there is a considerable difference between teaching a course that runs over several weeks with a small group of participants that you get to know, and in two hours present a method as well as its objectives to a large gathering of people whose backgrounds you can only guess at. Experience has taught me that most people, even inside the profession, have a rather warped idea about what film and TV editing entails, and script editing does not fare much better. Over the years I have had to answer some strange questions.

When I was regularly travelling between Toronto and New York with what looked like the same old roll of film under my arm, a customs officer who had started to recognise me once asked what I was doing. 'I am a film editor.' 'What sort of profession is that?' I explained that when you make a film you end up with much more material than is in the final film, and my job consisted in cutting out all that was superfluous. I had really hit the nail on the head; an accusing index finger came up wagging in front of my nose: 'I see, you are the one who takes out the naughty bits I want to see!' Oh, the difficulty of pleasing everybody! But first prize for misapprehension still goes to the producer in Toronto who contracted me as a film editor for an upcoming production. There was nothing unusual about our negotiations, but finally, when I was already standing with my hand on the door knob, he blurted out: 'Remember, I do NOT want a Bergman film!' What the poor man really meant, I suppose, was that he dreaded the possibility of having an 'art film' on his hands. I smiled my widest smile and assured him that if his director did not provide me with 'Bergman material,' he was surely not running the risk.

The National Screenwriters' conference gave me the opportunity to meet with, and listen to, Troy Kennedy-Martin and Frank Pierson among others. Troy talked with much enthusiasm about his very advanced ideas on television ads being 'the real plays of the near future.' He held forth that television and film on the whole only perpetuated outworn conventions and predicted that because of our present-day ability to quickly absorb what we see on the screens, a good part of the audience would very soon prefer the fast-moving 'mini-dramas' of pop videos and thirty-second commercials to a thirty-five minute play. Being Troy, he might have exaggerated just a trifle, but there *was* a great deal of truth in his perceptions, and I found it very refreshing that these ideas were voiced by a mature man with such excellent, although in form 'traditional,' writing as *Edge of Darkness, Reilly, Ace of Spies*, and

The Italian Job. At the same time the notion was also frightening. Would our lives in the long run really be bettered by us being indulged not to make any efforts of concentration longer than thirty seconds? Did and do we really need an even greater fragmentation? To be even more 'dumbed down?'

Praise has rarely felt as good as it did when Frank Pierson complimented me on my lecture. I had always greatly admired his work, not the least the screenplay for *Dog Day Afternoon* that after two earlier nominations[30] for an Academy Award finally earned him the trophy. His versatility was not only impressive but also rather unusual in the USA film and TV industry where he had edited, produced, written, and/or directed for film and TV for a very long time. He had taught, given master classes in screen writing, been the president of the Writers Guild, and in 2001 was, at the age of seventy-five, elected president of the Academy of Motion Picture Arts and Sciences! His scope was phenomenal, and much of this was already achieved when I met him, but there was not even the slightest tinge of stuffiness or self-importance. He was warm and direct, and after the conference he came to Sydney for a couple of days. Small groups of young and not so young filmmakers and writers spent hours with him listening, discussing, and learning while uncorking numerous bottles of wine.

Among other words of wisdom, Frank pointed to the importance of laughter and the need for sending a cinema audience signals that it might be okay to laugh even if they are not looking at a comedy. In front of their TV, most people laugh unembarrassed but in the cinema the rules are different. Sitting in the dark surrounded by strangers, only the most incorrigible will laugh when others are silent, and the cinema public need, Frank argued, the encouragement to laugh. I could attest to that, for when the first *Star Wars* played, a European friend and I had gone to the sold out, late afternoon show at a big cinema in Montreal. The great wardrobe ideas to dress the 'baddies' in uniforms that looked like the ones worn by Hitler's cohorts and the takeoff on Wagner's Brynhilde in the princess's hairstyle was not lost on the two of us, and we shrieked with laughter until people started to turn and stare. The rest of the audience who lacked our European references did obviously not see the jokes.

Frank took the beginning of *Dog Day Afternoon* as an example. We are watching a slice of life on a bad-hair day, but even such days can have brief hilarity. There was, in itself, nothing even remotely funny or unusual about a man entering a bank carrying what looked like an expensive florist's box of long-stemmed roses, but when Al Pacino starts to unpack his parcel you begin to wonder. Was he going to present the tellers with flowers? That *was* unusual, and he also did the unwrapping in such an awkward way that you could not help but laugh. It really was the most inept way imaginable to start a hold-up, but you soon realised that *that* was what you were watching. Part of the film's delight was that Pierson more than once interspersed the serious action with ridiculous and amusing details that allowed us to laugh as a relief from the tension.

We were also treated to small slices of typical Hollywood. Frank had always seen Al Pacino in the role as the character who, based on a real-life event, held up a Brooklyn bank to get the money he needed to pay for his lover's sex change. The actor, assuming that playing a homosexual would not do his reputation any good, declined. When the grapevine reported that the part had been offered to Dustin Hoffman, he however changed his mind. Still Al Pacino's fear of having a dash of an unwanted paintbrush was not put to rest until his refusal to appear on screen in the same frame as the lover was accommodated. Pierson had to change the originally scripted sequence, where the lover came to the bank, as he had done in real life, into a telephone conversation. Frank told us of his interviews with some of the people who had worked in the bank during the real hold-up, but the bank robber himself had, from his prison cell, steadfastly refused all contact, and Frank still regretted it!

A FLAVOUR OF THE EAST

Kuala Lumpur

Martin Hadlow, the director for the Asian-Australia Media and Information Program, had heard about my work and, during what was to be my last year in Australia, came to Sydney to interview me for the job of conducting screenwriting courses in Kuala Lumpur, Malaysia, and in Bandar Seri Begawan, the capital of Brunei. The host country was allowed four participants and the others — The Philippines, Thailand, Brunei, and Singapore — could each send two participants. Martin told me that the director of CDIS, the Education Department in Singapore, had called insisting on twelve places in the course in Kuala Lumpur! She was politely but firmly told that she could only have the regular two, so if she wanted more she would have to run her own course. He would be pleased to give her my co-ordinates.

Malaysia was the first place where I saw the results of positive discrimination on a grand scale, and I did not like the concept any more than I have done before or after. If victimising another, the betterment of one group amounts to nothing more than a new injustice, and among Malaysia's 23 million, the ethnic Indians — at nine per cent not only a minority but also the one with the weakest economy — had been hit the hardest by the promotion of the Malays. At the TV station in Kuala Lumpur, all but one Indian employee had been replaced. The screenwriting course was hosted by the station, and each day I would see this tall, sari-clad, very dignified woman walk from one building to the next, always alone. In the lunchroom nobody ever came and sat at her table, and there was an aura of abandonment and sadness around her that was truly heartbreaking.

The Chinese had, to some degree, met a similar fate, but thanks to their economic strength and know-how, they were still in every sense better off. Their numbers at the station had also diminished, but not in the same drastic way. Experiencing the laziness and ignorance among the Malays, I could not help but assume that in order to function, the station's necessity for self-preservation had been stronger than their need to be politically correct. A secretary of Chinese origin was nominated as my assistant, looking after bookings and other practical needs, and she was infinitely dependable, efficient, and pleasant, but her story was a sad and typical one. A couple of years earlier, she had come to the station as an apprentice director, but was never given the promised training and eventually found herself classified as a secretary. For financial reasons she stayed on but used her free time to learn new skills, hoping to eventually have a more fulfilling life.

Hosting the course seemed to bring some glory to the station, but the willingness to accommodate our needs was not impressive. Providing a TV and a VCR in a space where we could discuss and screen our tapes undisturbed, I would not have thought to be unreasonable at a TV station, but in Kuala Lumpur it was. We had to work in the main theatre and endure the constant interruption of people who walked through using it as a shortcut in the corridor system. Big *Do Not Disturb* signs on the doors were completely ignored. My secretary was for once unable to change the status quo; my own and finally Martin's complaints all went unheeded. No wonder I never took very warmly to Kuala Lumpur, but it was more than these irritations that blocked my usual interest in new places and my usual openness to meet what they could offer. If the place had attractiveness, it somehow escaped me.

The students were not an outstanding bunch either, and the only ones who have stayed in my memory are Karen, a Singaporean TV script writer, a somewhat mysterious Malay, and Suporn from Bangkok, Thailand. Karen, at twenty the youngest in the group, was the brightest student I ever had in any of these courses. She soaked up information and processed it in a quick, intelligent, and imaginative way that was sheer pleasure. When eventually I went to Singapore, we spent a couple of evenings together, and although she put on a brave face, it was obvious that she was not all that happy in her work. The course in Kuala Lumpur had opened up new horizons, and she did not think much of the scripts she had to write, but if she tried to present anything slightly brighter it was refused. For several years she used to send me Christmas letters. Eventually I learned she could not stand the tedium any longer and had left the station and gone to university.

The local Malay was, to all appearances, a film editor with directorial aspirations, but his connections to the TV station remained a mystery to both Martin and myself. He intimated at simultaneously holding down two different editing jobs in the private film industry; at least that was his excuse when not attending classes. When present he did well and obviously took what he learned to his friends in the film community. After a while he introduced me to a couple of young, bright filmmakers eager for my company. From then on — while constantly talking shop — we shared numerous tasty meals in small local restaurants where banana leaves replaced ordinary plates. I was invited to their editing rooms, and we looked at their work and had more discussions, but I never saw anything that my 'student' presented as his own work! He was a mystery and remained one, but thanks to his friends in the film community, my time in Kuala Lumpur was brighter than it otherwise would have been. If his real function was to keep an eye on what I did and said — the possibility did pass through my mind — and if that was the truth, and he was the TV station's choice, it had more ingenuity than anything else I saw coming from them.

Suporn was a scriptwriter at a TV station in Bangkok, and I remember her for two reasons: her never-ending perseverance and her unfailing grace, elegance, and superb cooking skills. Her English was rather limited, and as the sole participant from Thailand, she lacked the language support of a compatriot, but she made a Herculean effort and never seemed to go anywhere without carrying a big fat dictionary. Her homework was always done to satisfaction, but she must have worked well into the small hours every single night. Toward the end of the course, the TV station hosted a Saturday outing to the famous Batu Caves, but Suporn choose to stay home and go to the market instead. An attaché at Thailand's diplomatic mission in Kuala Lumpur lent her his kitchen, and she spent the day preparing a truly exquisite dinner.

At the time I was not familiar with Thai cuisine, but Suporn's cooking made it into a lasting passion. The whole evening had a dignity as well as a charm and grace that made it truly memorable among the numerous farewell dinners I have been honoured with.

The course in Kuala Lumpur and the one in Brunei were separated by the Christmas holiday, and I had been looking forward to spending it in Hong Kong with some Australian friends. Unfortunately, an emergency forced them to go back to Australia so I stayed in Kuala Lumpur where Martin, his wife, and two children kindly made me part of the family. They had been in the city long enough to have made local friends there. It was good fun visiting with them, carrying the gifts of the mandatory three oranges or mandarins, admiring the decorations in the temples, and most of all participating in the street life. The drums and the firecrackers gave your ears a battering, but the agility of the dragon dancers, their antics, and the whole street scenario were absolutely delightful. I had not found everyday life in Kuala Lumpur very colourful, but now, suddenly, the drabness was gone, and all was abundance, colour, and noise, and more noise!

Bandar Seri Begawan

Martin Hadlow accompanied me to Brunei, and in Singapore, without any explanation for the delay, we sat on the tarmac for a very long time. Martin, a frequent flyer on the route, did not have much difficulty divining the reason: the flight was delayed in order to ferry back to the Brunei capital some of the royal princesses who had gone to Singapore for a day of shopping. Equally despised by flight crews and passengers, this was a recurring event and only one of the royal families' capers. Eventually a number of black limousines came driving over the tarmac, and the women, loaded with shopping bags, boarded. We flew on to the capital, Bandar Seri Begawan, and in the recently built airport I got a first taste of bureaucracy, Brunei style. I had sent in advance a list of the video tapes I intended to bring, and somebody at the Brunei TV station, after the list had been duly scrutinised, was supposed to have arranged for an import permit. The papers could not be found, and the station employee, who was there to meet us, was of no help. Martin went in search of some higher authority. After lengthy discussions, I was finally allowed to provide my own copy of the list. The box was unpacked, the tapes ticked off, counted and recounted, and then reluctantly we were let through with my worrisome cargo.

Nothing had prepared me for Brunei with its incredible mix of East and West. It was a fusion that made it twice as difficult to remember not to automatically use my second-nature Western criteria as a yardstick. The incident at the airport was symptomatic for an all-embracing bureaucracy's severe control, but in Brunei I also met the most comprehensive welfare system since living in Sweden. The present Sultan's father had introduced social reforms that gave free health care and a non-contributory pension scheme providing monthly allowances to the aged, the blind, the disabled, lepers, the mentally ill, and their respective dependants. There were no visible slums, no beggars on the streets, and no children running wild because they were all in school at no cost to the family. Deserving students got scholarships to higher institutions abroad for courses that were not locally available.

The reigning Sultan — thanks to oil deposits, one of the richest men in the world — was British educated and had a passion for Western technology, which he imported on a big scale. While I was there, the communications system was being upgraded, and miles and miles and more miles of fibre optic cables were being put down in the jungles. This modern Lord Absolute — with two wives, the first very popular, the second less so — ruled with an iron hand and, at the time, was not only the head of State but also the Prime Minister and the holder of the portfolios of Home Affairs and Finance. He did not share his father's genuine warmth for England, but when it served his intentions and tastes, he had obviously no hesitation to use either specialists or technology from the United Kingdom. A British architect had designed his new palace where a massive onion-shaped golden dome crowned a streamlined, low building of considerable extension. It was very beautiful and was rumoured to be equipped with an electronic communication centre surpassing any in the region.

Training courses testified to a concerted effort to keep at least some of the old crafts alive, and it did seem to be more than an aesthetic whim that had properly sanitised and left in place the ancient stilt houses in kampong[31] Ayer. If the modernisation and cleanup had made the centre look somewhat bland, the kampong and the river with its intense traffic of small, colourful boats lent the area some welcome colour and liveliness. A government building next to the harbour housed the media course, and the TV station wished to send a car to take me there every morning. As my hotel was barely a ten-minute walk away I declined the offer, to much consternation. Even more than this minimal exercise, I wanted the daily pleasure of ambling through the market and along the canal where the sampans anchored in the early mornings. Weighted down with fruit and vegetables, that in the beginning I did not even know the names of, they conducted their business as long as they had something to sell.

In stark contrast to the streets with their heavy traffic, the harbour was a much more attractive place, but on the first day I already understood what a stir I had unwittingly created — and not only at the station. People stared at me through car windows. I seemed to be the only adult using her legs in this city, but after a week, I thankfully seemed to have become part of the landscape and hardly anybody noticed anymore. What I could not get over was the mass of visibly used cars. In no other place have I ever seen such a quantity of moving, battered metal mixed into the traffic flow.

The working conditions were much better than they had been in Kuala Lumpur, and the students were livelier and more committed; or maybe I had become better accustomed to the demands of teaching a group with very unequal levels of knowledge and skills. Even so, I discovered a new problem which was purely cultural, namely the way the four local participants had been selected. Two were young directors / scriptwriters who could well do with some education, but the two others must have been chosen for ulterior reasons: their standing at the station and their seniority! One was a distant cousin to the Sultan, although the man himself never alluded to it, nor did he seek any advantages. He seemed to enjoy the course, but as his films were already in a class of their own, I am sure the station could have found another participant in greater need of development. I soon discovered that, since his youth, he had had a keen interest in photography and it had taught him about light and framing, but he also seemed to have a knack for telling interesting stories within the confines of the system. His film education was no different from the others' at the station, but his camera work had a fluidity that theirs lacked.

Unfortunately his middle-aged compatriot was a different kettle of fish and unteachable: in his own mind 'Mr. Important' could do no wrong. As patiently as I possibly could, I pointed out the muddle and lack of logic in his scripts; he heard me out with impatience and invariably ended the discussion with, 'I think it is good.' Although he infuriated me, far worse was the fact that, in this culture's rigid value system, his attitude made his younger colleagues less mindful — not necessarily by what he said, but because his senior position lent some weight to his platitudes. He also set a bad example in more than one way. Because Friday morning was prayer time the course did not start until after lunch, but 'Mr. Important's' religious ferventness always seemed to last the whole day and some weeks even spilled over to Saturday. His absence was such a relief that I kept very quiet about it.

The two female participants came from the Philippines and were among the most attentive and vocal. One was in her forties, married, and a grandmother and had, since birth, lived her life in a wheelchair. With dwarfish arms and legs she was still an indomitably independent, clearheaded woman. We seemed to share the belief that there is a great need for more than just technical education inside TV. She was also very outspoken about what she saw as its educative impact and its informative possibilities. Well before the course was over, she inquired if I would be interested in coming to the Philippines if her TV station could find the money; sadly they did never seem to be able to. Her colleague, who was younger and considerably quieter, was all the same a very active participant, but little did I expect that she was the one who would give me a real surprise at the end of the course.

As could be expected, there was tightly maintained censorship in the sultanate, and I learned that all scripts at the TV station were vetted before going into production. You had better not in any way criticise the royal family, the police, or the army. Something as innocent as an inept policeman was enough to cause the demise of your script. During the course all participants had to show a program that they had written and directed, and they were all made in their local languages. That left some of us at a disadvantage that quickly was turned into anything but: was there enough visual readability and coherence to roughly tell us the story without it being propped up by dialogue or commentary? After a first screening, we told what we thought the piece was about, and that brought to light a number of misconceptions. We then repeated the screening, but now with a running translation in English. Some of the mistakes in understanding could be attributed to cultural unknowns, at least on my part, but most of the time the exercise was a telling example of how language had been favoured and image was almost a second thought. The writer/director was then invited to think of images that better represented the idea behind the program and encouraged to suggest ways of cutting down on the audio. As this demands a different and, for the most part, new way of thinking, I did not expect that a course of this limited duration would show any great immediate improvement. However, when we came to the end of the *One Flew Over the Cuckoo's Nest* exercise and the students had to write their own synopsis, at least some of them demonstrated an attention to their images that earlier had not been there.

The dualism that surged through this country really came home to me while looking at a locally produced musical, aired live once every two weeks. My class and I were prominently placed among the audience who clapped and cheered as directed by the prompter. The lyrics were sung in a careful, sedate language, and the dancing girls' skirts modestly went below their knees, their sleeves covered their elbows and white gloves their hands. There was no need for guessing the roots:

this was America in Brunei! The program was very well liked I was told, and having spent some evenings looking at the available TV menu, I did not doubt the accuracy of the statement. Whatever else on the screen might have been informative, or indoctrinating, or both, but how much of a parade of talking heads can you enjoy in an evening? Brunei was not hermetically sealed off from the influence of the rest of the world, and as history shows, even draconian laws and censorship have their limits. The beauty of the place could not disguise all its contradiction; Brunei to me felt like a political powder keg.

During the whole course, the two Philipinas had shown not only a great interest but also an unusually quick ability to adapt to this new way of thinking, and both their synopses confirmed it. The older one had opted for a 'based upon' version, but the other had turned in an 'inspired by' paper that was not only skilled but also in some disturbing way had the weight of the experienced. It was a prison story with torture and a climactic risky escape. Was this pure imagination or had it, at least in parts, some anchorage in a reality? At the end-of-the-course dinner, the writer came and sat next to me, and she was the one who broached the subject. It *was* personal and very much so: she had been a university student during the time when Marcos and his wife, still in power, were laying waste to the country. She had joined an underground opposition group, was eventually caught, thrown in jail, and tortured. That her father was one of Marcos's cronies did not change anything, and she speculated that he might not even have tried to get her out. Since starting university, she had no longer lived at home, and although she saw her mother, she had refused all contact with her father. Finally, after a hellish time, she had been helped to escape and guessed that her mother, behind her father's back, had bribed a prison guard. More dead than alive, she had been smuggled out of the Philippines and sent to Holland where she got lengthy medical and psychological treatment. Once Marcos was gone, she had returned, finished her studies, and started to work in television in Manila. She saw herself as capable of handling her life reasonably well in spite of what she had gone through, but also added that this was the first time she had been able to write about it. Her relief at having finally managed to flush the last remnants of the horror out of her system was a shared joy, and I only wished that Ken Kesey also had been able to listen to her. He might then have been less negative about the film he so steadfastly rejected, feeling that his important 'message' had been lost in it.

BECOMING A KIWI

While I was away the Australian economy had taken a new battering and unemployment, not the least in my field, was rampant. The economy in Canada was not good either and news from their film and TV industries precluded a return to Montreal. I started to look south. Back in 1982 New Zealand had been a very pleasant experience, and although the country had some economic problems, the fact that the government already had taken drastic steps, much too drastic some said, to stop the overspending, it made the opportunities more predictable. Several of my friends had already moved there. Richard Thomas and his family were now in Auckland where Richard had his own company. He not only strongly encouraged the idea of my moving there, but also kindly undertook to solicit letters of support to be added to my request for a work permit. Although in terms of age I was past the cut-off point, the permit was still granted, and at the end of 1987 I moved to Auckland where I found a half-renovated house in Ponsonby. I continued the renovations in stops and starts, as my economy directed, and when all was said and done, I lived in the nicest of houses — probably *the nicest* of all the houses that over the years I had lived in.

Once more I started to lay out a garden. The mild Auckland climate allowed me to try my hand at plants I had earlier not been able to cultivate, and this time I also had the practical help of one of the most gifted gardeners and woodworkers I have ever met. He built me a beautiful pergola where climbing roses in the second year gave a pleasantly shaded space. With tar-smelling railway ties, so heavy that I could barely lift my end, he terraced an impossibly steep slope which somebody, who probably did not have to push the lawnmower, had covered with grass. When all the roots finally had surrendered to my tools, we brought in new soil, laid out drop-lines for watering, and filled the space with ground-covering roses. From what I hear they are still thriving.

Helene Wong and her husband had relocated to Auckland, and they offered friendship, introductions, and practical advice. One of the private film companies that had used my services as a script editor during my first visit to New Zealand had maintained contact after my return to Australia, and now even more frequently used me in the same capacity. I also renewed the contacts from the earlier visit. Michael and Peggy Stedman were also back and lived on the South Island in Dunedin, where Michael was the head of the National Film Unit. The unit, a division of TV New Zealand, was the part that — with their Natural History documentaries — laid a number of golden eggs in the form of sales and festival prizes. Michael's entrepreneurial talents also secured co-productions and brought not only money but also the participation of some outstanding cameramen from the BBC's Natural History Unit in the UK. The unit itself had several good camera people as well as a number of natural history specialists turned documentary makers. One was the director / producer and eminent photographer Rod Morris who had documented a New Zealand primitive reptile, the tuatara, a strange little dragon with a vestigial third eye. Michael wished to send the film to a festival, but was not satisfied with its present form. A whirlwind assignment as a film editor was my introduction to Dunedin. The assignment was to turn the material into a saleable documentary in a week.

Both as a natural history specialist and as an outstanding cameraman, Rod, whom I had never met, had a profound sense of how dramatic, showy, and wonderful this rare little relic was. Understandably, he wished to make a dramatic film, but with no overt dramatic action in the footage, his and his editor's efforts to create a drama had not been very successful. I had never heard of the tuatara, let alone seen one, so to me the film was only a jumble with much repetition. This sort of rescue work is nobody's dream job — you tread on another editor's toes, and you are forced to make a perfectionist accept what he sees as less than sterling images! There are very different ways of taking the medicine, and Rod's was remarkable: without ever showing any hostility, without complaining, when his darlings were killed — I discarded four of his six full-moon-beauty-shots — accepting takes he had earlier disregarded as less than perfect, but now, out of necessity, were used in what was not the drama he had hoped for, but a documentary that in essence told of a particular landscape and one of its rare, strange, and wonderful inhabitants. After five days of almost round-the-clock work we emerged, physically exhausted but with a film Michael was happy to send to the festival —and Rod and I were still friends! He thanked me by showing me his favourite nursery. Some people *are* loveable.

I had now established my credentials in Dunedin and from then on had regular stints at the station as supervising editor, and finally was asked to direct a documentary about the Tasmanian devil, a carnivorous, ferocious marsupial.[32] Although small numbers were said to still exist in the wild, it was well on its way to extinction. However, to me and my film crew it already appeared to be extinct: endless waits in what were supposed to be the right locations and all the tricks of wildlife photography did not reward us with even a single glimpse of the black, ugly-looking devils. Finally, we had to resort to some uninspired footage shot in a 'wilderness park' where a couple were kept as a tourist attraction. I turned to another 'rarity' — the Tasmanian tiger,[33] a tan-coloured, black-striped carnivorous marsupial. This wolf-like creature, not related to a tiger at all, had once roamed on the island off Australia's south coast but many, many years back had been hunted to extinction. The misnomer probably had its origins in the black stripes on its back, resembling those on a tiger, but in more recent days the French painter Henri Rousseau might unwittingly have helped it along with the painting he called *Tropical Storm with a Tiger*. More than one souvenir shop in more than one museum, which I think ought to know better, sold paperweights with Rousseau's painting of a real tiger but with the enticing, additional label 'Tasmanian Tiger.'

According to the scientific community the creature was for all intents and purposes extinct, but all the same it still had a lingering presence in the minds of the population. Not a single year went by without sightings being reported. The ones made in the dark shortly after last call were not even worth spending time on, but I came across one that, for a short time, had excited even the specialists. A family on a tourist trip had stopped for a picnic lunch somewhere on a forest road, and their twelve-year-old daughter had ambled away among the trees and shrub. She came back telling about 'this dog' she had met, describing its size, its tan colour and the black stripes. The parents told her to make a drawing, and she made a child's picture of the Tasmanian tiger! When somebody local got sight of it, all hell broke loose. The parents denied any prior knowledge of the animal, and the girl maintained that she had neither heard of nor seen any pictures of a Tasmanian tiger. The forest was kept under observation for a while, but no footprints or animal was ever found, and another item was added to the archive.

> 'Tiger! Tiger! burning bright
> In the forests of the night.'[34]

My hunt at least turned up something material although not alive, and I had to go to the museum before I caught sight of the elusive beast. In a big old-fashioned glass jar, a small pup sat preserved, not in the commonly used formaldehyde — which is not ingestive — but in alcohol! A curator with a taste for the drink had shared his supply with all his specimens, and although I am unaware of how well it preserved *him*, it did not destroy the DNA in his collection — as formaldehyde would have done. So if somebody with enough money, expertise, time, and a burning desire to see *thylacinus cynocephalus* again roam in the wild there is still the chance!

When I arrived at the film school in Sydney, one of my first-year students was married to an artist named Bronwyn Oliver. Her husband had fooled me in his interview and time would tell that in the couple, there was sadly only one genuinely gifted person — Bronwyn. We quickly became friends, and an invitation to her first exhibition revealed an interesting artist using Japanese rice paper as material to 'sculpture' small objects. With time the objects grew in scale, and the fragile rice paper was replaced by resins and metal. A yearly exhibition at the best-regarded art gallery in Australia showed an unusual artistic growth, but her broadened reputation did not go to Bronwyn's head. She kept the same warm, level-headed personality I had first met, and her delicate frame was in astonishing contrast to her larger and larger sculptures. With her rapidly growing reputation that eventually also became international, Bronwyn, after a couple of years, received the internationally coveted Moët & Chandon prize — usually given to painters. She was the first sculptor to be given the award consisting of one year's use of the winemaker's studio in France, living expenses, and unlimited crates of champagne!

We had always kept in contact but had not met for a couple of years, when she got an invitation from the Auckland Art Gallery to use one of their work studios for some time and then exhibit what she had made. Her residency in Auckland was added pleasure, as well as the birth of the idea for a documentary about the creative process. Bronwyn had always had the rare capacity to talk about the development of her work in simple, concrete terms, and she now gave me permission to be in her studio with a video camera while she sculptured. The Art Gallery was enchanted with the idea of having a documentary film to show together with the exhibition, but not so the Film Commission. My application for a miniscule grant, covering the cost for camera rental and tape for a small documentary, was refused. They declined any assistance, with the motivation that neither I, nor the subject of the documentary were New Zealanders!

With the stepping stones of time and the experience of permanently living in New Zealand, my earlier impressions did come down a peg or two, but it was still in many important ways a very likeable and interesting place. The frightfully high travel costs and its enormous distance from Europe and North America were strong disadvantages, but if they were negatives, they were factors that *you* at least had some control over. When the question was nationhood, regardless of the irrationality of the decision, you had no sway whatsoever. In the final choice between staying for good or going back to Montreal, *that* was what tipped the scale. While I worked in Paris, I had seen prejudice exercised in

Sweden, but at the time, although it was a blow, I had never looked upon it as aimed specifically at me. In New Zealand the dig, when it came, had a much deeper, personal impact. I finally realised that I was no longer the luxe immigrant I had been at first. It had taken me a mighty long time to come to the insight that I was not an immigrant at all, but only a traveller. Before me lay the unmasking of where 'here' is in a world that has become a much less generous place. At long last I had learned that we speak different languages and we have vastly different habits, but also that what we carry in our heads and souls is, whether good- or black-hearted, much of a muchness.

EAST MEETS WEST — SORT OF

Singapore

Martin Hadlow's advice to the Singaporeans eventually bore fruit, and they decided to arrange a course of their own. The same woman from CDIS — the Education Department — who once had pestered Martin was now on my telephone. The negotiations were lengthy, did not go very smoothly, and we were both equally unhappy with each other. I refused to give in to her all-pervading insistence on efficiency, or more to the point *her* kind of efficiency, because *how* something was done seemed less important than *that* it was done. She steadfastly refused to pay any attention to my argument that there is a relationship, positive or negative, between class size and teaching time. At some point I refused to continue to negotiate: the group was too big, and the allocated time too short, and I could not see anything worthwhile coming out of such conditions. She ultimately came back and then revealed that, in reality, I would be dealing with two groups, a smaller one of about eleven ethnic Chinese with poor knowledge of English, and a larger group who spoke the language fluently. The course time had also been slightly lengthened and, she assured me, was now ample, especially as I did not have to spend much time with the ethnic Chinese. When expressing some puzzlement, I was brazenly told that this group was not important. It was of no consequence if they did not learn much! A prompt lesson in one of the the finer points of Singapore politics: as long as you acted in a politically correct way, i.e., you provided the opportunity for learning, how it was carried out was obviously an entirely different story. My threats to withdraw had evidently had some effect, and I was assured, on my insistence in writing, that my course plan and my way of teaching would not be interfered with. At this stage my knowledge about Singapore and its political realities mostly came from reading. Once there, I would realise that, without this relentless drive for efficiency, the woman would probably never have occupied her high administrative position. I only met her twice: she greeted me when I arrived and then, unannounced, turned up in the classroom one morning. She did not last long before marching out, loudly declaring, 'This is too slow!' However, as she had already interrupted three times, thereby paralysing at least some of the students. It took me more than the rest of the day to repair the damage she had created.

The political iron hand that undoubtedly existed in Singapore was not felt in daily life, and I had been unprepared for how little of it was really noticeable. It was also quite clear that I was being 'watched' by one of my male students, who did very well in class and seemed to be suitably familiar with all the nice rooftop cocktail places. He made some not-so-subtle publicity for all his freedom — 'If I wish to travel, I only have to ask for a passport and I'll get one!' — but he also appeared to feel genuinely satisfied with his existence, unless I was too gullible. My other 'watcher' was a woman in the administration. She was in charge on weekends and holidays when she took me sightseeing to parks, where oddly enough, there always seemed to be some sort of gathering with speeches and singing — none of it in English, so totally lost on me! The city was spotlessly clean, and I quickly found my two favourite places; one large park where dozens of stationary animals resided. They were all topiaries grown and trimmed on surprisingly accurate net models. The other place was an immense aviary where the netting was so cleverly covered up by palm trees and other greenery that it felt like an open space with a great, colourful, very talkative avian population.

When told about the two groups with their different language efficiency, I redesigned the course dropping the *One Flew Over the Cuckoo's Nest* exercise. More emphasis was put on discussions around the participants' own work. Keeping in mind the ethnic Chinese weakness in English, both groups would have the good luck to be treated to the most visual masterpiece I know of. Prized but hardly praised, the BBC's first broadcast of *The Singing Detective* dates back to 1986, but there is still nothing dated about this magnificent TV series that went on to win a gold medal in the TV entertainment and mini-series section of the New York International Film and Television Festival. Through a pre-sale, ABC shared a co-producer credit but was unwilling to let the series go to air because they thought it 'too intelligent for the audience.' Thank you, ABC! Humiliating and debasing as the judgement was the majority of networks shared the prejudice. Time seems to have occasioned a re-evaluation — otherwise the recent remake is unlikely to have seen the light of day, but it does in no way live up to the original. That highly entertaining and very accessible masterpiece is the delightful proof of one of those rare occasions when a whole group of outstanding talent has come together.

The script was written by Dennis Potter; some scatterbrained critic labelled it *'Pennies From Heaven* revisited.' Much of Potter's genius had already shown in that script, but if *Pennies* had been a mighty boulder on a generally very flat TV landscape, *The Singing Detective* is nothing less than a pyramid. Jon Amiel, an already skillful director, went to new heights, and actors Michael Gambon and Patrick Malahide — both formidable — led a long list of excellent performers. It would be unfair not to mention the makeup designer, Francis Hannon, who in order to transform Gambon into a psoriasis sufferer, every morning applied layer after layer of dyes, sealants, gels and other concoctions. The actor had to be absolutely immobilised during the four to five hour process — starting long before the cocks crowed.

Amiel, preferring to use low-profile actors, regarded Gambon as one of the top five British actors and was pleased that at the time he had rarely been on TV. Patrick Malahide, on the other hand, was well known from *Minder*, but no echoes linger in any of the three roles he inhabits in *The Singing Detective*. With voice, posture, gesture and the bare minimum of makeup, he creates three different characters. Hardly any work I had ever seen, before *The Singing Detective*, had so effortlessly taken me from present to past, from reality to zones of nightmarish fear, real or imagined injustices, and I never lost my footing in either time or space. Several parallel stories developed without ever confusing me, I hooted with laughter and cried for the child. My normal critical defences were down, and I had fallen head over heels in love. It had taken me several viewings before I could start to calmly and logically analyse the work, but even that did not diminish the splendour. After more than three decades and endless screenings and lectures, my respect, admiration, and love are still unconditional.

In Singapore all my students were trained teachers and academic achievers, commissioned to make educational films. They had been given some basic technical training in the use of camera and sound, but that seemed to be it. The upper echelon, who had created the unit, clearly had had no understanding of the complexities of filmmaking and with the veneration for scholarly achievement, so typical for this part of the world, mistakenly seemed to have believed that if the candidates had top grades the rest would miraculously fall into place. Unfortunately it does not work like that, and deeply insecure in their job as directors, the teachers fell back on what they knew best — facts and more facts. With an avalanche of explanatory help, their documents were usually very heavy on audio but poor on the visual side. Their misery was no doubt also increased by the indisputable fact that the kids, who suffered their uninspired presentations at school, later went home, without any memorable images in their heads, turned on the TV, and marvelled at slick, visually exciting music videos and commercials.

Surprisingly, the small group of ethnic Chinese, although their use of the camera was often clumsy, produced documents with superior acting and much more visual life. This difference between the two groups mystified me at first, but the explanation lay in the large-scale unemployment among ethnic Chinese actors so, even if the pay was poor, good ones still participated in the making of educational films. They seemed to use their experience, generously giving suggestions and advice. The bigger group did not have the same advantage because they, for talent, were in competition with commercial TV and mostly had to make do with less skilful actors and/or amateurs. No doubt intellectually well-endowed, my students on the whole were not only poor directors but their visual imagination was also untrained. I could only detect four females and one male among the Singaporeans, who by their documents and their reasoning, stood out as the most likely to come away from the course with a better understanding of their jobs. The rest showed varying degrees of interest and sadly seemed to live with the notion that they could do no better or, even worse, that what they did was good enough.

Once in Singapore, I discovered that the slightly prolonged course time had a trade-off that had not been revealed during the negotiations. The participants were supposed to, simultaneously with the course, continue their production work! My complaints fell on deaf ears, and to get a handle on the situation, I broke the English-speaking group in two: a smaller one, with what I estimated to be the most promising participants grouped together with the ethnic Chinese, and the rest formed the second. By teaching one group in the morning and the other in the afternoon their need for production time could be accommodated but I was adamant that they could not be absent a whole day. However inconvenient, it was up to them to reschedule their production work in half-day periods. As I never heard from management about this arrangement, I assumed that the students had realised that it was to their advantage and quietly arranged things among themselves. Some of the Singaporeans were perfectly bilingual and always helpful with translations when image language was not enough for the ethnic Chinese, but the need was not a frequent occurrence. This group was scheduled for the afternoons; I then had them for an hour longer, and there was always the possibility to go into some overtime at the end of the day. The students seemed to appreciate the opportunity, and if at times they were forced to leave at five o'clock, they were very apologetic. At the end of the course, I was pleased to find that none in the mixed group had missed a single day. My assumption that visual language would override any linguistic problems proved accurate, and the screenings of *The Singing Detective* were usually the high point of the day. Once we had looked at the series as a group, the students constantly asked to borrow the cassettes so they could look at them again. My self-elected challenge to run the course in such a manner that it became worthwhile even for the ethnic Chinese made for a very heavy workload, but with their more dynamic responses, this group was at least easier to teach. Nevertheless, together with the duplications of the morning lessons it was a gruelling experience.

At the beginning of the course, I had introduced the elements that make writing for the page different from writing for the screen, and I had also explained the mechanisms of transposing an idea from one medium to the next. Previous experience had showed that the necessary rethinking was the toughest part, but these students were surprisingly quick to grasp the concept. Was it their academic training or was it rooted in their cultural background? I never found an answer, but looking at classical Chinese paintings and poetry, one can see a respectful awareness of the difference between the concepts of translate and transpose that makes me suspect that it might be a mixture of the two. Their old regard for textbook fidelity naturally lingered, and they needed constant reminders. When those in preproduction brought in their scripts, I could, however, clearly see that some rethinking was already on its way. The students had been asked to read *One Flew Over the Cuckoo's Nest* before I arrived, and I had brought a tape they could borrow and look at in their own time. Most of them made good use of the opportunity and seemed to watch the film with both delight and deductive faculties. When we pulled their own works apart, it was regularly referred to and thus became a very useful role model. While I had not expected to find thirty-two sensitive filmmakers, it was disappointing that so few showed any real promise. My final report to CDIS stressed the point and suggested that, if they wished to see progress in the unit, they would have to test the applicants differently and also provide ongoing training. I suggested that a better way of producing good educational films might be to bring in professional documentary directors and use a small pool of teachers with visual inclinations as sources. Without specifically spending time on it, the professional filmmaker would act as a role model, and that probably would help the students to acquire some direction skills.

Realising that this was my first time in Singapore, several students from the afternoon group kindly offered their company in the evenings and on weekends. They brought me to places beyond the general tourist confines, and this was definitely more fun than the outings with my 'minder.' An always very smartly-dressed woman took me shopping and then brought me to her dressmaker — all the time closely watching that I got *her* prices and not the tourist ones.

Another student took me to a performance of one of the very few remaining classical Chinese street theatres. One evening directly after class, we hopped into her car and first drove to a museum to fetch one of her friends, Miss Wong, who was an expert in the field. While being directed to one of Singapore's suburbs, we enjoyed a lively exposé of the tradition of this very special kind of theatre. Eventually we arrived at our destination and made our way to a big open space where at one end a stage on stilts had been erected with a good number of tables and benches in front of it. At the opposite end was a makeshift kitchen where cooking was in full swing. The scene was empty, but at the tables people were eating, drinking, laughing, talking, making quite some noise. Miss Wong, who knew some of the main actors, went backstage asking permission to bring us to see them. We climbed a high, rickety ladder at the back of the stage, passed an altar with burning incense sticks, and went along a narrow, draughty corridor to be introduced to the leading lady. She only saluted us very briefly before continuing to put on her elaborate makeup with great concentration. Her heavy costume hung on the flimsy canvas wall; its colourful embroideries and richness of sequins made an incongruous, florid splash in this drab, chilly little cubicle. We stood silently watching how, layer by layer, she built the enlarged features of the mask we would later recognise on the stage.

Eventually we clambered down the ladder, got ourselves some tea, and found a place to sit while the din swelled as more and more people arrived. There was no admission, and some people sat at the tables without eating, some seemed to have brought their own food, while others bought theirs from the kitchen. The local community provided the space and paid the theatre company out of their yearly budget for communal education and entertainment, but it was up to the group to erect the stage and arrange the spaces behind it. This theatre group still had a small collection of stock plays, but it got smaller every year as they could not carry the high costs of replacing old costumes. Each play told a slightly different story — often taken from ancient Chinese history — but at the same time they were all moral allegories.

After a considerable wait the play started, but the actors' appearance on the stage did nothing to calm the noise, and they struggled on for a while until finally ceasing to speak. The lead actor came to the ramp, admonishing the audience and demanding silence. They never got total stillness, but the noise level diminished somewhat and eventually the play continued. With big gestures, that could be seen from even the remotest seats, and voices that carried as far back as the kitchen, the stylised performance was acted out as it had been since its beginning. Although I did not understand a single word, what took place on the stage was visual enough. After three hours the play was still in full progress, but when it started to rain, some folks got up and left, while others stayed huddled under their umbrellas.

Although I had quite a number of opportunities to see much more than the beaten tourist track, nothing compared to this evening. The glimpse of an ancient culture that, from what I understood, risked slipping into history any day soon added to the puzzle that was Singapore. The economic hub built on both sides of the river was Western looking with its glass and steel high-rises, wide, immaculately clean avenues, and elegant hotels — all surrounded by well-kept greenery. But not too far away, if you knew where to go, blocks of old but preserved low, dark wooden houses on narrow, often pot-holed streets were still common enough. Flowers in tin containers placed on windowsills gave some colour, but the further out from the centre you got, less and less verdure was visible and the more nondescript and drabber the big housing blocks became. And in this human anthill the millions worked relentlessly.

TWO SOLITUDES

'One's destination is never a place
but rather a new way of looking at things.'[35]

When, in 1968, I walked across a gangplank of an ocean liner destined
to sail me to Montreal for a temporary stay of three or four months, all
I knew about the future was that I would then continue to Cyprus. I
eventually did, but over the years I discovered that the timekeeper was
not a very trustworthy fellow — in the first instance 'a few months'
became nearly twelve, and from then on time would stretch and recoil
in a pattern of its own. It was near the end of 1992 before I finally
arrived back in Montreal for good; my cargo was a smattering of different languages, some knowledge of very particular places and habits,
the treasured opportunities of some fabulous company, and constant
surprise at human strength and frailty. Over the years I had always, if
at all possible, arranged my travels so that I could spend a little time in
Montreal, catching up with friends and luxuriating in the city's atmosphere. Now, once installed in my new-found apartment next to Mount
Royal, I started to take in the changes in a more accurate way. Here
and there new buildings — some ugly, some very beautiful — had
somewhat changed the cityscape but even more noticeable was how the
relationship between the Two Solitudes had evolved. In the film industry the language wall had come down; most francophone companies
now worked in both languages —if for love or money is of course open
to discussion. Noticeably, the ever-diminishing NFB had stuck to its
guns and maintained two separate language entities. More anglophones were undoubtedly by now bilingual, but from those who were
not, you heard complaints about unhelpful taxi drivers and shopkeep-
ers. When I first came to Montreal, I had never been berated for not
speaking French, but now, in a different landscape, new trenches
seemed to have been dug.

During my absence the idea of a francophone film school had taken root, but an unstable economy had also kept it from being a reality. A stable economy was still in doubt, but an emerging, much stronger political will to engineer a separation from the rest of Canada was clearly felt. In that climate the hope for a francophone film school was rising and INIS was born. A committee, headed by Fernand Dansereau, had for several years looked abroad at different schools and finally designed a model they believed applicable to Quebec. L'Institut nationale de l'image et du son was finally in an active planning phase. I sent my CV to the administration and after six months got a not very gracious letter confirming its reception. That it never was put to the scrutiny of the people selecting the teaching staff, I do not think had much to do with me personally. Importing specialists had been a necessity in and before 1968, but by now Quebec had developed its own, and no longer felt the need for foreigners.

When eventually I became employed during the school's first tumultuous year, it was due to a chance meeting with Mark Beresford, the elected head of the school. I had gotten to know him in the 70s when he was in charge of CBC's small anglophone unit in Montreal and had commissioned me to direct a couple of documentaries. I had liked working for him, and he had at the time produced some quite interesting programs on a very meagre budget. He had then been, and still was, a flamboyant personality, always full of ideas. When he asked why I had not applied to teach at the school, it became clear that my CV had never reached his desk; he now asked me to send it to him personally. When eventually interviewed by the INIS selection committee, I met more familiar faces; a couple had worked at the NFB when I first arrived in Montreal, and they now held important functions in the industry. There was also Rock Demers, the president of Les Productions La Fête. After my homecoming, he and his producer Kevin Tierny soon started to use me as a script editor; working with those two was always one of life's pleasures. Rock was not only highly respected and had a very special place in the Quebec film community, but he was also such a likeable person. Knowledgeable and extremely well-travelled, he never boasted but always listened carefully and having an opinion different from his did not destin you to the dog house. I had an equally good rapport with Kevin, and the fact that I was working for them, I am convinced, helped both to open doors to other companies and to smooth my way through the selection committee.

Mark and his assistant were, besides some clerical staff, the only people who were employed full-time — all the teaching staff were freelancers from the industry and came in to teach their specialities on course contracts. The selection committee, or at least part of it, also acted as a watchdog and were called in when the train left the rails, which it did with irritating regularity. That we all survived that first year was only due to Mark's assistant, an eminently able and persevering person. Besides being head of the school, Mark was also supposed to teach 'filmmaking' and suggested that the two of us should co-teach the subject, an 'offer' I politely declined, alleging time constraints. However, the real reason was that our discussions had shown me a man even flakier than I had suspected: he had no course plan, and his definition of 'filmmaking' was all over the map. I was not prepared to carry his load as well as my own, but some of it fell on me anyway. After a couple of months my students solicited my help with technical knowledge that Mark had not been able to give them! To the relief of most people, he left his position at the end of INIS's first year.

Having had the pleasure and the pain of involvement in three individual film schools, created in vastly dissimilar cultures and performing in different languages, makes me wonder about the overall relevance of such institutions. All you can *teach* are technical skills, but if you do that competently you might be lucky enough to facilitate the birth and growth of creativity. Save for some local traits, INIS's first year was a mirror image of what I had already assisted at twice: the disproportion between supply and demand for qualified *and* suitable teaching staff and, in the planning, the absence of an evolving, modernised look at industrial and cultural needs and expectations. I think it is safe to say that without the impetus of the likelihood of a positive outcome in the referendum, INIS would not have come into being, and I do not think it can take much glory either from the well-made, funny, stirring, human feature films made in Quebec. Some were made before INIS was even thought of, and some have been made since. Pray it may continue!

My own experiences had been extended over almost thirty years, and the INIS students were a generation who had grown up in a very changed society and had vastly altered expectations. They were, on the whole, pleasant to deal with. When I got to know them a bit better, I could also see that they were somewhat less 'cultured,' in the sense of being less interested in, and knowledgeable of, what surrounded them in the world. Globalisation did not seem to have done much for them. They did not live in McLuhan's world village although they loved its tools, and but for two or three who showed more depth and talent, they all had a hankering for Hollywood — even the unilingual French ones!

As script editor and sometimes lecturer, I made a couple of good friends at Radio-Canada,[36] but on the whole the place was a tower of stress and unhappiness. It was almost impossible to conduct any analytical work; for almost everybody I met, analysing was akin to criticising, and for fear of their future, almost nobody dared to do it. Yearly budget cuts made the upper echelons constantly exhort their employers to 'make more with less.' In what had been a very wasteful institution, you could probably have done that if some initial constructive thinking had taken place, but each budget cut only created more panic and only restarted the inflexible and deeply ingrained old thinking. When yet another budget cut precluded me from getting any more contracts, it was a financial loss but also a considerable relief.

I have no explanation as to what once motivated the francophones not to make a distinction between their radio and TV divisions by naming them differently. This is surely not the only reason why Radio-Canada, over time on an increasing scale, has resembled filmed radio, but there *is* much to a name. It is also perceived as less costly to invest in words than in thought! Not that their anglophone counterparts are paragons of programs worth spending time on, but, from time to time, they do appear. I can not even remember the last time Radio-Canada afforded me that pleasure. That they can not find inspiration inside their TV tower in Montreal is all too evident, but that Radio-Canada also seems incapable of taking any inspiration from the Quebec culture outside its walls, is a great worry. Is the reality that the Two Solitudes are as solitary as when I first met them in 1968? The walls do not seem to have the same shape, but they are still there.

With sad regularity my dealings with Radio-Canada brought Horace Wolpole to mind:

'This world is a comedy to those that think, a tragedy to those that feel.'[37]

AT LONG LAST

A photographic exhibition of 503 pictures from 68 countries presented by The Museum of Modern Art in New York in 1955 was called *The Family of Man*. The show also begot a book that an American friend sent me as a Christmas present. It was a fabulous gift indeed, and the passage of time has only slightly yellowed the pages. The impact of the human conditions they portray is still as strong as they were when the cameras clicked and when I first opened the book. I still marvel at its richness that for me has also connected it to Russia and China in a very special way. In the 60s I had stood at a street corner in central Moscow observing the tide of humans that came and went. I was mesmerised by the dissimilarity in faces, and the disparity in dress, and for the first time really became conscious of the enormity of the Asian part of Russia. *The Family of Man* came to mind, and wishing to find its Russian equivalent, I made my way to a bookshop, in my excitement forgetting that I was in a totalitarian state with scant interest for the individual. I was also in a place where most people had a fear of foreigners; even an innocent question for directions would seldom be answered. The woman in the bookshop was vexed by my stupid request and made it clear that the sooner I left the better. Her assistant, a short elderly man, had listened and suddenly flung open the doors on the lower part of a bookcase behind the counter and dove into it. It must have been deep for he almost disappeared; all that was left to see were the soles of his slippers, like two rabbit ears, at each side of his bottom. After a muffled victorious call, he backed out, waving a smallish brown envelope and exclaimed: 'I knew we had it, I knew we had it!' He had misconstrued 'face' to be 'mask' and on the counter spread ten small envelopes, each containing the most delicate paper cuts of the ten main characters in ten classic Chinese operas. They were exquisite in their double-sided colouring printed on the thinnest of rice paper, and I of course could not resist buying them.

Back in Stockholm I brought them to the Museum for Asian Art, and the Director generously offered to let an ethnic Chinese employee help me to transcribe the envelope text that I could not read. A while later the Director called, regretful that he could not help me: his Chinese employee was a child of the Cultural Revolution and refused to have anything to do with 'that old stuff.' I tried the Chinese Embassy, but the outcome was the same although they expressed them-selves in a slightly more diplomatic form and also offered me the gift of some 'modern' paper cuts — machine stencilled on some plastic-coated white paper! Over the years I have made a couple of equally unsuc-cessful attempts to get some help, and the beauties have stayed in their envelopes following me on my travels.

A couple of years ago, Montreal's icy winters finally outdid the charm and sophistication of this in so many ways unique city. Not with-out reluctance, but in the necessary search for a gentler climate, I left Montreal and moved out west to Vancouver Island. With surprise, I met a variation of the Two Solitudes: the larger Canadian one between East and West. As with all solitudes, it has its given ingredients of lan-guage and ethnic mixtures, but British Columbia, being a geographical outpost with an old history, as well as Victoria's relative smallness, combined with its diminishing — but still lingering fondness for things British — have together created a character that it has taken me some time to decode. The Capital has a high influx of 'weather-refugees' like myself, and those from Montreal, that I have met, all say the same: 'We miss it.' I can warmly attest to that, although Victoria has one thing that Montreal lacks. It has a spring season! As a rule in Montreal you go from winter to summer almost overnight. The Victoria spring does sel-dom respect its arrival date, as stated in the almanac; it mostly comes early, and suddenly the first cherry blossoms or an opened magnolia stops you in your tracks, putting a smile on your face. In contrast to this laudable haste, the powers that be have an infuriating habit of dis-cussing social problems ad nauseam, creating committees who contin-ue to do the same. In the meantime we all live, as best we can, with the same ills that plague most cities these days.

In 1999, when I still lived in Montreal, Dr. Marc Gervais — former teacher and one of the many Jesuits with a staying interest in Bergman's films — published *Ingmar Bergman Magician and Prophet*. In my copy he wrote:

> 'to Ulla
> who really knows
> but still smiles...?'

Although he seemed to have his doubts I still *do* smile, but do I really know? I do not think so.

When I moved to Victoria I lived on a street next to Chinatown where I went to buy my fruit and vegetables. As I had in Brunei, I found greens and tubers I did not know the names of — or how to cook — and not speaking English, the Chinese women in their shops were of scant help. Their men usually have some English, but they — on the other hand — do not seem to be cooking; I did not get very far until I discovered Chinatown's community centre. There I got more than I had hoped for. A very enterprising woman, who worked with elderly Chinese in an effort to keep them stay active, introduced me to the group. It forced them to try out their English — I got cooking advice and learned the names of these mysterious vegetables. From time to time we ate together and for my first potluck meal I brought the most typical Swedish dish of all: Mr. Jansson's Temptation. Its smell was foreign but the taste was a success! At the table I sat beside a Chinese couple — he a medical doctor, his wife a former opera singer. I had taken along the brown envelope with the Chinese opera 'masks,' and as the rest of the group admired them, the singer *knew* what she was looking at! She was initially shy, but her husband talked her into promising to help me translate the Chinese writing that for such a long time had stayed decorative lines, but had not told me anything.

A new project is on the worktable.

EPILOGUE

In its original form for piano, Maurice Ravel's *Pavane Pour une Princesse Défunte* was composed in 1899 and dedicated to the Princess de Polignac. Eleven years later Ravel orchestrated it, and that version became extremely popular — and very sentimentalised. A pavane is a dance, its tempo brisk. That is how it should be played to my ashes.

ACKNOWLEDGEMENTS

I wish to express my deep gratitude to Judith Brand, my editor. With a firm but gentle hand she guided me through all the intricacies of the English language and her sensitivity to voice and style has earned her my profound respect. Her never lacking cheerful support has also been a big comfort.

Lynne van Luven has been helpful well beyond the call of duty and at just the crucial moment said: 'Do not give up just yet!' Thank you Lynne.

Vivian Smith has my thanks for telling me, without circumlocutions, why an earlier draft was so misshaped. I left her a forest and got back some important notes about the trees!

Last, but not least, I wish to thank Katherine Tweedie for her delicate handling of the first pages I asked her to read a long time ago. She could — and rightfully so — have aborted the whole enterprise.

NOTES

1. The negative cutter uses the finished work-print as the model when cutting the negative but has no creative input.

2. Rushes: all the uncut film footage shot on a single day or in a specific location.

3. Lewis Carroll: *Alice in Wonderland*

4. You define this hypothetical circle by drawing an imaginary line between your object and your camera in its initial position.

5. As quoted in: Vilgot Sjöman: *L 136, Dagbok med Ingmar Bergman*, page 69 (my translation from Swedish)

6. A board where scene- and take-numbers are noted and filmed for identification each time the camera is turned on.

7. A professionally used recorder for the sound tape.

8. A fade is obtained by exposing the negative to more light = fade up, or to less light = fade down.

9. A superimposition is a double exposure of a fade down of the outgoing scene and a fade up of the incoming one.

10. Vilgot Sjöman: *L 136, Dagbok med Ingmar Bergman*. Kungl Boktryckeriet P.A. Norstedt & Söner, 1963.

11. Played by Ingrid Thulin.

12. Liv Ullman

13. Bibi Andersson

14. Wit that escapes you until you are on your way out: i.e., on the stairs.

15. *The Black Woman In The Wardrobe*

16. *Woman Without a Face*

17. *The Necklace*

18. *Together with Gunilla Monday Evening and Tuesday Morning*

19. Published scripts often conform to the final edit and if that is the case, there is no way of telling what was really happening in the editing room.

20. Thomas Stearns Eliot: from 'The Love Song of J. Alfred Prufrock'

21. The Food and Agriculture Organisation of the United Nations

22. H. C. Andersen

23. *Le Chagrain Et La Pitié* (1970)

24. The French language TV station.

25. *Ingenjör Andrées Luftfärd*, 1982

26. 'Cher Caillois, il m'arrivera encore de penser à vous en m'efforçant d'écouter les pierres.'

27. *Den Enfaldige Mördaren*, Sweden 1982

28. *Et Des Chansons Pour Les Sirenes*

29. The Maori word for the white settlers.

30. For *Cat Ballou* and *Cool Had Luke*.

31. A village built on stilts in the water.

32. *Sarcophilus harrisii*

33. *Thylacinus cynocephalus*

34. William Blake: *Songs of Experience*: 'The Tiger'

35. Henry Miller

36. French language TV

37. From Letters to the Countess of Upper Ossory, 16 Aug. 1776.